Patricia Posner is a British-born writer who has collaborated with her husband, the author Gerald Posner, on twelve non-fiction books, including *Mengele: The Complete Story* – a biography of Dr. Josef Mengele; *Hitler's Children* – a 1991 collection of interviews with the children of Nazi perpetrators; and most recently, *God's Bankers* – a financial history of the Roman Catholic Church. Her work has appeared, among other places, in the *Miami Herald*, *The Daily Beast* and *Salon*. She lives in Miami Beach.

THE PHARMACIST OF AUSCHWITZ

The Untold Story of Victor Capesius

PATRICIA POSNER

First published in the United Kingdom in 2017
by Crux Publishing Ltd.

ISBN: 978-1-909979-41-3

Also available as an ebook:
eISBN: 978-1-909979-40-6

Requests for permission to reproduce material from this work
should be sent to:

hello@cruxpublishing.co.uk

To Gerald, who encouraged me to channel into this book my passionate belief that the crimes of the Holocaust never be forgotten.

CONTENTS

INTRODUCTION

by Rabbi Abraham Cooper

I had the honor and privilege of knowing and working with Simon Wiesenthal, the Nazi hunter, for nearly thirty years. As a result of losing 89 members of his family in the Nazi Holocaust, and due to the unspeakable barbarity and cruelty that Simon suffered and witnessed during the Shoah, he dedicated every day from May 5, 1945 when US soldiers liberated him—more dead than alive—from the Mauthausen Concentration Camp, to pursuing and tracking down the mass murderers of his people. He would help hunt down some 1,100 Nazi criminals, including the man who arrested Anne Frank and her family.

"Justice, not vengeance" was his credo. "We need convicted criminals, not martyrs for the neo-Nazi cause," Simon would tell us at the Simon Wiesenthal Center, which he established in 1977. He was a crusader for justice, who toiled virtually alone and without significant support during the Cold War years to ensure that memory would be preserved and justice would be served.

"Every trial will be an inoculation against hatred and a warning to generations yet unborn of man's capacity for evil against his fellow man," he would tell audiences on American campuses in the 1970s and 80s.

How right this crusader for justice was. We live in a world where Holocaust denial is state policy of the Mullahocracy in Iran, where Holocaust terms and imagery are inverted and abused by extremists who hate the Jewish state; where words like Genocide and yes, even Auschwitz, are cynically co-opted by politicians, pundits, and even academics. Worse still is the instinct 70 years later to view the Shoah in the rearview mirror of history, to claim that Auschwitz has lost its relevance to our day.

That is why Patricia Posner's *THE PHARMACIST OF AUSCHWITZ: The Untold Story of Victor Capesius*, is such an important and relevant work. It traces the path of an educated man, Victor Capesius, who was trained as a pharmacist, who was a well-liked salesman for IG Farben and Bayer, who knew and socialized with Jews in his native Romania before World War II. That same man would end up standing alongside Auschwitz's Angel of Death, sometimes sending people he knew in peace time, including young Jewish twins, to their immediate deaths in the gas chambers. He also safeguarded the Nazis' stash of Zyklon B and provided drugs that would be used by doctors to perform horrific and deadly experiments on pregnant women and children. This was a man who picked through cadavers of murdered Jews in search of gold fillings and, driven by greed, dragged away heavy suitcases of gold extracted from thousands of victims.

As important as tracing Capesius's Auschwitz career, is Ms. Posner's reconstruction of the group trial of Nazi criminals in a West German court in the early 1960s. It included the chief aid to Auschwitz's commandant, and also doctors, dentists, even Kapos, along with Capesius. Throughout the trial and even after his conviction and sentencing to nine years, Capesius and the other defendants never showed remorse. Survivors who dared testify in the German court were greeted with stares of contempt by surviving Nazis who seemed disappointed that any of their victims had survived. In Capesius's case—the liar, thief, and robber of the dead—he always denied his crimes, refused to take responsibility for his actions or to apologize to the Jews he murdered. He saw himself as the victim, a good person who was just following orders, a small cog who never should have been jailed in the first place.

On January 24, 1968, less than two and a half years into his nine-year sentence, Capesius was released from prison by Germany's highest court. After his release, Capesius's first public appearance in Göppingen was with his family at a classical concert. As he walked into the music hall the audience broke spontaneously into enthusiastic applause. To many, including perhaps some of the ex-Nazi judges who had freed him, Capesius deserved sympathy and support. After all, to them he was just a good German who was just following orders.

Patricia Posner makes sure that new generations can understand that the path he, and others like him, chose led them straight to the gates of hell and beyond.

Rabbi Abraham Cooper
Associate Dean
Co-founder
Simon Wiesenthal Center
Los Angeles, California
August 2016

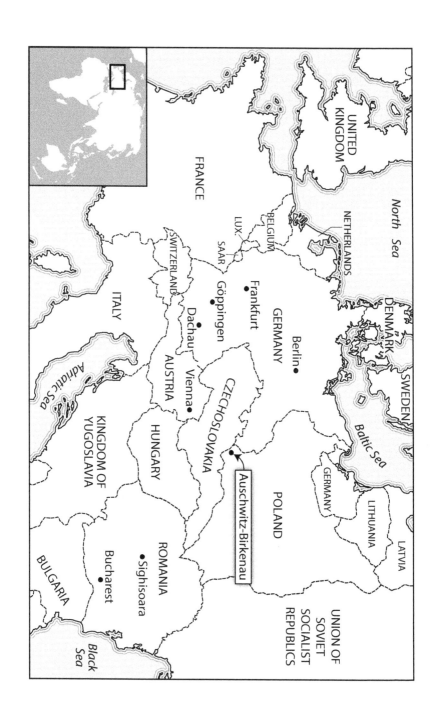

AUTHOR'S PREFACE

In the spring of 1986 I went to New York's Plaza Hotel for a meeting that my husband, author Gerald Posner, had arranged at Trader Vic's, a Polynesian-themed restaurant. It was for research we were conducting into Dr. Josef Mengele, the infamous 'Angel of Death' responsible for gruesome medical experiments at Auschwitz, the largest Nazi concentration camp. What had started as a pro bono lawsuit by Gerald on behalf of two surviving Mengele guinea pigs had turned into a biography of the Nazi fugitive. During those intervening years we had traveled to Germany and South America, pursued the story in long-sealed archives, and also penetrated postwar neo-fascist circles that had helped Mengele stay one step ahead of Nazi hunters.

The meeting at Trader Vic's was with none other than Rolf Mengele, the only child of the notorious doctor. Gerald and I waited in a dimly lit corner booth for 42-year-old Mengele to arrive. As a British Jew, I knew that if my maternal Polish grandparents had not emigrated to the United Kingdom at the turn of the twentieth century, it was likely they would have ended up at a Nazi death camp. Maybe they would have died at Auschwitz where men like Mengele reigned supreme. Little wonder that much of our Mengele research had seemed surreal to me. There had been that extremely uncomfortable and testy exchange Gerald had had in Buenos Aires with Wilfred von Oven, a top aide to Nazi propaganda chief Josef Goebbels and also the publisher of a virulently anti-Semitic postwar journal in Argentina. Or the time I saw a collection of Nazi memorabilia, 'gifts' from one of Mengele's sponsors for citizenship in Paraguay. But that all seemed quite distant now that I was about to meet Rolf Mengele.

Gerald and I had discussed it many times. A child is not responsible for the sins of the father. And I knew from our work that Rolf condemned what his father did at Auschwitz and was trying hard to make amends by allowing Gerald to use his father's diaries and letters free of charge in the upcoming biography. The New York visit was in part to discuss whether Rolf might agree to talk about his father on live television (he did, with Gerald, on the *Phil Donahue Show* that summer). Still, while my brain's rational side understood that the man I was about to meet bore no responsibility for the bone-chilling crimes committed by his paternal namesake at Auschwitz, I was nevertheless a jumble of nerves and conflicting emotions. Gerald had already met with Rolf in Germany over several weeks and the two had developed a good rapport. I was the one now on the spot.

My apprehension dissolved though soon after Rolf arrived. It seemed that he was as nervous as I, and that skittishness somehow helped reduce our shared anxiety. I was impressed with his sincerity in denouncing his father's crimes. And in the coming days I discovered that Mengele's atrocities had burdened his son with a legacy he did not fully understand nor embrace, and which he badly wanted to avoid passing to his own children.

At one point, while discussing his father's escape from justice, we talked about the chaotic months after the war had ended in May 1945. Mengele was still in Europe and American and British forces were hunting him. It turned out he had many lucky breaks. But one that made a lasting impression on me was that in September 1945, eight months after fleeing Auschwitz only steps ahead of the Soviet Red Army, Mengele showed up unannounced at the Munich home of a pharmacist and his wife. That unidentified pharmacist had served with Mengele on the Russian front in 1942, before Mengele's transfer to Auschwitz. But, said Rolf, the Munich pharmacist knew about his father's crimes because they shared a mutual acquaintance who had worked with Mengele at the death camp: another pharmacist, Victor Capesius.

"Capesius," said Rolf. "That's the pharmacist of Auschwitz. My father and Capesius were friends."

I remember that moment as if it were yesterday. My first thought was "Auschwitz had a pharmacist?"

Over the years, between my own book projects and the many shared with Gerald, I hoped someday to write about Capesius.

My desire to do so grew over time as I realized that his story – and the role he played at Auschwitz with some of Germany's biggest pharmaceutical firms – was largely untold, lost largely in the coverage of more infamous Nazis. As I gradually compiled information over the years, I discovered a compelling tale of perverted medicine and greed. Those few words thirty-one years ago from Rolf Mengele planted a seed that is now realized. What follows is the singular, disturbing, and at times maddening, story of the pharmacist of Auschwitz.

Chapter 1

"PHARMACIST UNCLE"

May 1944. Auschwitz, the Nazi high temple of industrial-scale genocide, was operating at full capacity. In a frenzied climax in its war to eradicate European Jewry, the Third Reich had set about deporting up to 800,000 Hungarian Jews to Auschwitz's gas chambers. The place that would become synonymous with mass murder was struggling to keep up with the flood of new victims. It was this chaotic setting to which Mauritius Berner, a Romanian doctor, and his wife and children, arrived. The Berners and eighty of their Jewish neighbors from Hungarian-controlled Transylvania got there just before sunrise after a torturous three-day journey packed inside a cattle car.

"Outside, the locks and chains were taken off and the door opened," Berner later recalled. "There were huge masses of suitcases, thousands of pieces of luggage in unimaginable disorder."

A phalanx of SS troops with barking Alsatians added a surreal silhouette against the backdrop of ultra-bright spotlights.

"I could not comprehend where we are, what has happened, why this picture of total devastation. As we look up ahead between the two pairs of train tracks, a few hundred meters away, we can see two factory chimneys with tall flames shooting from them, pillars of fire. . . At first we had the feeling of being in a bombed-out station . . . those huge columns of flames coming out of the chimneys made me think we had arrived at some ironworks or the entrance to Dante's Inferno."

Despite his fear, Dr. Berner reassured his wife and children. "The main thing is, the five of us will stay together . . . but we won't let anyone separate us."

An SS officer stepped in front of them at that moment.

"Men to the right, women to the left."

"In an instant I was separated from my wife and children," recalled Berner. They shuffled forward in two parallel lines only feet apart.

"Come, my darling, and kiss us," his wife yelled out.

"I ran back to them. I kissed my wife and my children, with tears in my eyes and my throat tightened up with grief, and I looked into my wife's eyes, wide, sad, beautiful, and filled with the fear of death. The children looked on in silence, following their mother. They could not comprehend what was going on."

A soldier shoved Berner back to the men's line. In a few minutes another shouted: "Doctors line up here." So Berner joined a small group assembling near several Red Cross trucks. There he watched as an immaculately groomed SS captain wearing white gloves stood at the front of thousands of new arrivals stretching a quarter mile along the tracks. As each approached, the SS officer gestured with one thumb to the right or left, splitting the crowd again. Only later would Berner learn that the officer was Josef Mengele and that being sent to the left was an immediate death sentence.[1]

Standing a few steps behind Mengele was another SS officer, a short and stocky man with his back to Berner. He directed the prisoners after Mengele had made the selection. At one stage that SS officer turned around. Berner was startled and shook his head and rubbed his eyes to be certain he was not mistaken. The SS major at Auschwitz's railhead was none other than Victor Capesius, a pharmacist from Berner's hometown.

In the 1930s, Capesius had been a likable enough sales rep for I. G. Farben, the giant German chemical and industrial conglomerate. He had sold drugs for Farben's pharmaceutical subsidiary, Bayer.[2]

"Once the war started I lost track of Capesius," recalled Berner, "until my family and I arrived in Auschwitz. And who was there? The same Dr. Capesius."[3]

Berner slowly worked his way close enough so Capesius might hear him. The words spilled out fast.

"You remember me!?" He pleaded with Capesius to be reunited with his wife and 12-year-old daughter and 9-year-old twins.

"Twins?" Capesius seemed interested.

Capesius and another SS physician, Dr. Fritz Klein, retrieved Berner's wife and daughters. They took the family to Mengele, who was intently focused on the long lines of new prisoners.

Klein told Mengele about the twins.

Mengele was obsessed with sequestering twins for his experiments. But since the war had recently turned against the Reich, he knew he no longer had the luxury of taking every set of twins.

"Identical or fraternal?" Mengele asked.

"Fraternal," Klein said.

"Later," Mengele waved him away. "I don't have any time right now."

"They will just have to go back to their group," Capesius told a sobbing Berner. "Don't cry. Your wife and children are just going to take baths. You will see them again in an hour."[4]

Berner was, in fact, dispatched to one of Auschwitz's slave labor sub-camps. It was only after the war that he learned his family was gassed within an hour of their arrival.

Two others recognized Capesius at the selection ramp that same day. Dr. Gisela Böhm, a pediatrician, and her twenty-four-year-old daughter, Ella, had arrived on the same train. Ella had comforted Berner's twins during the horrific journey. Both were startled to see Capesius at the railhead.

Dr. Böhm also knew Capesius from when he was a Bayer salesman. He had run a pharmacy in her hometown of Schässburg and made sales calls on her husband, also a doctor. Once he even showed them a Bayer promotional film.[5]

Ella had fond memories of Capesius from when she was twelve and her father had introduced him to her as her "pharmacist uncle." He had given her a Bayer notepad as a gift. "I was very proud of my Bayer pad," she recalled years later, "I bragged about it at school."[6] Capesius sometimes relaxed with her family at a public pool and Ella recalled he had been "sweet to me."

When Ella saw him her first thought was that he might help separate her and her mother from the thousands of others. But she could not get his attention. "What is he doing here?" she wondered. "What is a pharmacist doing at a forlorn place like this?"[7]

Chapter 2

THE FARBEN CONNECTION

The answer to Ella's question was not simple. To understand what a pharmacist like Capesius was doing at Auschwitz, it is necessary to know first how the camp itself came to exist as a profit center for medical experimentation, slave labor, and extermination; the deadly spawn of a military-industrial-political partnership between the Nazis and I. G. Farben, Germany's largest company. For Capesius in particular, that was more than merely a matter of understanding the dark history that led to Auschwitz. That is because before the war Capesius worked for Farben and its pharmaceutical subsidiary, Bayer. It was an affiliation that enhanced his standing among many of the Nazis who served with him at the camp.

Interessen-Gemeinschaft Farben (Syndicate of Common Interests Farben) was founded in December 1925, only eight years before Hitler became Germany's chancellor. Six leading chemical and pharmaceutical companies had merged to form the huge conglomerate. Among them were the world's largest synthetic dye makers, Bayer, Hoechst, BASF, and Agfa.[1]

In the 14 years from its inception to the start of World War II, Farben boasted a record of four Nobel Prizes in chemistry and medicine. It had a virtual monopoly on innovative patents at the forefront of manufacturing synthetic raw materials including rubber and oil, as well as revolutionary medications to treat syphilis and malaria, patents on morphine and Novocain, even the exclusive rights to Aspirin as a painkiller. Farben also boasted leading-edge research on thousands of wildly diverse products, from the artificial sweetener saccharine to potent poison gases and promising rocket fuels. Its quarter million employees were better paid and more skilled than those in competitive industries. In record time, with its complex web of partnerships and subsidiaries, Farben had become the world's biggest chemical company and the fourth largest industrial conglomerate, close on the heels of General Motors, U.S. Steel, and Standard Oil. It was by a wide margin Germany's most profitable firm.[2]

Even before Hitler came to power he shared an unshakeable belief widespread in Germany: the country had lost World War I largely because it had few natural resources needed to fight a prolonged military battle. Its vital industries ground to a virtual halt during World War I because a British naval blockade had strangled supply lines and prevented rubber, oil, steel, and nitrates from reaching Germany. This resulted in persistent shortages of everything from gunpowder to fuel, hobbling Germany on the battlefield. Ultimately it was the raw materials shortage coupled with a widespread civilian hunger that had broken the German will to fight.[3]

Hitler, who was a decorated World War I soldier, was convinced the country had to be militarily self-sufficient. Farben technologies offered Hitler a singular opportunity to rebuild Germany while no longer depending on other countries for oil, rubber and nitrates. But the marriage between the two, the up-and-coming rightwing nationalist and the monolithic company, was troubled early on. That was because many of Farben's best scientists, and about a third of its executive board, were Jewish. So there was a schizophrenic quality to the mating dance between Farben and the Third Reich. Nazi literature and commentators denigrated Farben as an "instrument of international finance capital," code words for the Nazi view that a small Jewish cabal controlled and manipulated worldwide financial markets and industries. Sometimes Farben was mocked as I. G. Moloch, a reference to a Canaanite god to whom children were sacrificed. That was intended to conjure the centuries-old libel that Jews killed Christian babies and used their blood in religious rituals. The virulently anti-Semitic weekly *Der Stürmer* ran cartoons of "Isidore G. Farber," an offensive caricature seemingly a mixture of Shylock and a prostitute.[4]

Some of the harshest Nazi criticism was directed at Farben's pharmaceutical divisions since they routinely used laboratory animals for testing medications. Top Nazis were surprisingly hardcore animal rights activists and Hitler was a vegetarian who hoped one day to ban all German slaughterhouses. The Nazis even passed laws to protect animals from hunters, to prohibit their use in films or circuses, and to outlaw Kosher butchers. Germany was the first country to outlaw vivisection. The punishment for laboratory experiments with animals was commitment to a concentration camp or in some cases, the death penalty. One of Farben's premier medical scientists, Heinrich Hörlein, argued that animal experimentation was critical to the safety testing of life-saving medications. Nazis thought that such an opinion was merely further evidence that Farben was "an international Jewish organization."[5]

Carl Bosch, the Nobel prize-winning chemist who ran the company, was no fan of Hitler. Bosch considered the Nazis little better than political thugs who had no appreciation for the scientific innovation that was the backbone of Farben. But, as Hitler started his climb to power, Bosch knew the company had to morph from an untrusted outsider to an indispensable partner.[6] So Bosch opened up Farben's coffers and became the Nazi's biggest financial backer in the 1933 elections in which Hitler gained nearly six million votes and solidified his position as chancellor.[7] Bosch also dispatched Farben's press secretary, someone who boasted solid Nazi connections, to make the case in Berlin that the company's leadership was mostly "Christian self-made men."[8]

Hitler meanwhile took an intense personal interest in Farben's patents for synthetic oil. When he met two senior executives, the Führer surprised them by saying that Farben was at the heart of his plan to make Germany self-sufficient.[9] When Bosch and Hitler had a summit in late 1933, the two initially bonded over a shared passion for a costly crash program for fuel independence. But the meeting ended on a sour note when Bosch raised concerns about the Nazi's accelerating exclusion of Jews from the sciences. Bosch was blunt. Both chemistry and physics would be set back a hundred years if Germany forced its Jewish scientists to leave. That suggestion infuriated Hitler. "Then we'll work a hundred years without physics and chemistry," he yelled.

It put the two at odds. That year the Nazis passed the Enabling Act which gave Hitler the authority he would use to ban Jews from science and technology, teaching at universities, civil service jobs, and providing services to the government. Against the advice of his fellow directors, Bosch continued crusading for Jewish scientists. Small wonder that Hitler never again agreed to be in the same room as Bosch.[10]

The Nazis might have dismantled a company with less power and influence, but Hitler and his henchmen knew they needed Farben's knowhow and muscle. So, starting in earnest in 1937, they did the one thing that would make it palatable to the Third Reich: Farben was Nazified. Hitler appointed Robert Ley, a Bayer chemist, as head of the German Labor Front. All Jewish officials were dismissed. A third of the supervisory board of directors were forcibly removed from its headquarters and banned from any contact with the firm. Leading Jewish scientists in the research divisions were shunted aside and summarily replaced.[11] By the time Jews were expunged from Farben's top ranks, Carl Bosch had become the firm's honorary chairman, a position with little influence (when he died three years later, in the dual clutches of alcoholism and depression, he predicted to his doctors that Hitler would lead Germany to destruction).

By July 1938, when the Third Reich decreed that even a single Jew on a board of directors made it a "Jewish company," the tensions and backbiting between the Nazis and Farben were history. Many company officials had become Nazi party members and some had even joined the SS. Farben successfully applied for a certificate that certified it was a "German firm" in full compliance with the race laws.[12] To demonstrate how seriously it viewed the directive to become an Aryan firm, Farben even dismissed 107 Jewish department heads that worked in international divisions outside Germany.[13] And Farben had successfully converted its wholly- owned American I. G. subsidiary into one of the Nazi's most effective spying resources in the U.S. With its ownership of film companies Agfa, Ansco, and General Aniline, its "salesmen" obtained everything from photos of secret military installations to copies of classified army and air force strategies.[14]

Hitler's annexation of Austria in March 1938 provided the first evidence of the extent to which the Farben-Third Reich partnership was in full bloom. Within weeks Farben had seized control of Skodawerke-Wetzler, Austria's largest chemical company, in which Europe's preeminent banking family, the Rothschilds, owned a controlling interest. Farben moved in Aryan technicians and managers as all the company's top Jews were forcibly removed (Isador Pollack, Skoda's general manager, was literally kicked to death by a gang of Nazi Storm Troopers).[15]

Farben's takeover of Skoda became the template it used in other countries that were the victims of Hitler's aggression. In 1938, during a standoff between Germany and Czechoslovakia, Farben used the threat of a Nazi invasion to buy Aussiger Verein, the largest Czech chemical company, at a fire-sale price. By the time the Nazis began their blitzkrieg into Poland on September 1, 1939, Farben adjusted its loyalties inside the Third Reich to maximize its wartime spoils. Before the war Luftwaffe chief Hermann Göring had been Farben's biggest supporter. When Poland fell to the Nazis, Farben allied itself most closely with SS chief Heinrich Himmler, who carried ultimate power when it came to the disposal of companies and properties there. That ensured it swooped up the three most significant Polish chemical and dyestuff firms.[16]

By June 1940 the Nazis had conquered Belgium, Denmark, Norway, the Netherlands, Luxembourg, and had stunningly brought France to its knees during a ferocious six-week assault. Many senior Farben executives had bitter memories of how the French had exacted huge reparations from German industry after World War I. Moreover, France's chemical industry had long been Germany's biggest competitor. The French firms were quickly Aryanized and through a new holding company Farben took control of France's prized chemical industry.[17]

Farben's ambitions grew in pace with the German battlefield victories. Directors drew up plans for carving up the chemical industries not only of occupied nations but also of future conquests, including neutral Switzerland, then-German allies Italy and the Soviet Union, and even Britain and the United States. By now the company provided a stunning 85% of the military goods the Nazis used in the war effort.[18]

The fall of France was to mark the zenith of German military success. Although the Nazis conducted a relentless air blitz against England, the British remained unbowed. Hitler then ignored the advice of his top generals and prepared to launch a second front in the east by invading Russia. The Nazi high command knew that the first year of fighting had already consumed large supplies of fuel and munitions. Even rubber, needed for everything from tires to combat boots, was running low, and a two-front war would put exponential demands on resources. Hitler demanded that Farben guarantee it could double its production of synthetic rubber and oil, requiring the construction of two new mega plants. Farben dispatched two teams to scout locations, one to southern Norway and the other to western Poland. Both were solidly under German control and safe from Allied attack.

Thirty-nine-year-old Otto Ambros, a chemist widely recognized as Farben's synthetic rubber expert, had overseen the construction of the company's first large rubber plant at Schkopau in eastern Germany. After visiting Poland, Ambros returned to the Frankfurt headquarters with news that he had found the ideal site to build both plants. It was in Polish Silesia, near the juncture of three rivers. Synthetic rubber and oil production required huge supplies of water for the high-pressure chemistry at the heart of both technologies. Three rail lines served the area. It was not far from a highway and large mining districts were within a twenty-mile radius. Another advantage, argued Ambros, was that it was next door to where the Nazis were turning an abandoned cavalry depot into a concentration camp. That meant Farben could have access to a steady supply of cheap inmate labor.[19]

Ambros's fellow directors quickly ratified the site, followed by an approval from the Third Reich. Farben decided to use the name of the small Polish village next door to its installation for its new corporate division: I. G. Auschwitz.[20]

Chapter 3

I. G. AUSCHWITZ

F arben had big plans for I. G. Auschwitz. Not only would it be the company's largest complex but for the first time would include an enormous hydrogenation facility to produce record amounts of synthetic rubber and fuel. The company expected I. G. Auschwitz to be a tremendous profit center. Farben was so confident that it declined the German government's offer of financing. If it had accepted Third Reich money, the Nazis would automatically have become Farben's partner. Instead, the directors wanted to assume all risks and reap all the profits.

Farben set aside almost a billion Reichsmarks (about $55 billion in 2015) for its ambitious construction.[1] The plans called for a sprawling facility several square miles in size, one that required more electricity than Berlin. SS chief Heinrich Himmler considered the success of I. G. Auschwitz so important that he appointed his trusted chief of staff, SS Major General Karl Wolff, as the Farben-SS go-between.

On March 20, 1941, Wolff met in Berlin with a Farben chemist and director, SS Lieutenant Colonel Heinrich Bütefisch. They wanted to sort out the details of how the neighboring concentration camp at Auschwitz might help Farben. Many skilled workers were serving on the front lines as Nazi troops so the company faced a shortage of experienced laborers. It planned on bringing in not only Germans, but what it euphemistically called "free workers" – employees from Holland, Belgium, France, as well as Poland, that were paid drastically reduced wages. Himmler ordered the Inspector of Concentration Camps to provide upwards of 12,000 camp inmates. Since camps like Auschwitz were SS profit centers, Bütefisch knew that Himmler would insist on compensation for any inmates Farben used.

After a half day of tough negotiations, Farben agreed to pay four Reichsmarks (then about $1.60, $20 in 2015) a day for skilled inmates, three for unskilled prisoners and one and a half (60 cents) for children. For that money – which eventually totaled more than $5 million – the SS agreed to provide transportation to and from the Auschwitz barracks, some four miles away from the construction site, as well as all rations.[2] A few weeks after that deal was struck, several Farben directors gave Himmler a private tour of the I.G. Auschwitz construction site. He was impressed and promised a steady supply of camp inmates as laborers.[3] Farben's Otto Ambros wrote in a memo, "Our new friendship with the SS is proving very profitable."[4]

Farben knew that the project's immense scope was a great technical challenge and that the constraints of war would make it tough to get all the raw materials. However, the construction proved even more problematic from the start and the development quickly fell behind schedule.[5] But I. G. Auschwitz was also plagued by an unexpected problem: Farben had not anticipated the terrible consequences for its workforce from the SS's savage punishment of inmates.

Internal company memos cataloged the relentless abuses: they were "severely flogged on the construction site" and sometimes kicked and beaten, even clubbed to death. One director noted, "This [the beatings] always applies to the weakest inmates who really cannot work harder."[6] It not only kept the frailest ones from doing their work but it had a generally "demoralizing effect among the free workers as well as on the Germans."[7] What's more, the daily march inmates made from Auschwitz drained them of much of their strength before they even started the workday. Wearing only ill-fitting wooden clogs and thin, prison garb, they suffered in the extreme heat of summer and bone-chilling cold of the winters. Plant managers watched in dismay as it took three, then four, and finally five malnourished inmates to lift and carry 50-kilo bags of cement.[8] Company executives complained internally that the SS did not understand what was necessary to make "free enterprise" flourish.

But the obsessively bureaucratic Nazis demanded every forced laborer who left the main camp in the morning after a 4:00 AM roll call be accounted for at the evening one. That meant surreal scenes at the end of each workday when inmates dragged along the corpses of co-workers who had died during that shift to assemble at their cellblock so that the Nazis could count the dead bodies as "present." Several times a week the Nazis trucked the piled corpses to the crematoriums. The bizarre ritual was rooted in profit: the SS made money from each cadaver, from extracting gold from dental fillings to using hair to fill mattresses and make warm socks for U-Boat crews and Luftwaffe pilots.[9] Disposing of dead laborers at Farben's plant would deprive the SS of the final opportunity to rape the corpses.

Farben executives did not fret about the mistreatment of their inmate workers because of humanitarian concerns. Instead, they were frustrated that it took three prisoners to do the work that could be done by a single well-fed German worker. This kicked off a furious internal debate about how to jumpstart the stalled construction. Officials feared that if the synthetic rubber and oil plants did not fully supply Hitler's army, the SS would blame the company. No one wanted to risk incurring the wrath of Hitler and Himmler over wartime projects that were deemed indispensable. So in July 1942, a year into the fierce fighting on the Eastern Front, Farben's board approved a remarkable proposal that cemented its slide into moral bankruptcy: it decided the best way to resolve its I. G. Auschwitz labor problem was to build its own concentration camp at a cost of $20 million. The site selected was adjacent to its ongoing construction and just east of the original Auschwitz camp. Ernst "Fritz" Sauckel, the Reich's Labor Minister, gave Farben's proposal a green light, concluding that it was the best way to "exploit [the inmates] to the highest possible extent, at the lowest conceivable degree of expenditure."

The new camp was named Monowitz Buna-Werke, a combination of the Polish village, Monowice (Monowitz in German) that was demolished to make room for it, and *Buna,* German for synthetic rubber. Access to a steady supply of slave laborers would eventually encourage Farben and other German companies to build 45 sub-camps – coal mining, metal works, chemicals, light industry, and even food processing – in a thirty mile radius as the Auschwitz footprint spread across the Polish countryside.[10]

Monowitz seemed to any casual observer simply a knockoff of Auschwitz, encircled with electrified barbed wire, watch towers with machine gun-toting guards, patrolling dogs, and searchlights illuminating the camp nightly to prevent escapes. Monowitz had its own gallows, wretched solitary confinement cells, and a phalanx of former convicts who served as sadistic foremen of the slave laborers.[11] There was also a brothel (frauenblock), where female inmates were forced to work as sex slaves for the German workers. Farben even created a duplicate of the mocking iron sign that stood over the entrance to Auschwitz: *Arbeit Macht Frei* "Work Will Make You Free" (for many prisoners the stone inscription to Dante's Inferno was more accurate: "Abandon all hope, you who enter").

Besides spending millions to build the camp, Farben agreed to cover all costs of food and housing while the SS took responsibility for security. The company did everything possible to boost its profits by cutting its costs. On average, three laborers were forced to sleep on wooden stalls originally designed to hold only one. Five times as many Jews were packed into barracks as were free German workers.[12] The thin straw filling for the beds was a constant source of infection and illness.[13] And the company aggressively experimented to determine the minimum amount of food required to keep inmates from starving while allowing them to work. The mainstay of the Monowitz diet was a watery soup the prisoners mocked as *Buna* since it had a rubber aftertaste. The average forced laborer, existing on no more than 1,200 calories a day, lost about nine pounds a week before stabilizing as emaciated skin and bones.[14]

Company memos reveal that Farben officials figured that any inmates who died from the harsh work could be easily replaced with new prisoners on the next arriving train. Benjamin Ferencz, a chief American war crimes prosecutor after World War II, noted that, "The Jewish concentration camp workers were less than slaves. Slave masters care for their human property and try to preserve it; it was the Nazi plan and intention that the Jews would be used up and then burned."[15]

A problem Farben faced was that the SS sent most of the arriving prisoners straight to the gas chambers. Company executives griped, for instance, that in one shipment of 5,022 Jews, 4092 had been killed immediately. After a formal complaint, the SS agreed to a rare accommodation by which some of the trains would be unloaded near I. G. Auschwitz, with an eye toward finding fit workers. On the first train unloaded near Monowitz, half of the 4,087 prisoners avoided the gas chambers and became slave laborers. Still, Farben managers noted their disappointment that the train contained "so many women and children as well as old Jews."[16]

Despite the unusual hurdles, top executives considered Monowitz to be a model for future projects. Chairman Carl Krauch wrote to Himmler on July 27, 1943, saying that he was "particularly pleased" to learn that in a discussion about a new synthetic rubber factory, the SS would "continue sponsoring and aiding us . . . as was done at Auschwitz."[17]

Eventually some 300,000 slave laborers passed through I. G. Auschwitz. It was there that fifteen-year-old Elie Wiesel and twenty-five-year-old Primo Levi worked (both survived and later became acclaimed writers, describing what happened there). Levi wrote that the Farben factory was a "huge entanglement of iron, concrete, mud and smoke, [it] is the negation of beauty. . . . Within its bounds not a blade of grass grows, and the soil is impregnated with the poisonous saps of coal and petroleum, and the only things alive are machines and slaves – and the former are more alive than the latter."[18]

About 25,000 of those forced laborers were literally worked to death, averaging a life span of only three months.[19] By the end of the war, however, Farben's ambitious I. G. Auschwitz experiment was a strategic failure. Despite the enormous bankroll from Farben, and the incredibly high human toll, to the complete dismay of Hitler the plant managed to produce only a small amount of synthetic fuel and no Buna rubber. Its everlasting testament would be only of its murderous role in the Final Solution.

Chapter 4

ENTER CAPESIUS

Victor Ernst Capesius was in many ways someone unlikely to end up at Auschwitz. He was not a native German or Austrian, the nationalities that dominated the soldiers, doctors and officers who staffed the concentration camps. Capesius was born on July 2, 1907 to devoutly German Lutheran parents in Reußmarkt, a Transylvanian town noted only for its close proximity to Vlad Dracula's medieval birthplace. His father was a physician and public health officer.[1] Young Capesius had an unremarkable childhood. He was a quiet and unimpressive student at the local Lutheran school in Sibiu, a Romanian city with such a strong German character that most ethnic Germans called it Hermannstadt. Capesius finished in the middle of the 32 graduates. He earned his undergraduate degree in general pharmacology from King Ferdinand I University on June 30, 1930, located in the town of Cluj-Napoca, called Klausenburg by ethnic Germans.[2] His first job was as an assistant in his uncle's pharmacy, the Apotheke zur Krone (Crown Pharmacy), in nearby Sighisoara.[3] Capesius's mother told him that one day he might inherit that business.[4]

He was only there five months before the Romanian army drafted him in 1931 as a first lieutenant and assigned him to Bucharest as a pharmacist assistant. But he soon managed to get extended leave to study chemistry at the University of Vienna.[5] His time there overlapped with Hitler's rise to power in neighboring Germany, something that could not have been lost on the young ethnic German student. It was in Vienna that Capesius met his future wife, twenty-four-year-old Friederike Bauer. Fritzi, as Capesius called her, was also a student at the Institute of Pharmacology and they both studied for their doctorate under the same professor, Dr. Richard Wasitzky.[6]

Fritzi found Capesius charming. When they started dating, she told her girlfriends that he was delightful. She liked everything about him, from his brown hair turning prematurely gray to his deep-set dark brown eyes. Some of her friends thought he seemed ungainly, but she corrected them, noting he was a wonderful dancer.[7] They felt a common bond since both fathers were doctors. Their families were devout Lutherans, although Fritzi's father was a Jewish convert. In 1932, as their relationship flourished, she introduced him to her parents. Then Fritzi spent her semester break with him in Transylvania.

Meanwhile, Capesius's dissertation about chenopodium, an herb used to treat people with parasitic worms, had earned him a pharmacy doctorate from the University of Vienna on November 30, 1933.[8] When he returned to Sighisoara he soon became the manager of his uncle's pharmacy. It was a profitable business, earning some 200,000 Reichsmarks annually (about $56,000 at a time when the average annual income in the U.S. was $1,601).[9]

Many ethnic Germans in Romania were transfixed when Hitler became chancellor of Germany that same year. But Capesius showed little interest in the upheaval gripping Germany. Although he joined a local nationalist social club, he seemed motivated more by the chance of making business contacts than fueling any political ardor. In his free time, he steered clear of the daily news and relaxed instead with friends. On Sundays, he could often be found with the Mild sisters, two pretty girls his age, enjoying a picnic in a garden overflowing with wildflowers. He particularly liked traditional dishes such as stuffed peppers and vanilla cream cake and prided himself on being a good dancer, especially waltzes. Capesius and a good friend, Roland Albert, together with nearly a dozen others, spent some spring and summer weekends swimming at a popular brook outside Sibu. In the fall they went hiking in the Hargitha Mountains. Capesius talked about the pretty German medical student, Friederike, he had met in Vienna. But if he was hoping to make a few of the town's girls jealous it did not work. Behind his back they gossiped about how hairy he was, "beefy and heavy," one even thought "he's got Gypsy blood in him."

They cringed when he occasionally broke into song since his voice was strong but dreadful. [10]

Although working at the family pharmacy was safe and comfortable, it was not very exciting. He started looking for work elsewhere. In February 1934 he landed a plum job as a national sales rep for Romigefa S. A., the Romanian holding company for Bayer, I. G. Farben's most prestigious drug subsidiary.[11] The previous month he and Fritzi had married and were eager to start a family. In fact, before the end of the year she was pregnant. Both saw in Farben far more opportunity for advancement than staying tethered to his uncle's pharmacy.

The German pharmaceutical firm that Capesius joined was the most dominant in the world in the 1930s. In fact, the modern pharmaceutical industry was virtually a German creation. It had its origins over a hundred years earlier in 1827 with a family-run Engel-Apotheke (Angel Pharmacy) in Darmstadt, Germany. Heinrich Emanuel Merck, the founder's great-great-grandson, isolated the pure alkaloids that were the chemical building blocks for many drugs, including codeine and cocaine. At the same time, Ernst Christian Friedrich Schering created Schering AG as a tiny producer of chemicals and a handful of medical compounds in Berlin. A few years later, Friedrich Bayer founded a factory in Wuppertal to make dyes from coal tar. Within a decade he had patented low-cost technologies to mass-produce them. When Bayer discovered his dyes had antiseptic qualities he sold them as medicines.

German scientists were responsible for nearly all early pharmaceutical breakthroughs. A 22-year-old pharmacist, Friedrich Sertürner, purified the active ingredient in the opium poppy and named it *Morpheus* after the Greek god of dreams. One of his pupils while working for Bayer added two acetyl groups in 1898 to the morphine molecule and developed heroin (from the German heroisch, or heroic). The following year that same chemist isolated salicylic acid and, after a spirited internal debate, Bayer trademarked its new drug *Aspirin*.

Capesius was proud that Farben/Bayer was unrivaled at the forefront of drug innovation. He proved a hardworking and loyal employee, earning an amiable reputation promoting the company's products to doctor's offices, pharmacies, and medical clinics throughout Transylvania. He even sold Farben's dyes and chemical products to textile manufacturers.[12]

World War II, as it did for most of his generation in central Europe, interrupted what in all likelihood would have been a successful if mundane career. Romania had been neutral in 1939 when the Nazis invaded Poland. But the following year, in November 1940, it aligned itself with the Third Reich after a successful coup by an ironfisted fascist, Marshall Ion Victor Antonescu. After Hitler invaded the Soviet Union in June 1941, many Romanian troops were sequestered to do his dirty work there.

Capesius was fortunate. When the army ordered him back to duty he was posted briefly to a hospital pharmacy at Cernavodă in eastern Romania, not far from the Black Sea.[13] His major disappointment in being called to service was that it separated him from his three daughters, six-year-old Melitta, four-year-old Ingrid and one-year-old Christa. In January 1942 he was promoted to captain and, for reasons not made clear in his military records, he was granted leave to restart his civilian Farben/Bayer job. He traveled so much that at times he lived in both Klausenburg and Sighisoara before finally buying a sixth-floor condominium on Brezoiano Street in an upper-class Bucharest neighborhood. He moved his family there and his earnings were sizable enough that he invested spare cash into a modern apartment on Dr. Marcovici Street. Capesius was a regular at the city's best business clubs and a familiar fixture on the social scene.[14]

Although the frontline fighting had not reached Romania, there were signs of war everywhere, especially at the large railway hubs. Tens of thousands of German and Axis troops passed through them on their way to fight in Russia. It seemed odd, thought Capesius, that the trains headed east packed with soldiers but returned empty. There was no leave for anyone on the Eastern Front.

The country in which Capesius was raised and worked was caught up in the fervor of National Socialism. Its leaders and institutions had not only embraced Fascism but they were completely seduced by Hitler's virulently anti-Semitic ideology. During his rise to power, Hitler had blamed an "international Jewish cabal" for enslaving Germany after its World War I loss and said the country would only be great again if it was free of Jews. That inflammatory scapegoating played well in satellite countries like Romania, places that hoped to mimic Hitler and his muscular way of governing in order to boost their stature in Europe. Romanian Christians were susceptible to this demagoguery since many believed that Jews were Christ killers who exercised outsized influence on their own economies.

Capesius's Transylvania was home to one of Europe's oldest Jewish communities, tracing its roots back to 87AD. It had suffered historically from surges of anti-Semitism. Intermarriage between Jews and Christians was banned in the eleventh century. During the fifteenth and sixteenth centuries, Jews were barred from living in its major cities. In the second half of the eighteenth century, the ruling Hapsburgs imposed a series of draconian taxes on Jews and forced them into ghettoes. False rumors that Jews killed Christian babies for religious rituals spread like wildfire, sparking government sponsored pogroms and widespread vigilante violence. When the Russians conquered Transylvania in the nineteenth century, the invaders brought their own Slavic brand of anti-Semitism, including the idea that Jews were part of an alien race.

Although much of Europe had benefited from the liberalizing political and social theories that swept eastward after the French Revolution in 1789, Transylvania seemed somehow insusceptible toward modernizing its views of Jews. In 1866, a new constitution declared that only Christians were citizens and the legal and property rights of the country's stateless Jews were further curtailed. In 1940, Marshall Antonescu began *Romanization*, a program similar to Hitler's Aryanization. All Jewish capital was confiscated and distributed to Romanians in furtherance of the regime's goal to expel all Jews.

Some of Capesius's mentors and close friends were enthusiastic backers of the new hatred. A science teacher Capesius had "revered" embraced the National Socialist view that ethnic Germans had to be protected from "inferior peoples."[15] Roland Albert, Capesius's friend, had joined a neo-fascist militia when Antonescu took control in 1940.[16] And he soon parroted the harshest sentiments disparaging not just Jews but also the country's Gypsies and Armenians. "A regrettably high percentage of town fools, village idiots, and weaklings of various kinds were polluting our bloodlines," said Albert. [17]

In the new Romania, friends sometimes even had disagreements about seemingly innocuous matters. Albert recalled once that he and Capesius went to an attic where there was a gramophone. "Have you got anything classical," Albert asked. "Schubert or Beethoven?"

"No, I'd rather hear the Charleston or Strauss's waltzes," Capesius told him.

"Philistine," Albert said in earnest.[18] He later told a journalist that those songs "reveal the essential difference between us and the Jew. . . . All that jazz, that American 'asphalt music; they are poisoning the world . . . this nigger music."[19]

There is no evidence whether or not the young Capesius, crisscrossing the country for Farben/Bayer, embraced the prejudices of his teachers or friends. From the cultural and historical setting in which an ethnic German like Capesius was raised, educated, lived, and worked, a denigrating view of Jews was the best that might be hoped for. He later claimed that, "I was never hostile toward the Jews."[20]

Whatever his true feelings, he wisely put business first. Two of his early Farben supervisors were Jewish, but they had to leave the firm in 1939 because of the Nuremberg [race] Law.[21] Many of the doctors, pharmacists, clinicians, and factory owners that Capesius serviced for Farben/Bayer were Jewish. None reported him ever showing any overt sign of anti-Semitism.

In fact, Capesius's Jewish customers were undoubtedly a profitable part of his client list. His single-minded focus on making money trumped any hesitations he might have had about them being

Jews. When Josef Glück, a Jewish textile manufacturer, complained directly to Farben's Frankfurt headquarters about delays in deliveries of colorants he had ordered, Capesius visited him. He personally fixed the snags and then closely supervised the account to ensure Glück was satisfied moving forward. Capesius also went out of his way repeatedly to replenish the stock at short notice of one of his biggest customers, Albert Ehrenfeld, a Jewish pharmaceutical wholesaler. And he made a special effort to keep two Jewish physicians, Dr. Gisela Böhm and Dr. Mauritius Berner, informed about new drugs in Bayer's pipeline.[22]

Capesius's Farben job kept him free from the growing war against the Jews in his native country. But this changed in the spring of 1943 when, thanks to Allied bombers having the range to finally reach Romania, the Nazis accelerated their conscription of ethnic Germans (Volksdeutsche). Capesius's eighteen-month interlude as a Farben/Bayer rep ended.

Capesius was not totally surprised when he was called up on August 1, 1943, for service in the German army.[23] Only a few months earlier the Russians had turned the tide at the war's bloodiest battle, Stalingrad, and he and many contemporaries thought it only a matter of time before Soviet troops advanced towards Romania and the rest of Eastern Europe. Karl Heinz Schuleri, a classmate of Capesius who had served with him in the Romanian army, recalled that many of them were not happy with being drafted by the Germans.[24] Capesius, however, was in a minority since he had a low opinion of the Romanian army and thought it "more honorable" to serve directly for Germany.[25]

Fritzi was not as happy. Typical of many wives, she was grateful so long as he was in the reserves and far away from the front lines. But with his induction into the German army she feared he might soon see combat. Her fear was that she might become another war widow raising her three daughters, then ages 8, 6 and 3, alone.[26] That concern prompted her to move with them from Bucharest back to Sighisoara, where they lived with Capesius's cousins.[27]

Capesius was not worried about whether he would soon be in combat. He instead concentrated on proving his Aryan ancestry back to the eighteenth century, qualifying him for a six-week training with the Waffen-SS (the SS's combat unit). He wisely did not mention that Fritzi, by the Nazi interpretation of religion as blood, was half Jewish.[28]

"Because the SS tailor shop had been bombed," Capesius later recalled, "we waited around six weeks for our uniforms to be finished at the police tailor. A very pleasant six weeks in civilian clothes, lots of theater and cabaret. And we lived in the Hotel Zentral with its enclosed garden."[29]

On completing his training he received the rank of Hauptsturmführer (captain) and was given the permanent mark of SS status, a small black ink tattoo, near his left armpit, that indicated his blood type.[30] Once the uniforms arrived, Capesius said the recruits "were scattered to the four winds."[31] He and a dozen other ethnic Germans from Romania were dispatched to the SS Central Medical Station in Warsaw.[32] From there he served brief stints as a pharmacist in the SS medical dispensaries at two concentration camps outside Berlin and Munich, Sachsenhausen and Dachau. They were established for political prisoners but as the war progressed held ever-larger numbers of Jews. Although conditions were brutal at both, neither was an extermination center. Capesius, with his Bayer pedigree, was a natural pick since Farben ran all the camp dispensaries.

Capesius knew that ethnic Germans like him from Yugoslavia, Bulgaria, and other central and eastern European countries were considered "second class Germans" by Himmler and the top Nazis. "We had an inferiority complex about the Germans from the Reich, the real Germans," noted his friend Roland Albert.[33] What Capesius did not know then was that view among the SS elite meant that ethnic Germans got some of the least desirable postings, translating to disproportionate numbers assigned to the concentration camps.[34]

It was at Dachau that a physician, Colonel Enno Lolling, took a liking to Capesius. A former morphine addict who had been a concentration camp doctor for seven years, Lolling was the chief of Medical Services and Camp Hygiene by the time he met Capesius.

That meant he was responsible for all SS physicians at all the concentration camps.

Lolling had an obsession with the macabre. He had ordered hundreds of human skins with tattoos be gathered at concentration camps. Inmates who had tattoos judged collectible were killed with injections of phenol to the heart and their skin carefully removed and dried before being sent to Lolling in parcels marked "War Materials – Urgent." He forwarded some specimens to Berlin's Kaiser Wilhelm Institute, the Third Reich's preeminent research center on "Racial Hygiene" and the emerging discipline of eugenics. But the best samples he converted into ghoulish gifts such as wallets and cigar cases for his fellow officers.[35] Lolling even instructed SS physicians at the German concentration camp, Buchenwald, to research how to shrink human heads, one of his morbid fascinations. They scoured books about the practice from South Seas cannibals and Central American Indians, but their breakthrough came in a text about techniques aboriginal headhunters used to master the art. Of some 30 prisoners who were killed for their heads at Buchenwald, only three were successfully shrunk to the size of an apple (one of which the camp commandant used as a paperweight).[36]

In November 1943, Lolling informed Capesius that he was to be transferred to Auschwitz. Capesius knew that while the Germans had hundreds of concentration camps, Auschwitz was on its own for its grand size and brutal reputation. While serving at Dachau and Sachsenhausen he had learned about the notorious group of camps that operated under the single name *Auschwitz* some thirty miles west of Kraków. It had started in April 1940 as a backwater penal camp. Dilapidated military barracks at the edge of a small town – Oswiecim in Polish, Auschwitz in German – were converted to a prison camp. A year later it had 10,000 prisoners, almost all Polish political dissidents.[37] That was when I. G. Farben decided to build Monowitz only four miles to the east. Since the SS wanted to supply Farben with laborers it ordered an expansion of the original camp, tripling the number of inmates to more than 35,000.

The camp's grim reputation, however, was the result of two subsequent and independent events. The Nazi invasion of the Soviet Union in June 1941 had proved a spectacular early success. In only a few months, the Germans had nearly 1.5 million Russian POWs and needed places to put them.[38] So SS Chief Heinrich Himmler ordered the construction of an enormous second camp a mile away at the nearby village of Brzezinka, which the Germans called Birkenau. Located on the other side of the main railway line, it was intended to hold up to 200,000 POWs, many of whom were to be put to work for Farben, Krupp, Siemens, and other German companies that were clamoring to open satellite work camps fueled by slave labor. But the plan that Birkenau would be only a giant POW camp was short lived. By January 1942 the Nazis had decided officially on the Final Solution, their plan to murder all the Jews of Europe. It prompted the Nazis to create extermination camps elsewhere inside Poland – Treblinka, Majdanek, Chelmno and Sobibor. But those were not capable of killing fast enough the millions of Jews living in Nazi conquered nations. So Birkenau was remodeled as both a camp for laborers as well as a death camp, with its own state of the art gas chambers.

Capesius knew that Auschwitz, as it had morphed into its hybrid status as a penal, work and death camp, was unlike any other. It was also where SS doctors and German pharma companies had the largest number of human guinea pigs on which to test lab drugs in chilling medical experiments. By the time Capesius was told of his transfer there, the SS technically referred to the original camp, now mostly administrative, as Auschwitz I; Birkenau was Auschwitz II; and Monowitz was Auschwitz III.

According to Lolling, Adolf Krömer, Auschwitz's pharmacist since 1941, urgently needed a competent assistant. Krömer had joined the SS in 1933 and as a result had a prestigious low membership number. Notwithstanding his good pedigree, Krömer was evidently not capable of carrying out his full duties without help. What Lolling did not share with Capesius was that Krömer was losing a battle against depression.

Capesius did not want to go to the place that SS physician Heinz Thilo had called the "anus mundi" (asshole of the world).[39] He tried circumventing Lolling by lobbying a Dachau friend, Captain Dr. Hermann Josef Becker. Becker ran the SS Department for Aviation Medicine, responsible for brutal high altitude/low pressure experiments conducted on camp inmates, ostensibly to develop better flight equipment for German airmen. Becker was also a respected Nazi party member and had clout with Berlin. Capesius said he preferred to stay at Dachau. "I like it there," especially since the camp "was well run."[40] But Becker was unable to help.[41]

Capesius arrived at Auschwitz in December, just as the first snowstorm blanketed the camp. Dachau and Sachsenhausen might have been eye openers for the Romanian pharmacist but Capesius's baptism of fire was yet to come.

Chapter 5

WELCOME TO AUSCHWITZ

Capesius reported for duty to Dr. Eduard Wirths, a 34-year-old SS captain who was in charge of Auschwitz's 20 physicians. At the time, those doctors were responsible for everything from attending to the health of the camp's SS personnel to keeping alive the forced laborers to overseeing medical experiments. Capesius had learned from his colleagues at Dachau that Wirths was unlike any other doctor with whom he had served. An ardent Nazi, Wirths had fought on the Eastern Front but after a mild heart attack in 1942 recuperated by serving as the chief psychiatrist at the Neuengamme concentration camp outside Hamburg. After three months he was dispatched as the chief doctor to Auschwitz.

Capesius had heard that Wirths was consumed by research into both mass sterilization and cervical cancer. What he did not then know was that in pursuing those obsessions Wirths had authorized experiments on hundreds of female inmates, destroying their ovaries with radiation or removing them through crude surgery, resulting in an 80% death rate. Wirths' younger brother, Helmut, a noted Hamburg gynecologist, went to Auschwitz in 1943 to join in with the experiments, but the younger Wirths was so revolted at what he saw that he quickly left after an explosive argument with his brother.

Wirths was also passionate about eradicating typhus (spotted fever), a disease that infected not only the SS guards and overseers but also killed thousands of half-starved prisoners and had proved resistant to all efforts to control it. Wirths rolled out aggressive programs to delouse the barracks and inmates from lice and other pests that easily spread the disease in the pervasive unhygienic camp conditions. It evidently did not seem odd to Wirths that many of the inmates he worked hard to save from the scourge of typhus were likely to end up in the gas chambers.

Capesius knew Wirths had a reputation for eccentricity. He liked riding around in a car sporting Red Cross flags, his way of mocking the international aid organization that occasionally inquired about conditions in concentration camps. As a leftover of his two-month stint as an untrained psychiatrist at Neuengamme, Wirths provided free-of-charge marital and stress counseling to Auschwitz's SS personnel.

Six months before Capesius's arrival, Wirths had made a change that forever altered the history of Auschwitz and how future generations would judge the physicians who served there. Until early 1943, SS men appointed by Rudolf Höss, Auschwitz's commandant – a convicted murderer – performed the life and death selections of newly arrived inmates at the railhead. Most new prisoners deemed unfit for labor – including the elderly, children and pregnant women – were automatically directed to the left, which meant death in the gas chambers (ultimately 1.1 million of the 1.5 million deported to Auschwitz died immediately). However, since the workers inside the camp died at a fast rate from malnutrition, beatings, disease and executions, there was a constant need to replace them.

Those spared at the ramp were tattooed on their forearms in order to identify and keep track of them (Auschwitz was the only camp that did this). Beyond those assigned to Monowitz, forced laborers also worked as carpenters, electricians, barbers, and in the kitchen. Sometimes, under armed guard outside the camp, they were put to work in rock quarries, digging tunnels, shoveling snow from roads, and clearing debris from air raids. Women were mostly put to work sorting through the tons of personal goods taken from the arriving prisoners, preparing anything of value for shipment back to Germany. Some women were made to work as sex slaves. Medical professionals were often spared death and then assigned to perform some of the most gruesome tasks as inmate assistants to the SS doctors, pharmacists and dentists. Prisoner dentists were forced to pry the gold from the mouth of corpses. And the most able-bodied men who were selected to live were often assigned to the Sonderkommando, the prisoners with the ghastly responsibility of pulling the dead from the gas chambers.

Wirths wanted the selections of arriving inmates at the railhead to be under his control. As far as he was concerned, only physicians should make the life and death decisions. If Auschwitz was an unprecedented opportunity to advance Nazi science, Wirths contended, the doctors had to personally pick their own guinea pigs. That view had been reinforced by the arrival that spring of Dr. Josef Mengele, a decorated thirty-two-year-old veteran of the Eastern Front. Mengele was a protégé of Dr. Otmar Freiherr von Verschuer, one of Europe's leading geneticists at the forefront of the Nazi racial pseudo-science. While a medical student, Mengele had served as von Verschuer's favorite research assistant at the esteemed University of Frankfurt's Third Reich Institute for Heredity, Biology and Racial Purity.

Mengele's work with von Verschuer had put him at the epicenter of an emerging Nazi scientific philosophy that thought it possible to select, engineer, enhance, and thereby "purify" humans.[1] In his research, von Verschuer devoted most of his efforts to studying twins. He was by then the chief of Berlin's preeminent Kaiser Wilhelm Institute for Anthropology, Human Hereditary Teaching and Genetics. It was von Verschuer who influenced Mengele's appointment to Auschwitz and secured funding for some medical experiments. An inmate physician at the camp, Ella Lingens, who worked under Mengele, later concluded: "Under the leadership of Otmar von Verschuer, the final, fatal consequences of race-based science and research were revealed, to which, under National Socialism, there were no limits."[2]

Mengele wasted no time once he got to the camp. What he needed for his research were twins. Lots of them. But finding them among the thousands of exhausted, dirty and disorganized arriving prisoners was not something, he told Wirths, that could be left to the untrained eye of ordinary SS guards. This was further reason, thought Wirths, of why medical oversight of the selections was critical.

All the camp doctors, even Wirths, were assigned to perform the selections in round-the-clock shifts. Two physicians greeted each arriving train. Not all liked their new duties. Some, Hans König and Werner Röhde for example, got drunk. The notoriously sadistic Dr. Fritz Klein, Capesius later observed, "was mostly drunk." Another, Hans Münch, refused the assignment, was demoted, and delegated mostly to Farben's Monowitz camp where he processed blood samples. Dr. Johann Paul Kremer kept a daily diary during his several-month-long assignment at Auschwitz. He wrote that the camp made "Dante's inferno almost a comedy," and noted that "men compete to take part in such selections [because] they get additional rations – one fifth liter of vodka, 5 cigarettes, 100 grams of sausage and bread."[3]

Most doctors needed no extra incentive; for some it was simply their duty. But a few relished the "special actions." None more so than Mengele who even volunteered for extra shifts. It was at the railhead that he became the Nazi that tens of thousands of arriving prisoners first saw. The image of that immaculately dressed SS officer, occasionally whistling an operatic aria, carrying a polished riding crop with which he directed prisoners to the left and right, became an indelible memory for many of the camp's survivors.[4]

About 5,000 twins, many children, eventually passed through what inmates called Mengele's *zoo*, Barrack 14 of Camp F. There, he conducted some of the war's most gruesome experiments. Mengele had, as did the other SS physicians, a virtually unlimited supply of human "lab rats." His intent was to use them to unlock the secrets of twin births so that every good Aryan mother might have two children, helping to replenish quicker the German war dead. He was also curious about altering "inferior races," a quest to make gypsies and Jews look more Aryan. Mengele indulged any medical theory that piqued his curiosity, no matter how tenuous the science or cruel and deadly the procedure.

One time, an inmate, Vera Kriegel, was led into one of his lab rooms. She was stunned to see a wall covered with human eyeballs. "They were pinned up like butterflies," she later recalled. "I thought I was dead and already living in hell." Mengele sent those eyes to his mentor, von Verschuer, so that one of the professor's Berlin researchers could finish a paper about whether eye pigmentation was a useful biological racial marker.

Capesius then had no idea on his first day at the camp that his prewar employer, Farben/Bayer, funded many of the camp's medical experiments. Nor did he know that Farben also profited from Auschwitz's pioneering use of Zyklon B, a cyanide-based pesticide used to deadly effect in its gas chambers. Decades before anyone heard the name Auschwitz, Farben had purchased a controlling interest in the Zyklon B patent. Bayer was primarily responsible for sales and distribution.[5] It was originally used at Auschwitz to fumigate prisoner barracks and clothing. But it had assumed a more important and deadly role some eighteen months before Capesius reported for duty, when top SS officials and the Chiefs of Reich Ministries had met at a conference in the Berlin suburb of Wannsee. There they had planned how to coordinate the "Final Solution of the Jewish Question." The Nazis had abandoned all plans for expulsion and resettlement of European Jewry. SS chief Himmler summoned the camp commandant to Berlin and informed him that the Führer had given the order for complete extermination.[6] Shortly after the Wannsee Conference, Hitler gave one of his most infamous speeches on the fate of Europe's Jews. In a frenzied delivery, the Führer promised: "The Jews will be liquidated at least for a thousand years!"[7]

By this time, more than a million Jews had been killed by mobile firing squads (Einsatzgruppen), mostly in Poland, Ukraine and Russia. At the Chelmno camp northwest of Warsaw in September 1941, Jews had been gassed with carbon monoxide fed into specially constructed vans. At other early death camps in Poland such as Treblinka, Belzec and Sobibor, the Nazis also relied mostly on carbon monoxide, usually delivering it by diesel engines to sealed rooms. But at Auschwitz the technology of mass murder had advanced. After much experimentation Höss and his staff settled on Zyklon B. Its inexpensive bluish gray granules turned into a deadly gas when exposed to air. The first fully functional gas chamber at Auschwitz began operating in March 1942, only a month after Hitler had promised to liquidate the continent's Jews.

The patents for Zyklon B's chemical formula were held by a German company, Degesch (Deutsche Gesellschaft für

Schädlingsbekämpfung – German Corporation for Pest Control). Farben owned 42.5% of Degesch and controlled its executive board. Degesch's wartime chairman was a Farben director.[8] The company also had a separate patent on an eye irritant it added to Zyklon B, a way to warn people of the presence of the otherwise colorless and poisonous gas.

Kurt Gerstein, the SS's chief of its Technical Disinfection Division, insisted Degesch remove the warning irritant from all Zyklon B sold to the SS. When Degesch executives resisted, afraid that they might open themselves to generic competition, Gerstein shared the grisly details of how their product was used as the preferred killing agent. It was necessary, he informed them, to remove the irritant so that those about to be gassed would have no last minute warning that might cause mass panic. Instead of recoiling in horror that the SS wanted their insecticide to kill upwards of several million people, the Degesch executives agreed to remove the warning irritant and ramped up production to record levels. (It was around the time of the first large SS orders of Zyklon B that Gerstein, haunted by gruesome images of a botched gassing of 800 Jews by carbon monoxide, confessed to a German bishop the details of the Nazi mass murder underway in Eastern Europe. It was the first time a ranking SS officer had confirmed the Final Solution. Gerstein's confession was sent to the Vatican by sealed diplomatic pouch and stayed a secret through the war).[9]

Starting in 1942, as a result of the enormous orders from the SS, Degesch's profits from Zyklon B soared. Auschwitz alone ordered a stunning 23 tons of the insecticide. In 1943, Zyklon B accounted for a remarkable 70% of Degesch's earnings.

On his first day at Auschwitz, Capesius was yet to learn about the ingrained role of Zyklon B. Wirths gave him only a perfunctory overview of the camp. His full introduction to his medical role was left to Dr. Adolf Krömer at the pharmaceutical dispensary. That was the spot Capesius would call home for the rest of the war.

It did not take Capesius long to determine that the problem with his new boss was far more than a mild depression. Krömer, in fact, seemed on the verge of a mental breakdown. Although some doctors, including Wirths and Mengele, flourished at Auschwitz, a few were overwhelmed by the unending barbarity. Krömer was evidently one. An inmate pharmacist, Jan Sikorski, confided to Capesius that Krömer had said, "The war can no longer be won."[10] Capesius refused to believe that Krömer would be so foolish to say something so reckless to a prisoner, so he confronted Krömer.

"Yes, that was me," Krömer admitted.

Capesius soon discovered that Krömer talked loosely to many of the inmates working at the dispensary. "Your eyes will pop out of your heads, this is Sodom and Gomorrah," Krömer warned Capesius. "The inferno in the underworld is nothing compared to this." [11]

Capesius was at Auschwitz less than two months when Krömer was arrested, tried in a summary proceeding, and executed for "spreading defeatism." In a postwar account, Capesius gave a banal description of the tumultuous events: "I was detailed to Auschwitz by Sturmbannführer Lolling, since the pharmacist at the SS dispensary there, Dr. Krömer, had become ill. . . . I reported to the garrison doctor, Dr. Wirths, at Auschwitz. Dr. Krömer received me in the SS dispensary. Then he went into sick bay and died on February 18, 1944. I was appointed to succeed him." (In 2010, during the renovation of a private home near Auschwitz, a cache of original camp documents was discovered. Among them was Krömer's death certificate. The SS, not wanting to advertise that it had to execute one of its senior officers, innocuously listed his cause of death as a "heart attack.")[12]

Capesius was proud of his promotion as the chief pharmacist. After the war he would claim that "the horrible things" he had seen at the camp were "depressing, it makes you want to vomit. You feel like you will puke any second. At first. Then you get used to it."[13] But he never showed any hesitation or indicated any discomfort to his colleagues. In fact, they admired that Capesius seemed free of the second thoughts and guilty conscience that had smothered his predecessor. He was determined to make the most of his service at the largest Nazi death camp.

Chapter 6

THE DISPENSARY

Capesius's living quarters were in a wooden barrack near the officer's mess. He shared that space with most of the physicians, including Josef Mengele and Fritz Klein, with whom he struck early friendships. Capesius's workplace was the dispensary in Block 9 of the original Auschwitz camp, part of an autonomous network of SS hospitals and clinics. The first infirmary was built in 1940. The medical group had since added wards for prisoners, consultation and outpatient clinics for the SS, a dental suite, as well as the dispensing pharmacy. The hospital, nicknamed by inmates as a "waiting room for the crematorium," had started as a single large room.[1] By the time Capesius arrived, it had grown to occupy four block buildings, including one set aside solely for medical experiments.[2]

"The SS dispensary was located in a brick building outside the main camp area of Auschwitz," Capesius recalled after the war. "The building had a ground floor, a second floor, and an attic. The dispensary was on the ground floor, where there was also a room in which the medications and equipment arriving on the ramp at Birkenau were sorted through. Sometimes there were medical instruments as well. These items were meant exclusively for prisoners. This task was my responsibility, but the actual work was performed by the Polish inmate pharmacist named [Jan] Sikorski."[3] Sikorski, a long-serving prisoner, had arrived in June 1941.[4]

Capesius worked from a spacious ground floor office. It was spartan, three bare metal tables, a few chairs, and some filing cabinets and storage boxes stacked along the back wall. He shared the room with the dispensary's bookkeeper. An adjoining office was for his inmate pharmacist assistants. A third room to the rear was for the garrison physician and camp dentists. A small infirmary on the second floor had six beds for SS patients. And the top floor, an angled attic, was where medications and personal items taken from arriving prisoners were stored.[5]

"My job as Apotheker [pharmacist]," recalled Capesius, "was to order the medical supplies needed for SS personnel and prisoners from the central medical station in Berlin, by this I mean the central station of the Waffen-SS. And I had to order supplies for the main camp at Auschwitz and all the auxiliary camps, including Birkenau and Monowitz."[6]

Capesius kept medications he ordered in the basement. It was also where a thousand cans of the pesticide DDT, sent by the Red Cross for delousing, were stored. The basement had separate showers and lockers, as well as a barbershop, available only to the SS medical corps.

"I had about twelve prisoners working for me in the SS dispensary," recalled Capesius. "Except for the bookkeeper, all the prisoners were pharmacists of various types."

Sikorski, Capesius's chief assistant, oversaw the other inmate pharmacists. "I was a kind of Oberhäftling, a supervising prisoner," Sikorski later recalled. "The command was too small for a Kapo (a prisoner foreman). Sometimes they called me that, Kapo."

The office contained prisoners from all over Europe, what German writer Bernd Naumann called "a motley cast assembled by fate on the stage of death of Auschwitz."[7]

"Besides me there was a German Jew from Silesia working there named Strauch," recalled Sikorski. "He had been a school chum of the pharmacist Krömer before the war. There was also a bookkeeper named Berliner, an old man. And two women from Hungary, I only know their first names, Piroska and Éva. And then a well-built, good-looking young pharmacist from Transylvania, Grosz, also a Jew. And also a Greek, Aaron was his name. And another Hungarian, a big fat guy, Altmann. I think he was a wine merchant by profession. From Poland there were two more druggists, Prokop and Jozef Gorzkowski from Kraków. And two more pharmacists, Szewczyk and Swiderski. There was also a short, young assistant, Sulikowksi. He was a colleague of my brother's, that's how I knew him.

"People spoke in Polish, Russian, Hungarian, but also German and Yiddish, and also this special prisoners' language, the so-called lagerszpracha of Auschwitz. . . . Our pharmacist Capesius, the boss, acted as though he wasn't listening when his prisoners were talking lagerszpracha."[8] Besides calling him *boss*, behind his back, the prisoners called the 5' 10", 200-pound Capesius *Mopsel* (pug-face or tubby).[9]

In the Nazi bureaucracy Sikorski did not report directly to Capesius but instead to several SS officers who were also pharmacists and shared an adjoining office. One was Sergeant Kurt Jurasek, another First Lieutenant Gerhard Gerber, and the third was Boleslaw Frymark.

The dispensary was responsible for servicing all the sprawling Auschwitz complex. While Monowitz had a separate pharmacy, it ordered medicines and supplies monthly from Capesius. If he ran short, a specialist pharmacy on Józefińska Street in Kraków supplied temporary provisions.

Capesius focused first on having enough medicine for the SS. Yet in the bizarre world of Auschwitz, prisoners who had been spared at the railhead and were assigned to work details or used as guinea pigs in medical experiments were supposed to be treated as long as the SS wanted them alive. Given the constraints on medical supplies during wartime, however, there were few medications left over for prisoners. Ludwig Wörl, a German inmate nurse, charged that Capesius deliberately refused to set aside *any* of his medical supplies for sick prisoners. In that way, "he had many thousands of deaths on his conscience."[10]

Whether denying medications to inmates was a sadistic strategy or simply a result of making the SS personnel his top priority, what is indisputable is that many prisoners who were not immediately gassed died from treatable illnesses. The medications that would have extended their lives never found their way out of Capesius's pharmacy.

Shortly after becoming the chief pharmacist, Capesius decided to do a complete inventory of the dispensary since "it had not been turned over to my command in an orderly fashion."[11] That revealed a significant shortfall of essential medicines.

"Prior to then, medications and instruments were always being stolen in 'Canada'," said Sikorski, referring to the nickname for the large warehouses at Birkenau where all the personal belongings of arriving Jews were stored. The Polish prisoners considered 'Canada' a faraway land of riches. "The dispensary got only the very worst. For that reason, Dr. Capesius went to the commandant's office and got official permission to collect the suitcases himself."[12]

So several times a week Capesius's driver took him and two inmate assistants to the railhead ramp in Birkenau. Capesius described what he saw: "The apparatus of extermination ran smoothly. The staging and running of the transports was carefully prepared. The camp commanders were notified of the arrival of a transport via telegrams and radio messages, and they would then give further instructions to the detention camp leaders, the Political Department, the office of the SS garrison doctor, the truck drivers' unit, the guard detachment, and the work deployment office. Each one of these units involved with the 'handling' of a transport had a specific duty roster for its operation in 'special actions' on the unloading ramp."[13]

By the time Capesius arrived at the ramp, thousands of prisoners had been pulled off the trains. Each had been allowed to take 50 kilos of belongings for the journey, most of it their treasured items bundled into cloth sacks. All those personal goods were stockpiled onto an enormous clearing along the edge of the track. Capesius's duty was to be on the lookout for instruments belonging to doctors, dentists or pharmacists, as well as medications, particularly sulfamidic powder for wounds and iodine, both of which were in short supply. An SS security policeman usually conducted the search under Capesius's direction. Because those goods belonged to newly arriving prisoners many of whom were immediately gassed, no inventory was made.[14]

Sometimes Capesius said he found enough drugs to "stock a pharmacy."[15] He took everything back to the dispensary. "There we presorted and stored the luggage of those doctors and pharmacists arriving in the Jewish transports. . . . I poured the contents of any containers that bore a coded number or an illegible label out into a zinc vat. Anything still in its original container, or whose pharmaceutical effects were especially powerful, or whose effects I was not completely sure of, I kept in a large white crate in the basement. This crate was secured with two locks."[16]

Medications from the arriving prisoners were not all Capesius stashed in his dispensary. Phenolic acid, used by some SS physicians to kill prisoners, was also stored there. Sikorski later recalled that Capesius, who signed all requisition forms, was solely responsible for all orders from Berlin of *phenol pro injectione* (phenol by injection).[17] Ludwig Wörl, the inmate nurse, estimated that some 20,000 inmates were killed by phenol injections to the heart. In those instances, doctors wanted to obtain organ specimens from cadavers that were undamaged. Many of the injections were administered by a medic, sergeant Josef Klehr (after the war Klehr claimed that was "the biggest slander ever heard" and that he had only killed – "on orders of course" – 250 to 300 prisoners with phenol injections).[18]

But there was an even deadlier item at the dispensary under Capesius's control. One day a box arrived from Berlin. When Sikorski opened it he found it crammed with round can openers with sharp metal prongs.[19] He soon learned they had been designed to facilitate opening canisters of Zyklon B while minimizing the risk of the poisonous pellets spilling out.

Not long after the can openers arrived, a group of SS officers showed up at the dispensary with a shipment of sealed brown cartons from Berlin. Those contained dozens of 500-gram canisters of Zyklon B. Capesius, who by now was fully aware of how Zyklon B was used at Auschwitz, told Sikorski that he "wanted nothing to do with it."[20] Capesius's hesitation was not because he objected to the poison or its deadly deployment, but rather that he simply did not want the responsibility for such a lethal inventory. Handling all the camp's pharmacy needs had stretched him to his limit. He would have preferred returning it to the main administration but that was impossible. Instead, dozens of cartons containing the poisonous insecticide were placed into yellow cupboards in a locked bunker – that had earlier served as one of Auschwitz's crematoriums – directly across from the dispensary.[21] Other items kept there, according to

Capesius, included "petrol, creolin, carbolic acid, calcium chloride, and possibly other liquids in wicker bottles."[22]

The keys to that bunker were under Capesius's control, locked away in one of his desk drawers where he also kept keys for all the rooms in the dispensary. When anyone from the SS wanted to get into one of those spaces, protocol demanded that they sign out the keys from Capesius.[23]

Although Capesius later denied having any role with Zyklon B, several witnesses put him and the pesticide together: According to Dr. Władysław Fejkiel, an early 1940 prisoner, "the camp pharmacist was in charge of the poison gas."[24] Nurse Ludwig Wörl confirmed that Capesius was responsible for the "storing, distribution, and application" of the Zyklon B.[25] Pharmacist Szewczyk saw some of the Zyklon B canisters in the dispensary's basement. SS officers Kurt Jurasek and Tadeusz Dobrzanski told him that Capesius had ordered them to retrieve the poison canisters and bring them to the gas chambers.[26]

Worse still, according to an account by Fritz Peter Strauch, a Jewish inmate pharmacist who was one of Capesius's most trusted assistants, the Zyklon B Capesius stored had no warning agents or labeling. It was the batch made by Degesch only for gassing humans.[27]

But Capesius was more than simply the key holder to the storage room for the poison. Other witnesses saw him play a much more direct role in the murder machinery by personally transporting the deadly pesticide to the gas chambers. Zdzislaw Mikolajski, a Polish political prisoner, once saw Capesius, and the SS dentists, Drs. Frank and Schatz, load cartons of Zyklon B into an ambulance and pack their own gas masks, before heading off to Birkenau and the gas chambers.[28]

Mikolajski's account was corroborated by two other witnesses. One, in a twist of fate, was Roland Albert, Capesius's childhood friend. Albert had also been posted to Auschwitz and was an SS Lieutenant in charge of a guard unit. He once witnessed an incident when a truck with Red Cross markings was parked near the gas chambers.

"Dr. Capesius and SS Sergeant Major Josef Klehr get out," recalled Albert. "Klehr has four green tin canisters in his hand. They both cross over the green strip of grass to the gas chamber, climb up onto the roof, put on their gas masks, and then Klehr lifts up the little trap door, but only after Capesius has given him the order to do so, because it has to be an SS doctor who gives the killing orders. Klehr breaks the seal on the canister, and shakes out the coarsely granulated contents, a violet-colored, crumbly mass, into the opening. The Zyklon B."[29]

On another occasion, Dov Paisikovic, assigned to the Sonderkommando, also saw Capesius arrive at a crematorium in a Red Cross truck. When he walked up to the gas chamber, SS Corporal Karl-Fritz Steinberg, a gas mask dangling from his hand, asked:

"Where is the canister? Where is the Zyklon?'

"I brought only one," Capesius said.

Steinberg started yelling at him to bring a second quickly.

"The people were in the gas chamber, not yet gassed," recalled Paisikovic.

Any delay in gassing these Jews would throw off the day's carefully timed killing schedule. Capesius ordered his driver to hurriedly fetch another Zyklon canister from the pharmacy dispensary. When the second canister arrived, Steinberg waited for Capesius to give the order before dropping in the pellets.

Each crematorium had a built-in gas chamber. At crematoriums I and II, Zyklon was fed into pipes that dropped into the sealed chamber whereas at Crematoriums III and IV, the SS had to climb a ladder and pour the pellets through a small window. When Paisikovic was asked after the war, "How often did you see Capesius at the crematorium?" he did not hesitate: "Many times."[30]

Despite his denials that he had any role in the gas chambers or crematoriums, in his postwar notes Capesius revealed an emotionless in-depth knowledge about them.

"According to the technical design the crematoriums were capable of incinerating 4,756 bodies a day. But this was really only a theoretical value, which included time for maintenance and the cleaning of the furnaces. In fact, up to 5,000 corpses were burned per day in Crematoriums II and III, and up to 3,000 in Crematoriums IV and V. The capacity of the pyres by the bunkers was unlimited. In the summer of 1944 during the deportations of the Hungarian Jews, the SS took over the operation of Bunker II again. In this period up to 24,000 people per day could be killed and incinerated. The ashes of the dead were used as fertilizer on the fields, for filling in swampland, or were simply dumped into the neighboring rivers and ponds. Mostly into the Soła River, which flowed right by."[31]

Wilhelm Prokop described after the war how he once overheard his boss talk about possibly using smaller amounts of poison gas to kill Jews.[32] One day Capesius went into the bunker where the Zyklon B was kept, accompanied by Sergeants Josef Klehr and Kurt Jurasek. Klehr was Auschwitz's chief SS officer in charge of the euphemistically dubbed Disinfection Command. At considerable risk, Prokop stood outside a slightly ajar door. Capesius ordered Klehr to get ready to receive "a great many canisters [of Zyklon B]." They were needed, said Capesius, since a "larger operation" was planned that day. The Zyklon B stock was always carefully monitored lest the camp run short. To stretch the existing inventory of the poison, and to reduce expenses since each canister cost five Reichsmarks (about $2), the SS had begun experimenting with using less at the gassings. Instead of the twenty canisters needed to kill upwards of 2,000 prisoners, the SS dropped the number to fifteen. No one seemed bothered that it extended by a stomach-wrenching twenty minutes the time for the last few to die.

One day, when Capesius ran into Dr. Miklós Nyiszli, a Romanian inmate physician who worked for Dr. Mengele, he learned about the moment when the Nazis realized they had cut the Zyklon too much.[33]

"Klehr, who was in charge of the gassing commando, came barging into Nyiszli's room," Capesius later recounted, "and told him in a very excited way that a teen girl had been found still alive beneath the mountain of bodies in the gas chamber, that she was still moving. And Nyiszli went running with his doctor's bag into the gas chamber, and right there next to the wall – still half covered with bodies – was this girl, naked like the rest, but wonderfully beautiful, like an angel breathing her last, just lying there."[34]

Nyiszli recalled the dramatic next few minutes. "We freed her body from beneath the corpses. I carried the light body of this young girl to the room beside [the] gas chamber where the gas kommando men changed. I laid her on one of the benches. She must have been around fifteen. I took a syringe and gave this panting girl three injections, instantly, one after the other. The men covered her frigid body with their thick coats. Someone ran to the kitchen to fetch her some tea or soup to drink. Everyone wanted to help as if they were fighting for the life of their own child."[35]

When the Nazis discovered Nyiszli treating the girl, they feared if she told others "everything she experienced, where it happened and what she saw, the news would spread instantaneously throughout the camp."[36] It was too great a risk, they concluded. "The girl was led," recounts Nyiszli, "or rather carried, out into the anteroom, and there she was killed with a bullet in the back of the head."[37]

Eventually, in the waning days of Auschwitz, as the supplies of Zyklon B ran low, one witness recalled that commandant Rudolf Höss ordered that children no longer be gassed, instead they "should be burned to death [alive] on fires fed by bodies taken from the gas chambers and sprayed with gasoline."[38] The I. G. Farben camp at Monowitz had to step up its production of methanol supplies to help burn all the corpses.[39]

Prokop recalled "it was only later that I heard it had been such a large operation that, owing to lack of space in the incineration ovens, the bodies of the gassed victims were burned in trenches and on pyres. The burning of so many bodies in the open air caused an unpleasant sweetish smell to fill the whole area. So they tried to find a means to neutralize this smell. Jurasek, himself a pharmacist, was assigned to work on this problem. I suspect that he did it on Capesius's order. Jurasek asked me, since I was a pharmacist, what naphthalene (a pesticide) was used for. I explained to him that it was a substance that could neutralize unpleasant odors indoors and outdoors."[40]

Capesius was emotionless when tackling assignments such as "neutralizing the smell" from the burning corpses. For him, it was only a technical challenge. Prokop was not surprised that his boss never seemed to flinch when they talked about how to better mask the smell of death. "I saw him as a man to whom a prisoner was nothing but a cipher, whose only purpose was extinction."[41]

Chapter 7

"GET TO KNOW THE DEVIL"

One day, in early 1944, SS doctor Werner Röhde walked into Capesius's office. With him was Dr. Bruno Weber and four emaciated prisoners they had pulled from the hospital block. Röhde told Capesius he was assigned the duty of figuring out how to best spike coffee or tea in order to knock out a British agent that German intelligence had identified and planned to kidnap. Röhde needed morphine and Evipan, a short acting hypnotic barbiturate. He knew both drugs could be fatal since they caused a rapid drop in blood pressure. In fact, another Auschwitz physician, Dr. Herta Oberhauser, regularly used Evipan injections to kill children in her lab before removing their organs or limbs for shipment to a genetic testing center in Berlin. (When Oberhauser was later transferred to the Ravensbrück camp she specialized in simulating combat wounds on inmates, using glass, nails and screwdrivers to inflict the lacerations. Shockingly, she served only a seven-year sentence after the war before opening a medical practice in Germany).

Röhde wanted to be certain there was no risk of killing the British agent. Capesius dispensed the morphine and Evipan. After all four inmates were given large doses, Röhde later reported, "They died a jolly death."[1]

Capesius was unfazed when he learned the prisoners had died of what the SS files listed as "heart attacks."[2] He seemed indifferent about his role since he considered himself merely a pharmacist who supplied the fatal drugs, not the doctor who killed them. He had learned that at Auschwitz medications were used in ways he could never have imagined when he was a Bayer salesman. He had also fully embraced the viewpoint of his SS physician friends that the camp's medical experiments were "really an important matter, as there was no other place where you could just perform research like that, no problem."[3]

The callous side of Capesius is in contrast to the way a few had described him when he first arrived at Auschwitz. Roland Albert, his good friend, said that the pharmacist "liked people, was kind . . . he was kindness itself."[4] Jan Sikorski, his inmate assistant, recalled "he had a good reputation among the prisoners. He was matter of fact."[5] But after Capesius was at Auschwitz for only a few months, there were no more good reports about him. He had, as he later admitted, "gotten used to it." And Capesius had also made the intellectual compromise to justify his service.

The most dramatic evidence of his moral decline was his participation in the selections that decided which of the arriving prisoners would live or die. In the late spring of 1944, Dr. Wirths summoned Capesius to his office and informed him that going forward one of his responsibilities would be to assist at the railhead selections. Auschwitz was gearing up for what would soon be its busiest time ever, massive deportations of Jews from Hungary and Transylvania. Capesius's pharmacological degree was medical training enough. In fact, Wirths had also put Capesius's assistant SS pharmacist, Gerhard Gerber, and both camp dentists, Drs. Frank and Schatz, on selection duty.[6] Even non-medical SS officers would have to occasionally assist, Wirths informed him.

Capesius had on some earlier occasions performed selections including a March transport of 5,007 Jews from the Theresienstadt ghetto in Czechoslovakia. Only fourteen had survived.[7] Erich Kulka, a Czech Jew assigned as a locksmith to Birkenau's maintenance crew, witnessed many of the incoming trains and fingered Capesius as one of the SS officers who performed the Theresienstadt selections.[8] Capesius, who had already tried to shirk the responsibility for oversight of the Zyklon B, was not happy that his new assignment made him a more accountable part of the camp's murder machine. His objection was not a moral one, he simply did not want the extra responsibility. It was abundantly clear, however, that Wirths was in no mood to make any exception. Within a couple of weeks of the directive, Capesius no longer traveled to the railhead simply to pick through personal belongings of the victims, but took his place alongside other physicians including Drs. Mengele and Klein.[9]

Once the transports packed with Hungarians and Romanians began arriving that spring, a remarkable event played out at the Auschwitz railhead. Many of the new inmates were startled to recognize Capesius at the ramp. That was because they had done business with him before the war when he was Romania's Farben/Bayer agent. Those individual eyewitness accounts are notable because after the war Capesius incredibly denied having performed a single selection.[10]

That was the case for Romanian doctors Mauritius Berner and Gisela Böhm. Berner was with his wife and three daughters and Böhm with her daughter, Ella, who as a child had called Capesius her "pharmacist uncle." The same was true for Klausenburg native, Paul Pajor, a Jewish pharmacist, who arrived at Auschwitz on a Sunday in the spring of 1944.[11] "When I got to the front [of the line], I saw an officer pointing people to the left and right. . . . This officer was Dr. Victor Capesius. I got to know him prior to 1940. At that time, he was the chief sales representative for Bayer and visited us frequently. He came into my drugstore several times, was always quite nice, chatted with me while his driver arranged his sales displays of Bayer products. Sometimes, he would say: 'I will leave you some Bayer packing paper, so you won't have to lay out anything for things like that,' and so on. It seemed unbelievable to me that it was him."

Capesius looked at him for a moment and then asked, "Aren't you a pharmacist?"

"Yes, I am, I am a pharmacist," Pajor said.

"Don't you have a pharmacy in Oradea?"

"Yes."

Capesius motioned with his hand for Pajor to move to the right. Pajor had no idea that in that brief encounter Capesius had spared his life with a simple wave of his hand. [12]

Exercising the power over life and death at the railhead may have been something Capesius initially had wanted to avoid. But controlling who would live and die quickly became intoxicating. At Auschwitz, the default decision was to send most arriving prisoners to their death. Real power, however, was the ability to sometimes play God, to spare a life, even if it was only a temporary and brutal respite from the gas chamber.

Adrienne Krausz witnessed firsthand the capriciousness of how Capesius chose who would live or die. She arrived in June 1944 with her parents and sister. Her parents, doctors, had known Capesius from his Bayer work.

"When my mother saw the officer carrying out the selection process, she said, 'Well, that's Dr. Capesius from Klausenburg over there.'

I think he recognized my mother as well, because he waved at her. My mother and sister were sent to the left by him, into the gas, but I went to the right and I survived. Later I met a friend who had been with my father during the selection. He told me that my father had said hello to Capesius and asked him where his own wife and eleven-year-old daughter were. Capesius supposedly answered: 'I'm sending you to the same place where your wife and daughter are, it's a good place.'"[13]

At times Capesius seemingly split families for no apparent reason other than his own whim. That was the case for Sarah Nebel who arrived at Auschwitz with 5,000 Hungarian Jews during the middle of the night in June. She knew Capesius from Bucharest before the war (1935 to 1938). "We lived in the same building," Nebel later recalled. "I on the ground floor, Dr. Capesius on the second floor. He was a representative of Bayer. Sometimes I spoke to him and his wife."[14] In 1939, just before the start of the war, she had coffee with Capesius and Friederike in their Transylvanian home.

"I recognized him right away – Dr. Capesius. I was happy to see him. When I stood in front of him all he said was: 'How old are you?' and sent me to the right."

Capesius sent her father, sisters and brothers to the left. Nebel did not know what the difference in directions meant but she did not want to be separated from her family. So she tried to get back to Capesius and plead they stay together. But an SS officer blocked her.

"Isn't that Dr. Capesius?" Nebel asked the SS officer.

"He looked at me with surprise. 'That's the pharmacist Dr. Capesius. How come you know him?'"

She said she knew him from Romania. But he pushed her back into the crowd of prisoners.[15]

Sometimes Capesius had to decide which spouse lived. Dr. Lajos Schlinger, a Klausenburg native, had known Capesius since 1939, when as a Bayer rep Capesius called on him and the two also ran into each other socially. Schlinger was part of the last group of Jews deported from Klausenburg. "There were twelve of us, doctors, and we took the ghetto hospital with us," he recalled.[16]

When their cattle car arrived in June, it was kept sealed at the rail ramp for several hours as other cars were emptied. Around 4:00 AM their doors were opened.

"We were driven out violently," recalled Schlinger. "It was a hellish situation because we had brought along the hospital patients – about 200 to 300 – among them many who were critically ill and couldn't even stand up. . . . The sick people were lying or sitting on the ground; women were crying, children screaming. It was a terrible situation."[17]

It was then that Schlinger saw Dr. Capesius.

"I ran up to him happily and greeted him. 'Where are we?' I asked."

"In central Germany."

Schlinger, who had noticed signs in Slavic, did not believe him.

"What will become of us?"

"Everything will be all right," Capesius assured him.

Schlinger told Capesius that his wife was not well.

"She isn't quite well?" Capesius asked. "Then she should stand over here." He pointed to a cluster of very ill people. Schlinger's teenage daughter accompanied her mother to the infirm group.

"I never saw my wife and my seventeen-year-old girl again," said Schlinger.[18]

Few among the arriving Jews in the spring of 1944 knew Capesius better than Josef Glück, a textile manufacturer from Klausenburg. He got to Auschwitz on a transport of 2,800 Jews on June 11. Glück was the businessman who had complained to Farben's Frankfurt headquarters about delays in deliveries of colorants needed for his factory. And Capesius had visited him to resolve the problem and afterwards stayed in touch to ensure the account was satisfactory. They had not seen each other in more than two years but now met again at the ramp at Auschwitz.

Glück was with his wife, their two-year-old twins, his own mother and sister-in-law and her two children. By coincidence, two other Jews deported with Glück in that same transport were Albert Ehrenfeld and Wilhelm Schul, former customers with whom Capesius had cultivated special prewar business relationships.[19] The three men stayed close together.

"We had to parade before one SS officer," recalled Glück. "He sent the individuals either to the left or right. To my astonishment I recognized the SS officer! It was Dr. Capesius. As I marched past Capesius, I was in the company of Schul and Ehrenfeld. We all immediately recognized Capesius on the ramp. At first, we thought that was good fortune for us."[20]

Although there were other SS officers on the ramp, Glück saw that "Capesius alone decided who had to go to the left or the right."

The fifty-four-year-old Schul was the first to reach Capesius. All were certain by Capesius's expression that he recognized them but gave no indication. Before Schul reached the head of the line, Capesius had not said a word to any of the new arrivals, instead simply gesturing with his hand for them to proceed to the left or right. But for the three men who had been his prewar customers, he had questions.

"Do you like to work?" Capesius asked Schul in German.

"I can no longer work," Schul said, "I'm too old."

Capesius pointed to the left side.

Ehrenfeld was next.

This time in Hungarian, Capesius asked, 'Well, you are also here? You like to work?"

"Yes," Ehrenfeld responded.

Capesius directed him to the right.

Next came Glück.

Again in Hungarian, Capesius asked "Do you like to work?"

"Yes."

"Capesius said nothing else," Glück later remembered, "and sent me to the right."[21]

Glück and Ehrenfeld joined a group of about 130 men (of the 2,800 that arrived on that Romanian transport only 350 were spared).

After the selection of the men, it was the women's turn. Although Capesius sent Glück's wife and sister-in-law to the right, Glück never again saw them. As for Glück's twins, they were dispatched immediately to the gas.

"I had no idea where we were going," said Glück.

Capesius's cold-heartedness at the selection ramp surprised Jan Sikorski, his chief inmate pharmacist who said his boss had "treated me like a human being." The accounts of him at the railhead was evidence, thought Sikorski, that Capesius was simply a "kind of Jekyll and Hyde."[22] Sikorski was the equivalent of a Kapo, a hand-selected enforcer and, in fact, was the only prisoner who later had anything good to say about the pharmacist. But for those Capesius spared at the railhead, they saw only Hyde.

After he dispatched Adrienne Krausz's entire family to the gas chamber and saved her, she joined hundreds of other women in the baths, "our hair was shaved . . . while we were still naked standing in line, Dr. Capesius walked through. I was standing next to Frau Stark, an elderly woman who had also known Dr. Capesius from back home. She spoke to him, and asked, 'Doctor, what will happen to us?' or something like that, I can't remember exactly anymore what it was. He pushed her away, so that she fell down on the slippery floor. That was the last time I saw Dr. Capesius."[23]

Ella Böhm saw her "pharmacist uncle" when he came to her prison block.[24] She tried using some straw to hide a pregnant girl's baby bump. "He pushed me aside and swept the straw away from the pregnant woman with his stick; I never saw the expectant mother again."[25]

Textile manufacturer Josef Glück later saw Capesius on "a number of occasions," often with Dr. Mengele, "selecting in the camp." Once, Capesius and Mengele and two other SS officers showed up at the infamous prisoner Block 11. It was home to many Jewish teens between the ages of sixteen and eighteen.

"They probably sensed what they were up to and dispersed," recalled Glück. "Thereupon the camp leader rounded them up with dogs. That happened on a Jewish holiday. After two days, vans came and these boys were put on the vans and taken to the gas. This was done amidst laughter. They probably were very amused because these children cried out for their mothers."

Glück's sixteen-year-old nephew was seized. Before the SS took him away he had managed to cut his arm and with blood from that wound write on a back wall of the barracks: "Andreas Rappaport – lived sixteen years."[26]

Glück was also a witness on August 6, when the SS liquidated the "Gypsy Family Camp" by sending 3,000 women, children and elderly to be gassed. Two of the chief selectors, according to Glück, were again Mengele and Capesius.[27] That autumn, Glück was fixing a water pipe in the women's camp when Mengele and Capesius again arrived for a selection. "Eighty-five women were sent to the gas chamber [including]my wife."[28]

Magda Szabó, a Romanian Jew, who arrived at Auschwitz with her family in May 1944, may have encapsulated best the Capesius prisoners knew. As she marched toward a group of SS men she overheard one speaking Hungarian. She learned his identity later in the camp. "The face of Dr. Capesius wasn't to be forgotten so soon," she recalled after the war. "It was not a typically German face."[29]

Szabó ended up in Block 27 of the C Compound, from which sick and feeble prisoners were frequently selected for gassing. The two SS officers who did the selections there were Mengele and Capesius. "Always the same," she recalled. When Szabó was transferred to the kitchen detail she worked with several prisoners in making the "nasty taste . . . camp-flavor soup," a mixture mostly of water, with a few potatoes, some flour and "and a bit of margarine." One day, some extra margarine was found on one of the inmates. Capesius came to investigate. He ordered all the prisoners to grab rocks from outside the barracks and hold them while hopping around in what he called "exercise" until they dropped from exhaustion.[30]

"I am Capesius from Transylvania," he bellowed at the inmates. "In me you will get to know the devil." [31]

Chapter 8

"BAYER'S POISON"

Since the SS doctors considered themselves an elite cadre of professionals it might have seemed that a simple pharmacist like Capesius would be held in lower esteem. In that case he might not have been expected to contribute very much to the camp's frenzied human experimentation. But Capesius had a special qualification that could not be underestimated: his longtime work for Farben/Bayer. At Auschwitz the companies had reached their diabolical zenith. All the physicians there were indebted to their generosity in funding many medical experiments and the camp presented the ultimate human laboratory for Farben and Bayer.

A longtime Bayer employee-turned-SS Major, Dr. Helmuth Vetter, oversaw the company's programs that utilized prisoners for testing unproven drugs. Some Farben executives predicted the company's future was not in chemicals but rather in the emerging field of modern pharmaceuticals. "The experiments in the concentration camps with IG [Farben] preparations," SS physician Waldemar Hoven testified after the war, "only took place in the interests of the IG, which strived by all means to determine the effectiveness of these preparations. . . . Not the SS but in fact the IG took the initiative for the concentration camp experiments."[1]

The SS, of course, did not simply turn arriving prisoners over for Farben sponsored experiments. The company bought its human guinea pigs the same as it paid the SS rates for its slave laborers at Monowitz. Bayer haggled in one instance with Auschwitz's commandant about the price for 150 women on whom it wanted to try "a new sleep-inducing drug." The SS wanted 200 Reichsmarks for each prisoner (about $80). Bayer complained that was "too high" and countered with 170 RM, an offer the SS accepted.

"Please prepare for us 150 women in the best health possible," a Bayer executive wrote in a memo confirming the purchase.

After Bayer took custody of the female inmates it noted to the SS, "Despite their macerated condition they were considered satisfactory. We will keep you informed of the developments regarding the experiments."

A few weeks later, a Bayer executive sent the SS a memo that was strikingly similar to most others that marked the end of one of its concentration camp pharmaceutical trials.

"The experiments were performed. All test persons died. We will contact you shortly about a new shipment."

In another round of experiments Farben documents reveal in chilling detail the failure of Preparation 3582, an untried drug targeted for typhus. SS physicians took fifty human guinea pigs at a time and infected them with typhus before administering the experimental 'treatment.' Side effects ranged from blistered mouths to uncontrollable diarrhea, vomiting and exhaustion. After three brutal phases over a couple of months in 1943, about 55% of those "treated" died. That was about the same number as those who survived when left untreated. Farben went back to the drawing board to reformulate its drug. Meanwhile, the prisoners who had survived the typhus were sent to the gas chambers to avoid the possibility they might infect others.

Another group of female inmates died from what is only described as "experiments with unknown hormonal preparations." And an entire ward of prisoners infected with tuberculosis in Block 20 was unsuccessfully treated with an unmarked Bayer injectable.[2]

In one experiment, Dr. Vetter tested Bayer anti-bacterial medications by injecting the lungs of two hundred women with streptococcus bacilli. All died painful and slow deaths from pulmonary edema. Vetter presented his findings of the drug's failure to the Wehrmacht Medical Academy.[3]

Mengele, undoubtedly the camp's most energetic experimenter, also used untested Farben medications labeled B-1012, B-1034, and 3382 (1034 was Methylene Blue, an experimental typhus cure).[4]

Wilhelm Mann, a Farben chemist who was also the chairman of Zyklon B manufacturer, Degesch, wrote in 1943, "I have enclosed the first check. Dr. Mengele's experiments should, as we both agreed, be pursued."[5]

As opposed to other doctors who mostly searched for some experimental cure of an existing illness or underlying medical condition, Mengele administered many of his drugs – via enema, hypodermic, intravenous or pills – to otherwise healthy patients. His lab notes were lost after the war so no one is certain what he really intended with the Farben drugs. Theories run the gamut.

Some believe Mengele had access to Farben's cutting-edge Sarin and Tabun gasses, colorless, odorless powerful nerve agents the company had discovered in the 1930s. Tabun was greatly feared because a single drop was deadly. The Third Reich's chemical warfare division was pushing Farben to develop Sarin and Tabun into easily distributed mass production weapons. Hitler twice seriously considered using the nerve agents, once at Stalingrad and the other time after the Allies landed at Normandy. In both instances the Führer decided not to after Farben's top chemical warfare expert, Otto Ambros, incorrectly warned that the Allies and Russians had their own stockpiles of nerve agents and would retaliate against the Fatherland in kind.[6] Whatever the reason for Mengele's quackery at Auschwitz, what is undeniable is that most of the prisoners he experimented on with Farben compounds died.

After the war, Capesius tried justifying Mengele's experiments with a flat-out lie, claiming that "the Americans eventually got all those studies, all that . . . research on twins and genetics. . . . And the Americans paid the Poles a lot of money for that, since that was really an important matter, as there was no other place where you could perform research like that, no problem."[7]

At times in the camp, Capesius was more than just a cheerleader or pharmacist who supplied the company drugs for experiments on others. Internal SS files indicate he was present and helped direct human trials about untested types of anesthesia.[8] When the Gestapo commissioned the former I.G. Farben psychiatrist Bruno

Weber, director of Auschwitz's Institute of Hygiene, to study how pharmacological agents could enhance brainwashing, Weber in turn tapped Capesius for assistance. The two concocted experimental compounds mostly consisting of morphine and barbiturates.[9] They also used mescaline, a naturally occurring psychedelic, the same drug that was used in similar experiments in Dachau.[10]

Zoe Polanska was only thirteen when she was deported in 1941 from Odessa to Auschwitz. During her three years in the camp she got to know Capesius all too well. In the presence of other doctors, and occasionally on his own, Capesius ordered Polanska stripped naked and fixed to a bed with iron rods. Sometimes IV liquids were administered. At other occasions Capesius gave her pills from bottles whose only marking was a Bayer label.

"They never asked you [to] take drugs, they were simply shoved down your throat," recalled Polanska. "I did not ask what they were giving me."[11] After the war she discovered she was sterile since her ovaries had failed to develop. She surmised that the experiments to which Capesius had subjected her were a botched effort at sterilization or an early birth control pill, what she called "Bayer's poison."

Chapter 9

"AN UNAMBIGUOUS SMELL"

It might surprise many that as horrific a place as Auschwitz was, the SS assigned to the camp tried their best to create a semblance of a normal life for themselves. For some that meant moving their families there. Commandant Rudolf Höss lived with his wife and five children in a stucco house encircled by a white picket fence. The garden was filled with thick reddish hedges and begonias in powder blue flower boxes. After the war Höss recalled the peaceful setting that served as his family home: "Every wish that my wife or children expressed was granted them. The children could live a free and untrammeled life. My wife's garden was a paradise of flowers. . . . The children were particularly fond of the ones [prisoners] who worked on the garden. My whole family displayed an intense love of agriculture and particularly for animals of all sorts. Every Sunday, I had to walk them all across the fields and visit the stables, and we might never miss out on the kennels where the dogs were kept. Our two horses and the foal were especially beloved. The children always kept animals in the garden, creatures the prisoners were forever bringing them. Tortoises, martens, cats, lizards: there was always something new and interesting to be seen there. In summer they splashed in the paddling pool in the garden or in the Sola [river]. But their greatest joy was when daddy bathed with them. He had, however, so little time for all these childish pleasures."[1] ("I did not know that, next door, these atrocities were taking place," Ingebirgitt Hannah Höss, one of his daughters, told *Stern* in 2015. She was six when she moved to Auschwitz. "I never asked why there were fences and watchtowers. When you are nine and ten years old, your mind is filled with other thoughts."[2])

Auschwitz had a German kindergarten and primary school, football stadium, grocery store, photographic lab, theater, library, SS swimming pool, and a prisoner symphony orchestra. Many of the

SS joined a sports club. They boasted about their Christmas parties. There was a sex-slave brothel called "The Puff," frequented by SS men and some Kapos. In an effort to maintain the façade of *normalcy* there were even traffic regulations and traffic lights. Speeders and red light runners were investigated by the SS traffic court.[3] (Mengele got a ticket early on, noted disapprovingly in his SS file).[4]

Höss was not the only officer whose family either lived at or visited Auschwitz. Among many others, Dr. Werner Röhde raised his daughter there before he was transferred to a camp in the Alsace. Dr. Horst Fischer, the dentist Willi Frank, and SS Lieutenant Ernst Scholz were a few of the others who brought along their wives and children. Gertrude, the wife of Lieutenant Roland Albert, lived at Auschwitz and taught primary school for the children of other officers. Their son was born there. "We planted a vegetable garden," Albert later recalled, "kept bees, planted flowers, went hunting and fishing, there were afternoon coffee parties, birthdays, Christmas parties with Commandant Höss . . . and the kids would recite their Christmas poems."[5] (Albert himself spent some of his off-duty time teaching religion at the school, his prewar career).

Mengele did not move his wife, Irene, to Auschwitz, thinking it safer for her to stay in the southern German town Freiburg. But Irene visited him. Her first time was August 1943. A quarantine because of a spike in typhus infections caused her to stay longer than planned.

"What's this stench?" Irene once asked.

"Don't ask me about this," Mengele replied.[6] (Gisela Böhm, an inmate physician, described it as "an omnipresent sweetish odor of burnt human bodies, it penetrated everything, invisibly, like a finely dispersed corpse inside of everyone.")[7]

On a second visit, in the blistering heat of August, 1944, Irene stayed again at the SS barracks on the camp's perimeter. According to her diary, her first three weeks were spent picking berries and bathing. She even visited Solahütte, an SS recreation camp 18 miles south of Auschwitz on the Sola River. (A photo album kept by the camp adjutant, Karl Höcker, was recovered in 2007, and shocked many for its photos of SS personnel on leave at Solahütte, lighting Christmas candles, having boisterous sing-a-longs, sunbathing, and otherwise enjoying themselves as one might expect any soldiers on leave during the war).

On this visit, Irene was again aware of the peculiar "sweet stench" she had noticed the previous year. And she had little doubt that Auschwitz, ringed with barbed wire and guard towers, was a concentration camp. From the SS barracks she wrote in her diary "the incoming trains were clearly visible."

Just as she was set to leave on September 11 she fell ill with diphtheria. The next six weeks were spent in the camp's medical clinics, shuttled between one or another depending on air raid alerts. This was when Capesius came to know her well, assuring Mengele that his wife had a priority on any medications needed to control her high fever and relieve her distress. When she was finally released from the hospital on October 18, she moved into a more modern apartment in the SS physician's barracks. As she wrote in her diary, she felt "once again as a newlywed."[8]

As for Capesius, he had decided not to bring his wife Fritzi and their three daughters to Auschwitz. Instead, his way of holding on to some semblance of a normal life was to slip away many weekends to the nearby country estate of an ethnic German Romanian couple, Hans and Hildegard Stoffel. Capesius and Hans Stoffel had first met in 1935 when they invested in a couple of cooperative apartments in Bucharest.[9] Stoffel later joined the German war effort. The small estate in Przecischau, nine miles from Auschwitz, in the Beskidy Mountains, had belonged to a Polish family before the war but was part of a program the Nazis had instituted to distribute Polish and Jewish owned property to ethnic Germans that had been early supporters of the fascist movement in their native countries. It was thought in Berlin that the free land giveaway might encourage more ethnic Germans to enthusiastically back the Reich. The Stoffels had been friends with Captain Fritz Fabritius, the hardline founder of Romania's original Nazi offshoot, Nationalsozialistische Selbsthilfebewegung (National Socialist Self-Help Movement). Both Fabritius and the Stoffels were given large lodges and grounds that were ideal for hunting.[10] The

Stoffels moved to their new property in October 1943 and it was not long before their estate became a regular haunt for weekend parties and get-togethers by some of the Auschwitz SS men.

Fritz Klein, a doctor from Transylvania, had also known the Stoffels before the war. Klein was a fierce anti-Semite who told the couple that, "The Jews are the enemies of mankind, not just ours." He was one of the few physicians who volunteered for extra selection duty at the railhead ramp as well as assignment to the camp's "Black Wall" at Block 11 where prisoners were executed by firing squad. He personally selected the prisoner girls for the Auschwitz brothel. The girls were forced to have sex at least six times nightly and the SS waived any "racial limitations or prohibitions." After the war Klein shamelessly claimed those sex slaves "did so voluntarily."[11]

With their Transylvanian roots as a common bond, Capesius and Klein were quick friends. It was not long after Capesius's transfer to Auschwitz that he began regularly visiting the Stoffels' mountain retreat. He made his way there sometimes by bicycle, occasionally by train, and once in a while on his favorite motorcycle, a DKW 100.[12] One of Auschwitz's dentists, Dr. Willi Schatz, frequently joined Capesius as did his friend and pharmacist, First Lieutenant Gerhard Gerber. And Capesius's childhood friend, Roland Albert, was a regular. "Well, we had to take breaks," Albert recalled after the war. "To rest. To forget. Maybe on Sunday go hunting [to the Stoffel estate]." By going there, Albert said, it was a way from the oppressing smell of "Burnt flesh. Burnt skin. Burnt hair."[13]

Capesius arrived most weekends with some of the best clothes he had stolen from the personal belongings of the new prisoners. "I often took such clothes with me in the fall when I went hunting in the Beskidy mountains," Capesius later recalled. "And I gave them out to our Polish beaters and their children, with whom I was very popular."[14]

The "beaters" were local Poles who cleared the brush so that the SS men could hunt small game. Dr. Schatz brought along his dog, Treff. Capesius, an avid hunter, considered Treff "an excellent hunting dog." The SS men were traumatized when during one weekend of hare hunting the dentist mistakenly shot his dog when aiming instead for a rabbit. They frantically tried digging the buckshot from the wounded dog but it died.[15]

Capesius usually stayed over Saturday night in one of the Stoffel guest rooms. Sunday was when a dozen or so SS men and women came to the estate for a boisterous meal before heading back to the camp late that same night.[16] Saturday, June 7, 1944, a particularly large group from the camp came to celebrate Hans Stoffel's birthday.

When Hildegard Stoffel had problems with her teeth, she discovered that the Polish dentists in nearby Oswiecim did not have the x-ray machines or skill to treat her. So she went to Dr. Schatz, who shared the Auschwitz dispensary with Capesius. Years later she had only benign memories of her four to six visits there, "The entrance where I used to go in . . .that was all very beautiful. There were flowers planted, there were nice clean barracks. . . . I saw no prisoners [but in] the dispensary where Dr. Capesius worked . . . those people didn't look like prisoners. They were well nourished, well dressed, always very positive and happy. So I didn't see anything bad about their environment. . . . They all looked very good."[17] Her husband, Hans, noted that the inmate pharmacists "spoke very highly of Capesius."[18] And he said he did not know what was taking place in the camp since he incredulously claimed he never looked outside any window and never asked Capesius questions.

What is without question is that the Stoffels afforded Capesius a place where he could be himself, far enough away from the camp's SS hierarchy that he occasionally felt free to even talk about the stress of the war. In late May, 1944, for instance, he had traveled to Berlin's Central Military Hospital to place some large pharmaceutical orders. On that trip he witnessed firsthand the great destruction of a massive two-day Allied bombing run that began on May 28. When he returned to Auschwitz, he took off after a few days to relax with the Stoffels. There was a large hunt underway, and Capesius found "everyone was still in a festive mood, even dancing, despite the rain coming down in sheets." But he could not stop talking about how unsettled he was from the power of the Allied bombers. The others found his nonstop chatter depressing. It was not long before they "asked me to keep quiet about it," which he managed to do. Hildegard Stoffel later recalled that she and her husband were "always reluctant to have upsetting conversations like that."[19]

The Stoffels were not Capesius's only social release outside the camp. He frequently visited Armin Rump in Oswiecim, the adjacent Polish town. Rump, a Transylvanian ethnic German, was the pharmacist there. He and his family, also friends of the Stoffels, had moved to Poland from the town of Dorna Watra in northern Romania's Bucovina province.[20] That was a place that had earned an ignominious listing in the elimination of European Jews. Bukovina had one of Romania's oldest Jewish communities and in the last prewar census about 92,000 Jews made up about 10% of the population and enjoyed prominent positions in transportation, lumber and finance.[21] Starting in 1941, Romanian militias and police squads started murdering Jews.[22] Armin Rump's hometown was small, only 7700 residents, of which more than a quarter, 2,000, were Jewish. By 1942, only the midpoint of the war, and before Rump relocated to Oswiecim, only 21 Jews remained.[23]

Capesius said that he enjoyed "looking for company with the Rump family or on the Stoffel's estate . . . to get away from the concentration camp atmosphere." Still, Rump was close enough to Auschwitz that visiting him did not always provide much of a respite. As Capesius wrote: "[F]rom the pharmacist Rump's balcony at night you could see the light of a huge fire burning about four kilometers (2.5 miles) away, and everyone knew that human beings were being burned here, you could smell it too, when the wind was blowing in the wrong direction."[24]

Chapter 10

THE HUNGARIAN JEWS

It is undeniable that some of the SS assigned to Auschwitz and other concentration camps were pathological sadists who derived satisfaction from the barbarity. A few physicians, such as Mengele, were all too pleased to be there since they were obsessed with their pseudo-racial science experiments. But many other SS assigned to Auschwitz – of the 7,000 who served, 177 were women and 350 were Romanian Germans like Capesius – considered it a mostly undesirable and difficult posting. There was no extra pay for working in a desolate part of the Polish countryside that was brutally hot during summer and bitterly cold during winter. And the diseases that ravaged the prisoners – typhus, diphtheria, and pneumonia – did not spare the guards, officers and physicians. Dr. Johann Paul Kremer kept a diary during his three months at Auschwitz during 1942. He complained incessantly about the miserable conditions. "It is a week since I came to camp and still have not been able to get rid of the fleas in my room in spite of using all kinds of insecticides."

Kremer, as did all the others, received a series of inoculations in the hope of preventing typhus. Those shots had side effects including high fever and diarrhea. And despite those vaccines, Kremer's diary is filled with references to colleagues who fell miserably sick. In one instance "Sturmbannführer Caesar also ill with typhus, after his wife died of it a few days ago." Besides typhus there was a rampant "Auschwitz illness," a bacterial infection resembling a severe flu, accompanied by a spiking high fever, chills, muscle cramping, and debilitating headaches.[1] Mengele got fitfully ill with malaria two months after he arrived at the camp.

That is not to suggest that those who were unhappy at being posted to Auschwitz did anything less than their full duty in helping to murder millions of innocent civilians. But they looked for other ways to make it a better assignment. For many, the camp's mass murder operation presented a one-off opportunity to personally profit. In letters to family and conversations with colleagues, a surprising number of Auschwitz's SS thought they were entitled to something more than their salary (Capesius earned a working class 9,000 Reichsmarks annually there, about $3,600). That often translated into pilfering food and liquor stashed in the personal belongings of the arriving inmates. But others were not happy simply setting aside extra rations in the hope they saved enough for an occasional gluttonous feast.

Those who were greedy focused on accumulating jewelry and cash. And there was a lot of that at Auschwitz. The flood of Jews who arrived daily stuffed into cattle cars clung to the hope they were being relocated to work camps in the East. They had little doubt it would be a tough and bare existence. Despite rumors of death centers that had spread inside the ghettoes of the occupied countries, the new arrivals refused to believe their train journey ended at a gas chamber. So, in the hope they could start a new life, they took along as many valuables as they could hide from the Nazis. Cash, diamonds and jewelry were often sewn into the linings of overcoats, dresses, and suits, hidden inside bottles of lotions or creams, and even in secret compartments cut into suitcases. The Nazis soon became proficient at knowing where the victims stashed their valuables. All that plunder was stored in Birkenau's giant warehouses, dubbed 'Canada,' which acted as a way station before the loot was transported to Germany.

There was no chance for an inventory since too many people arrived daily and too much of value was taken from every trainload. The failure to catalog it created an opportunity that was ripe for theft.

"They [the SS] were taking home lots of gold and other valuables," recounted Libuša Breder, a Slovakian Jew assigned to 'Canada.' "Every piece had to be searched, underwear, everything. And we found lots of diamonds, gold, coins, money, dollars, foreign currency from all over Europe. . . . It was a bonanza for them . . . nobody counted it."[2]

Prisoners like Breder were not the only ones aware of the widespread SS theft. In 1943 a 22-year-old SS corporal, Oskar

Gröning, was put in charge of managing all the cash from the rail transports. Every couple of months he packed it into crates and accompanied it by train to Berlin.

"If a lot of stuff is piled up together, then you can easily stash away something for your personal gain," Gröning recalled after the war. "Stealing things for yourself was absolutely common practice in Auschwitz."[3]

It was not long after his posting that Gröning, like many of his colleagues, succumbed to that easy temptation and began stealing.

By October 1943, the SS hierarchy in Berlin acknowledged it had a corruption epidemic at the camp. Himmler dispatched Lt. Colonel Konrad Morgen, a lawyer and judge, to investigate and fix the problem. Days after he arrived Morgen led an unannounced search of the SS lockers.

"Examination of the lockers yielded a fortune in gold, rings, pearls, and money, in all kinds of currencies," he later recounted. "The conduct of the SS staff was beyond any of the standards that you'd expect from soldiers. They gave the impression of being degenerate and brutal parasites."[4]

Morgen knew he had to set a firm example if he had any chance of putting an end to the corruption. He ordered two of the SS ringleader guards arrested for stealing contraband. While awaiting trial, one hanged himself in his cell. Morgen reported to Himmler that the abuses were widespread. Rudolf Höss, the hard charging commandant who was widely credited with the nonstop expansion of Auschwitz and its killing capacity, had allowed the culture of corruption to flourish. In fact, Höss had set a poor personal example for discipline by having a widely rumored affair with a Jewish Czech inmate (when she got pregnant, he ordered her starved in order to abort the fetus). Himmler concluded he had no choice but to replace Höss.[5]

The commandant resisted the transfer. He appealed personally to Himmler, claiming that he alone could best clean up the mess. But Himmler was unmoved. Still, the SS chief softened the blow by promoting Höss to a desk job at the Concentration Camp

Administration headquarters. Remarkably, when Höss moved to Oranienburg, just north of Berlin, for his new posting on November 10, 1943, his wife and five children stayed in their Auschwitz home. Two months after Höss's departure, the camp warehouse where Morgen stored his growing archive of damning evidence, mysteriously caught fire and burned to the ground. That fire put an end to any further trials of SS personnel for corruption.

And if there was any doubt that Morgen's probes took a back seat to killing Jews, seven months after his investigation had begun, Höss was back in command at Auschwitz. Himmler knew no one else was capable of running the camp with the brutal efficiency required for the massive Hungarian deportations scheduled to begin in the spring of 1944. Höss's return, coupled with the stalling of Morgen's inquiry, emboldened those who were intent on stealing as much as possible.

Before 1944, three death camps in Poland, Treblinka, Sobibor, and Chelmno, had vied with each other for the dubious title as the leading Nazi extermination center. But starting in May, Auschwitz was about to earn the ignominious title as the top killing machine. The politics behind this were in part related to Capesius's native Transylvania. As a result of an agreement (Vienna Treaty) signed in 1940, Hungary had annexed Transylvania which became an ally of the Third Reich. The hardline fascists in power, however, had not embraced the Nazi exhortations to round up and deport their 800,000 Jews. When German intelligence reported to Hitler in March 1944 that the Hungarian leaders were secretly negotiating a surrender to the Allies, the Führer dispatched the German army to take control. One of the first Nazi officials to arrive in conquered Budapest was SS-Obersturmbannführer (Lieutenant Colonel) Adolf Eichmann, chief of the Security Services Sub-Department IV-B4. Eichmann was responsible for evacuating all Jews in conquered territories to concentration camps. He was the chief bureaucrat of genocide, sometimes called "death's traffic cop." In a frenzied climax to the Third Reich slaughter of the Jews, Eichmann organized a conference in Vienna in early May, during which expedited schedules to send Hungarian and Transylvanian Jews to Auschwitz were set. The transports started in mid-May, initially with four daily, each packed with about 3,000 Jews. It was wildly ambitious even by the grisly standards of the German killing machine.

Commandant Höss had ordered a furious expansion of the camp, moving train tracks, converting a large bunker into another gas chamber, completing several new incinerator ovens, and building five enormous trenches for burning the expected overflow of corpses. The Sonderkommando, the prisoner unit assigned to remove the corpses from the gas chambers, was expanded from 200 to 800 men.

Although the Nazis would ultimately boast that over a hellish ten weeks that spring they killed half of all the Jews ever gassed at Auschwitz, the flood of prisoners proved too much even for a place synonymous with mass murder. Soon tens of thousands of corpses were decomposing in sprawling makeshift pits waiting for the overwhelmed crematoriums to catch up. The eight inmate dentists who used pliers to pull gold from the mouths of corpses worked day and night. The hydrochloric acid bath used to remove any bits of flesh and bone from the extracted teeth was backlogged for weeks as a record of twenty pounds of gold was pulled daily.

Dr. Miklós Nyiszli, Mengele's inmate assistant, later recalled that the "transports of Jews from Hungary arrived just one after the other, frequently two trains at once. On such occasions people literally poured out of the boxcars like a river. What Dr. Mengele did on the ramp could no longer be called *selection*. His hand was pointing mostly only in one direction: to the left. Sometimes entire transports were immediately sent to either the gas chambers or the blazing ditches."[6]

Dr. Otto Wolken, a Jewish inmate doctor, remarked "that the Hungarian transports brought about a huge change in the whole business. Suddenly the [Adolf] Eichmann 'travel agency' was back in business, and day after day four, five, six, some days even ten trains arrived in Auschwitz."[7]

Capesius's colleague and friend, Lieutenant Roland Albert, was in charge of SS Company Four, the guard unit responsible for the main watchtower at Birkenau under which all trains arrived. From that perch, Albert and his men had a full view as the cattle cars were opened. They trained machine guns on the streaming prisoners in case one tried escaping. The arriving prisoners, exhausted from their brutal several-day journey jammed into cattle cars, and confronted at the railhead with intimidating guards and upward of 150 dogs, invariably had no strength or wherewithal to make a dash for the high-tension electrified barbed wire surrounding them.

"Yes, it was horrible," Albert recalled later. "I could see everything happening down on the ramp from up in the tower: when one of them after three days on a trip from hell had enough strength to speak, to move, then he would pray, I saw it when I had ramp duty. Tough duty. Many of them were dead in the cars, a fearful stink as the doors were opened, others were still breathing. The children cried, the women whimpered, and the men called out for their families."[8]

Years later Capesius recounted the camp's bloodiest period in his typically clinical and dispassionate terms: "Between May 14 and July 7 of 1944, thirty-four trains with 288,357 Jews arrived from northern Transylvania and Hungary, who all went through the selection process on the ramp; of that number, only about one third were declared fit for work and saved. Children below the age of fourteen did not fall into this category."[9]

Auschwitz's most murderous phase that spring is shocking on its own but is somehow even more remarkable in light of what was happening elsewhere in the war. The previous year, 1943, marked an end to what had seemed unstoppable Nazi momentum. The 5-month siege of Stalingrad resulted in a stunning Russian victory when more than a quarter of a million German troops surrendered. Field Marshall Erwin Rommel, the highly celebrated Desert Fox, retreated across North Africa before fleeing to Germany half a step ahead of American and British tank corps. Italy switched sides, abandoning the Third Reich and striking a deal with the Allies. And the Soviet Army repelled a German offensive involving the largest tank battle in history at the Russian city of Kursk. But if 1943 was the year in which the Nazi blitzkrieg became only a memory, 1944 was when the Allies turned the tide of the war in their favor.

January and February started with the much touted impregnable German air defenses being smashed by massive British bombing raids against Berlin, Frankfurt, Hamburg, and Leipzig. In fierce fighting, the U.S. Army established a beachhead at Anzio, just 31 miles south of Rome. That February, Stalin's army captured ten German divisions in central Ukraine, and the Allies were furiously preparing for the great land invasion at Normandy that summer.

Inside Germany, the rapidly mounting casualties and reports of the setbacks turned into an ingrained pessimism that the war might be lost. At least it was clear that Hitler's plans to conquer all of Europe were now simply a misguided dream that had instead mired the Fatherland in its second devastating war of the twentieth century. Yet at Auschwitz, those involved in history's greatest war crimes had no apparent second thoughts about aggressively expanding the murder machine. Instead of pulling back and wondering if one day they might have to answer for their sins, those running the camp seemed surprisingly oblivious to the changing wartime fortunes.

As for Capesius, some who worked with him in the dispensary noticed that he saw an opportunity to profit as the pace of the Hungarian convoys strained the camp's capacity. Wilhelm Prokop, an inmate pharmacist, said, "I got to know Capesius as a person who was always trying to turn the huge Hungarian transports to his maximum advantage."[10] Capesius initially used the pretext of searching for medications and medical equipment taken from new prisoners to look instead only for valuables.[11] Nyiszli, Mengele's assistant, said that Capesius quickly developed "a reputation as a great organizer" of arriving booty.[12]

Ferdinand Grosz, a Jewish inmate pharmacist who had known Capesius in his Bayer role, arrived at Auschwitz in June and was assigned to the dispensary. He saw his boss at the selection ramp several times a week and "as far as medications were concerned, his only interest in them was to have us all inspect the prisoners' jars of creams and tubes of toothpaste for hidden jewels. He came to us daily to check up on whether we had found anything. Just in those months that I worked in the infirmary he collected huge quantities of jewelry, which he viewed as natural and proper income for himself."[13]

Inmate nurse Ludwig Wörl knew Capesius was keen on looking for diamonds hidden in medications. "The valuables were much more important to Capesius than the life of the prisoners," noted Wörl.[14]

Capesius's theft was easy since under the rules at Auschwitz he took all the goods he personally seized at the ramp back to his dispensary without signing any document acknowledging their receipt. That was a major shortcoming in the otherwise stifling German bureaucracy that dominated every aspect of mass murder, a loophole that he regularly exploited.

After returning from one trip to the railhead, Polish pharmacist Tadeusz Szewczyk recalled that Capesius ordered him "to take some suitcases down from the ambulance. These were leather valises of various sizes, and I was to bring them into the storeroom of the pharmacy. There were fifteen of them . . . and I stayed there with Capesius and sorted the contents. Better things were packed into better suitcases. Dr. Capesius took everything." According to Szewczyk, "everything" included foreign currency, which Capesius put immediately into his cashbox, and jewelry and Reichsmarks, which he repacked into separate cases.[15]

One time, when Capesius wanted a diamond brooch for his wife, he "commissioned" his top assistant Sikorski to find one. When Sikorski eventually delivered it, Capesius rewarded him with twelve bottles of schnapps.[16]

Inmate pharmacist Prokop also witnessed first-hand what Capesius was up to.

"One day I was sorting out medicines in the attic storeroom when Capesius appeared. He previously had charge of the suitcases kept up there, which had belonged to the prisoners. Capesius brought these suitcases himself from the camp at Birkenau. I paid attention to his activities during my shift. I noticed how Capesius separated out the valuable objects and expensive items and packed them in the best leather suitcases."

The luggage was filled with "first class new suits." Prokop looked "dumbfounded" as Capesius started sorting it all. When Capesius noticed Prokop staring at him, he stopped.

"Prokop, you know why you are here. Sooner or later you'll have to die. It's up to you to decide when this time will come. If you notice things and talk about them then this time will come sooner than you expect. I hope you have understood me."

Prokop later stated "I knew that if I told anyone a thing about it, I was lost."[17]

Capesius ordered Prokop to hide two of the suitcases filled with the best clothing. The next day, when Prokop checked for them, they were gone.[18]

The pharmacist of Auschwitz had reached a turning point. He was now dedicated to stashing away whatever he could so that whenever the war finished, he would have enough money to start a new life.

Chapter 11

DENTAL GOLD

On August 20, 1944, the SS at Auschwitz saw for themselves how radically the battlefield momentum had shifted against the Third Reich. That day, Allied bombers tested the limits of their range and struck Monowitz. Fortunately for the pilots the I. G. Farben plant was so large that it was impossible to miss even in a single-pass bombing run. German employees and Farben executives, together with the free Polish and western European workers, scrambled into the factory's bomb shelters. Slave laborers and POWs had to fend for themselves.[1] That run killed 40 of the plant's 1200 British POWs (Farben had even arranged the transfer to Monowitz of skilled POWs). Air raid sirens blared out again twice the following month and on October 13 an air strike again hit Monowitz (The question of why the Allies did not bomb the rail tracks on which the Nazis transported hundreds of thousands of Jews to the gas chambers during this time is a much debated issue).[2]

Capesius was not there during the September bombardments since he was on a two-week long leave.[3] He had wanted to go home to Fritzi and their three daughters. She was still running the family pharmacy in Sighisoara. But any trip home for Capesius was extremely risky as the Red Army had seized Transylvania and Romania had abruptly switched sides from backing Germany to joining the Soviets in fighting the Nazis. Fritzi had sent him a letter informing him that their condominium in Bucharest had been destroyed in a retaliatory attack by the Luftwaffe.[4]

Capesius initially traveled north in the hope of finding safe passage home. He was accompanied by Lotte Lill, a nurse stationed at Auschwitz who was married to an ethnic German SS officer and friend of Capesius.[5] As they neared the Romanian border, Capesius recalled later, "It felt like something awful, like the end of the world.

The overriding emotion was fear."[6] Many Romanians had welcomed the Russians as liberators. The public mood had quickly shifted against ethnic Germans like Capesius who were still fighting for the Third Reich.

After several failed attempts, Capesius and Lill abandoned their quest of safely reaching Schässburg. Capesius returned to Auschwitz. According to Roland Albert, Capesius had to go back to Auschwitz to manage the execution of the Sonderkommando after an unprecedented uprising; "Since he was in charge of the Zyklon B, he had to report for duty," recalled Albert.[7] In his postwar notes, Capesius noted only, "On that very evening I served my good Hungarian apricot schnapps in the barracks" with "Drs. Fischer, Klein, and Mengele." Also omitted from his account was that he had returned to confront an intensely personal problem.

A well-placed rumor was that the thirty-seven-year-old Capesius was having an affair with Éva Citron-Bard, a twenty-six-year-old Jewish inmate pharmacist from Transylvania that he had casually known before the war. She had been selected during her summer 1944 arrival by Drs. Klein and Mengele, and after only five weeks had begun working in the pharmacy dispensary. After the war, Capesius wrote to friends about his "blond assistant, Éva" and noted that she "was a friendly creature with blond hair three centimeters (1.2 inches) long, which later grew into a ponytail, something normally forbidden in the concentration camp."[8] Hermann Langbein, the Austrian political prisoner who worked for the chief physician, had learned of the reputed liaison when word reached Dr. Wirths' office.[9] Fortunately for Capesius, the camp's Gestapo never opened any formal investigation.

Upon returning to Auschwitz on September 22, Capesius was startled when Éva told him in confidence that while he was gone someone in the SS command had decided she "knew too much" and should be eliminated.

"Thank God Hauptsturmführer, that you are back! Now I know, I will live," she said excitedly.

Capesius was initially suspicious that his nemesis, Dr. Wirths, was behind it. But he learned quickly it was other inmate workers who were jealous of Éva's elevated status.

"I then spoke with the doctors in the barracks about Éva," he recounted.[10] "I discussed the entire incident."

His forceful and rare intervention on behalf of a Jewish prisoner succeeded.

"Nothing happened to the female inmate Éva," he later told his friends.

In October, Farben ordered home all the German women and children at Monowitz. That the Farben executives no longer thought they could provide safety to the civilians there was a sign of how quickly the battlefield situation was deteriorating. And the pressure on Farben was growing, not just at places like Monowitz. The conglomerate's indispensable role in the Nazi war effort was now front and center for the Allies. Only the month before the Farben evacuation of the German women and children from Monowitz, President Franklin Roosevelt had sent a public letter to Secretary of State Cordell Hull, saying: "The history of the use of the I. G. Farben trust by the Nazis reads like a detective story. Defeat of the Nazi's army will have to be followed by the eradication of those weapons of economic warfare."[11] Company directors feared the firm would be under full assault once the fighting finished.

Mounting evidence the war was going badly added to the urgency for both Farben executives and the SS at the camp. It meant that window of opportunity for personal enrichment was rapidly closing.

Capesius saw a unique opening for further cashing in under the subterfuge of an order issued around this time by Dr. Wirths. According to Capesius, Wirths had directed that all the inmate assistants who worked in the dispensary, and were aware of the mass murder, should themselves be gassed. He claimed he kept his inmate pharmacists alive by having "them work on all kinds of pointless projects." The "pointless projects" were limited, he said, to "reinspect[ing] several times" an overflow of victims' personal belongings stockpiled at the dispensary. In fact, Capesius had little interest in saving their lives but was instead focused on putting them to work scavenging for valuables.

Capesius had embarked on his most gruesome war booty, a quest for the gold fillings extracted from the mouths of gassed prisoners. Dental gold harvested from corpses, together with gold coins, watches, cigarette cases, and jewelry taken from the arriving prisoners, was smelted into bullion. On average, the Nazis reaped between 65 and 75 pounds of gold daily at Auschwitz.[12] It proved a great source of profit for the SS. Shipments of gold stamped "Auschwitz" began arriving at the Reichsbank, the Nazi central bank in Berlin, as early as 1943. Most of that was pressed into bars, each stamped with a swastika and the words *Preußen Staatsmünze-Berlin* (the Prussian State Mint in Berlin). It is not clear how much gold was mined from the Auschwitz corpses since after the war the U.S. army captured the Nazi records listing the exact quantity of gold shipped from the camp to Berlin. The Americans failed to make copies before turning the files over to the West German archives, where they were later destroyed as part of "routine maintenance."[13]

Yakoov Gabai, a Sonderkommando inmate, recalled the grisly process of extracting gold from the dead: "There were two guys from Czechoslovakia, the so-called dentists, they yanked the gold from the victims' mouths. They were actual dentists . . . there was a large crate there, into which they tossed the gold. A large box, a cubic meter in size, with the word *Germany* printed on it. They threw the gold teeth in there."[14]

They operated from a bunker that served as a hellish way station for the twisted corpses between the gas chambers and crematoriums.[15] And they had trouble keeping up the pace with the flood of dead bodies from the around-the-clock Hungarian convoys. As the corpses piled up, Commandant Höss fretted that the backlog might even mean the camp would leave behind gruesome evidence of what had happened at Auschwitz. So in the autumn of 1944, as the Red Army marched inexorably westward, Höss speeded up the handling of the corpses. A new batch of inmates armed with pliers yanked out as quickly as possible the teeth from the piles of dead.

It was a twist of fate that put the dental gold at Capesius's dispensary. Back in 1943, one of the SS officers tasked to accompany a suitcase of dental gold to Berlin had absconded with the ghastly loot (he was arrested in Dusseldorf). After that theft, it was put under the jurisdiction of Auschwitz's chief of the dental clinic, Dr. Willi Frank, and his top dentist, Lieutenant Willi Schatz.[16] Much of the harvested dental gold was crammed into large trunks and sent across the camp from Birkenau to Schatz. As luck would have it, Schatz's office was in Capesius's dispensary. And that is how Capesius came to "volunteer" his inmate pharmacists to sort through those suitcases filled with thousands of teeth pulled from corpses. It was a grim collection.

According to Capesius, "these suitcases were sent to us, or to Dr. Schatz's dental unit, for the gold teeth to be melted from their mountings, and used in new prostheses for prisoners, but given our equipment, this was totally impossible." [17]

Even if such equipment had been available, Capesius had no intention of using any extracted gold to benefit inmates. In fact, he had personally arranged a transfer of a noncommissioned SS officer, Boleslaw Frymark, from his assignment in the "tooth extraction unit" to the dispensary.[18] He and his SS colleagues were by then convinced that all the remaining prisoners were destined to die in the gas chambers. The lure of greed was all consuming.

Pharmacist Prokop later recalled seeing between 50 and 100 suitcases, "overflowing with gold teeth extracted from dead victims' mouths, still with bits of flesh adhering to them. A horrible stink."[18] In a different room of the dispensary, he stumbled across "twenty-five to forty different bags with thousands of individually extracted teeth and whole sets of dentures." As with the grisly collection of trunks he had seen earlier, "these teeth came from the jaws of gassed inmates, often with bits of gum and bone still clinging to them."[20]

Capesius's assistant, Sikorski, recounted after the war that, "On the building's ground floor, where the SS dispensary was located, stood trunks filled with teeth. . . .The first time they turned up, Dr. Capesius showed them to me . . . I counted fifteen trunks [they] were brought from the crematorium."[21]

According to Sikorski, Capesius assigned a Polish prisoner, Maciej Sulikowski, to oversee a handful of inmates in "melting the gold down . . . it was a sideline for the boss." Sikorski saw the results of their work when "some inmates showed me gold bars of six to seven hundred grams each (21 to 24 ounces), made from the melted gold fillings and teeth."[22]

One day Prokop was with Capesius in the dispensary's attic. "Capesius would walk up to the suitcases," said Prokop. "Inside they were filled with teeth and pieces of jaw, gum, and bone still clung to them. Everything had begun to decompose. It stank terribly. It was a macabre sight."

Prokop told his boss that he thought this grisly collection should be stored in the dental office. Capesius ignored him and instead bent over the suitcases and "with his own hands began to dig around in this stinking mess. He pulled out a denture and tried to estimate its worth. And I ran away."[23]

Over time, as Prokop checked on those stored cases of teeth, "their contents were diminished from day to day."

Capesius's partners in this grave robbery of dental gold were his friends, the camp dentists Drs. Schatz and Frank. For his part, Capesius sent dozens of small packages filled with the looted gold to his sister in Vienna.[24] The instructions were clear: stash it all in a safe place since gold might be the only acceptable currency in the chaos of the end of the war.

Chapter 12

IMPENDING END

In November 1944, the realization that the war was lost had finally sunk in for Heinrich Himmler. The SS chief ordered an end to the mass executions. November 2nd was the last day Zyklon B was used at Auschwitz. Starting in late November, tens of thousands of inmates at Auschwitz and other death camps in Poland were forcibly marched westward, away from the advancing Russian army, toward Germany's concentration camps. Many thousands who were already weak and sick died during those marches. In the case of 4,500 Jews from Monowitz who started toward Bergen-Belsen, most were killed by their Nazi guards after they tried fleeing into a nearby forest in the chaos following an Allied bombing run.

At Auschwitz, the Nazis had picked up the pace of dismantling the evidence of mass murder. On December 1, a demolition unit composed of 200 inmates (half of whom were women) began destroying the crematoria. The Nazis were in a race to eliminate as much evidence as possible against the fast approaching day when they would have to abandon the camp.

By January, the Nazis realized it was impossible to evacuate all the inmates. The numbers were overwhelming. About 600,000 prisoners were still in concentration camps and about 250,000 were slave laborers for companies like Farben.[1]

In the second week of January, Farben sent home its remaining German employees. On Saturday, January 13, ninety-six Allied bombers hit Monowitz for an unbroken 15 minutes. It was a reminder that the evacuations had begun just in time. A skeletal staff stayed with orders to oversee the last stages of document destruction and to sabotage the plant so as to render it useless to the Russians.

Capesius and his colleagues were feverishly preparing their own departures. Each had different priorities about what was important before they fled. Mengele, for instance, went to the Jewish doctors' quarters and announced that everything movable was to be packed, even his marble dissecting table. He then stopped by the office of his inmate anthropologist, Dr. Martina Puzyna. It was there that hundreds of twins had been measured before being subjected to his medical torture. "He came into my office without a word," she said. "He took all my papers, put them into two boxes, and had them taken outside to a waiting car."[2] Most of the other SS physicians were in the final throes of vigorously destroying papers about their experiments.

As for Capesius, he scrambled to take as much gold as possible. His chief assistant, Sikorski, noticed that in the dispensary, "On the building's ground floor . . . stood trunks filled with teeth." During those chaotic final days, Capesius surprised Sikorski. "You are a prisoner and I am an SS officer. In two months it may be the other way around."[3] Sikorski did not answer and when he next checked on the trunks, although they were still there, "there was no more gold in them."[4]

Capesius urged his friends, the Stoffels, to flee westward. He told them that the German army in the east was in full retreat. On January 15, in the midst of a raging snowstorm, the Stoffels headed to Bad Tölz in Bavaria.[5] Capesius fled the camp three days later, January 18, traveling with four female inmate assistants, including Éva Citron-Bard. They made their way to Wodzisław Śląski, a medieval town in southern Poland, at the border with Czechoslovakia. There, he said, he let Éva and a couple of the other inmates stay at a weaving mill where they could continue working as prisoners.[6] As for Capesius, his new assignment was Mauthausen, a sprawling concentration camp 12 miles outside Linz, Austria. Gerhard Gerber, Auschwitz's assistant SS pharmacist, had been sent there over a month earlier. "He worked there until the very end in the pharmacy," Capesius later claimed "I did nothing in Mauthausen."[7] The records are not clear about how much time he spent there, but what is undeniable is that by April at the latest he headed to Berlin where he was attached to the Central Medical Station.[8]

Despite their furious last ditch efforts, the Final Solution at Auschwitz had been so grand it proved impossible for the Nazis to destroy all incriminating evidence before fleeing. The Red Army's battlefield advance had picked up momentum by mid-January. Those still in the camp could hear Russian artillery pounding weakened German positions around the clock. The Nazis had no doubts that the Russians, who had lost millions during the war, and whose POWs had been treated as mercilessly as the Jews, were out to exact revenge. It had resulted in a deep apprehension among the remaining SS and forced them to choose between their own freedom or staying to enforce Himmler's directive to eliminate all the evidence of the crimes. On January 19, the remaining SS staff roused a contingent of inmates to spend the morning piling together all the corpses that had been left lying about for more than a week. And during the afternoon, those same prisoners retrieved from the warehouses at 'Canada' as much as they could of hundreds of suitcases that had not even been searched for valuables. That night, the SS set fire to both the dead bodies and the luggage.[9]

When the Red Army entered the camp's perimeter on January 27 they found some 600 unburied corpses and nearly 15,000 prisoners alive. They were the ones too ill to make the march westward and with the gas chambers destroyed there had been no way during the final days to kill them. Even the hardened Red Army troops were startled at the sight of the half-dead, almost zombie-like skeletal prisoners. Within a few days of liberation hundreds died of complications from malnutrition and illness. At Monowitz, nearly half of the 800 prisoners left behind also died over a few days.[10]

In the warehouses of 'Canada' the Russians came upon some of the most stomach-wrenching evidence of what had happened at Auschwitz: 837,000 women's dresses; 370,000 men's suits; 44,000 pairs of shoes, and almost 8 tons of human hair.[11]

When word reached Farben's sprawling Frankfurt headquarters that the Russians had seized Monowitz, Fritz ter Meer – the plenipotentiary for Italy of the Reich Minister for Armaments and a Farben director – ordered the destruction of the company's paperwork.[12] As in Auschwitz, there was simply too much to destroy. Panic-stricken employees tossed out a stunning one hundred tons of documents from their windows into a massive courtyard. Some of the paper was burned in large bonfires while several truckloads crammed with files made their way to the vault of a nearby Reichsbank branch.[13]

Despite the last ditch effort, the Allies captured a warehouse full of papers when they seized Farben's headquarters. It was not the only place where the company left behind key evidence. At the Ludwigshafen plant, a British and American document recovery team discovered critical papers buried in a nearby forest. In another instance, Farben had not had the time to destroy its advanced chemical lab at Oppau, so the Allies disassembled it and shipped it back to England for specialists to pour over.[14]

Many of the soldiers who found the paper troves were disappointed they had uncovered documents rather than some of the missing European art treasures for which the Nazis had become infamous for plundering. But while the front line troops might have been looking for paintings, sculpture and gold, a team of British and American prosecutors and investigators who had been compiling war crimes cases since 1943, were ecstatic. They knew that any paper evidence that survived Himmler's "leave no trace" order would be indispensable to holding those responsible – from the guards who shoved Jews into gas chambers to the company directors who signed the orders to use slave labor – for the crimes of the Third Reich.

By April, American troops had reached Nuremberg and the Red Army was on the outskirts of Berlin. Buchenwald was liberated by the U.S. Army on April 11 and British troops entered Bergen-Belsen on April 15. Two days later, Capesius fled the Red Army and headed further north from Berlin to the northern towns of Flensburg and Husum in the German province of Schleswig-Holstein.[15] He traveled with other SS officers from the central medical office. Capesius was with a contingent that included Himmler. "At the end I was very near him," he recalled years later.[16]

General George Patton's Third Army got to the Flossenbürg concentration camp on April 23 and less than a week later liberated Dachau. The day after Dachau was freed, Hitler committed suicide in his Berlin bunker.

Chapter 13

"UNDER AUTOMATIC ARREST"

On May 5 the American 11th Armored Division liberated Mauthausen. That was the same day that British troops captured Capesius near Flensburg.[1] Two days later, the war ended when Germany unconditionally surrendered.

As the American and British combat troops waged the last fierce months of fighting, military support units behind the frontlines busily preparing for the expected flood of more than five million German POWs and upwards of ten million refugees. They had been converting hundreds of military barracks, schools, even prisons and former concentration camps, into hybrid detention centers.[2]

Capesius was transferred to detention center 2375, one of five camps Britain had set up hurriedly in and around Zedelgem in western Belgium. It was there that he learned on May 23 that SS chief Heinrich Himmler had taken his own life after his arrest by crushing a cyanide capsule hidden in his mouth.

The staggering numbers overwhelmed the Allies who quickly fell behind in processing POWs and refugees. An early goal was to repatriate refugees to their home countries as quickly as possible. That was simpler said than done. Many did not want to return to Eastern European nations under Soviet occupation and concentration camp survivors often had no place left to call home. Their families were dead, their homes had been confiscated, and their communities had been obliterated.

Another priority was to locate somehow in the millions of POWs those who were culpable perpetrators in the Third Reich genocide. Segregating the SS from ordinary German soldiers was a first step. So the Allies had all POWs first strip to their waist and check for the small SS blood-type tattoo. As it turned out for Capesius and the near one million other Waffen-SS, the tattoo that had been the symbol they were an elite Nazi troop had turned into the mark of Cain. Any POW with the tattoo was placed into a higher security portion of the camp and subjected to more intensive questioning. Because of the massive influx, many of those detained ended up spending the better part of a year in custody.[3]

Early during his detention, Capesius filled in a 'Fragebogen' a six-page questionnaire listing 131 questions that the British and Americans had jointly developed. Every German over the age of 18 was ordered to complete one. While the hope was that it might weed out the paper shufflers from the architects of the Final Solution, it was also fully expected that many Nazis would simply lie. So the answers of every questionnaire had to be crosschecked against Nazi party files, German war records, counter-intelligence archives as well as police records, civil service certificates, publications and occasionally even informants.[4] Since the answers were in German, the ability of the U.S. and British to process them was dependent on how many Allied military personnel fluent in German could be dedicated to just that task. Not surprisingly, there was very quickly a significant backlog. In the U.S. and British occupation zones there were some 17 million completed Fragebogens by the end of 1945. Nearly 10 million of those questionnaires, mostly from German POWs like Capesius, had not even gotten an initial review.[5]

Fritzi Capesius was not certain her husband was even alive until late 1945 when she received a postcard from him via the Red Cross. She was overcome with emotion that he was safe, although a hint of his service at Auschwitz unnerved her since she "had heard such horrible things about it." [6] The thirty-eight-year-old Fritzi thought the news of her husband's captivity was the best she had received since the war's end. In Communist-controlled Romania she was no longer the wife of a socially esteemed and successful businessman. Instead, the new government set about expropriating the property of those who helped the Nazis. The Capesius family-run Apotheke zur Krone (The Crown Pharmacy) was seized. Fritzi went from being an owner to a mere employee. She and her three daughters were forced to move to a smaller apartment and soon she was ironing shirts at a local cooperative in order to earn enough to support the family.[7]

While still in detention, in February 1946, Capesius met some ethnic Germans. He described them as "Saxons from Transylvania, country boys, who had done duty as guards in Auschwitz and in Bergen-Belsen. They had been asking whether anyone knew or had seen the druggist of Auschwitz.

"When this group was brought to me," Capesius later recounted, "they told me that Obersturmführer Dr. Fritz Klein had been with them in Bergen-Belsen. They had been charged jointly in the Bergen-Belsen trial."[8]

The previous September, the British had conducted the first war crimes trial charging 45 SS men and women and some Kapos who had served mostly at Bergen-Belsen. Thirty-one were found guilty after a three-month trial. Capesius's friend, Dr. Klein – made infamous when a postwar photo of him standing in a small mountain of corpses at Belsen was introduced into evidence – was hanged December 13, 1945.

Now, two months after Klein and ten of his SS colleagues had been executed, a few of the ethnic Germans transferred to Camp 2375 had asked for and found Capesius. This author has discovered the identity of one of those in the Belsen contingent, a twenty-eight-year-old ethnic German from Romania named George Kraft, who had been inducted into the SS the same month as Capesius back in 1943. Kraft had served as a guard at Buchenwald and Belsen, and possibly also at Auschwitz although he denied eyewitness accounts that placed him there.[9]

Capesius quickly discovered why Kraft and his friends were looking for him.

"Dr. Klein had given them one assignment: they were to look for Dr. Capesius, the druggist of Auschwitz, his compatriot from Reußmarkt, wherever they went," he later recounted in the third person. "They were supposed to tell him that he [Klein] is facing his death calmly, and he is just happy that he, Klein, by his intercession in Auschwitz, was able to shield him, Dr. Capesius, from guilt."

In addition, Kraft informed Capesius that Klein wanted him to know that his mistress, the Romanian inmate pharmacist Éva Citron-Bard, had survived the war. Klein had seen her after they were both transferred to Belsen, and when she contracted typhus, he had gone out of his way to get her food and medicine.

"This he had done as a last kindness for Dr. Capesius, because he knew that he surely would have wanted it that way."[10]

Shortly after his encounter with the former Belsen guards, the British transferred Capesius to Neuengamme in northern Germany. It had been a Nazi concentration camp that the British had converted into a large holding prison. On April 17, 1946, the British issued a decree that essentially categorized all conscripted ethnic-German Waffen-SS members, like Capesius, as ordinary German soldiers. It meant that simply being a Waffen-SS was no longer automatically cause for more intensive investigation or longer detention. Five weeks later on May 25, 1946, a little over a year after he had been captured, the British – unaware of how much blood he had on his hands – released him.[11]

After his release, the relieved Capesius moved to Stuttgart. The city was still in the early stages of recovering from having lost nearly 70% of its buildings from heavy Allied air raids. There, under his real name, he rented a small apartment at 48 Bismarckstrasse.[12]

Although he was longing to return to Romania to his wife and daughters, he abandoned the idea when he learned that a court in Cluj-Napoca, the capital of his native Transylvania, had tried him along with 184 other ethnic-Germans who had served the Nazis and charged them with war crimes.[13] That court had convicted him and sentenced him to death in absentia while he had been in British custody.[14]

He eventually learned from a family friend how it had come about. A Romanian Auschwitz survivor, Marianne Willner, had returned home after the war and had obtained work as an X-ray technician at a medical clinic in Sighisoara that had been used during the war by the Romanian and German military. In their hasty retreat from the Soviets, many documents were left intact. One day, Willner recalled, "I found two interesting documents in a drawer: an SS book and a Romanian military booklet with a photograph, and the signature of a Victor Capesius. I looked at the photograph and said to my husband, 'This man selected me in Auschwitz.'"

She distinctly remembered the "broad shouldered SS officer with a strong face who spoke flawless Hungarian." When she had arrived at Auschwitz in June 1944, she had marched with other women toward an SS man standing at the top of the rail ramp. He was "friendly and charming. He was cheery, laughed, acted jovial, and good-natured. . . . Whoever was tired should go over to the other side [he said]. There was a rest camp there. Everything there was nice and comfortable. We could meet our relatives there again. Many friends went. I did not, instinctively. I wanted to stay with my friends on the other side. Around a hundred of the women thus went to their deaths."

Later, a young medical student inside Auschwitz told Willner "that the officer in question was from Transylvania, that was why he could speak such good Hungarian, he was a druggist and was named Capesius . . . [she] knew that because her father was also a druggist."[15]

Willner knew that in her small Romanian town, "everybody was already talking about Capesius having been in Auschwitz." She thought he was likely dead. Still, she figured it best to "turn over the documents to the appropriate authorities which in this case was the Romanian state security authorities in Sighisoara."

Those two files were enough to jumpstart the stalled investigation that led to his trial and death sentence in absentia. Fritzi was devastated by that judgment. Not only did she steadfastly believe he was incapable of committing such crimes, but she knew also that it put an end to any chance they had of reuniting in their native country. And the Communist government did not allow its citizens to emigrate to the west.[16]

In addition to being a wanted man in his own country, Capesius learned that the Red Army that now occupied Romania had deported some ethnic Germans back to the Soviet Union in mid-January, 1946. It was a day his family and other ethnic Germans called "Black Sunday." Capesius's wife could not help thinking of how it reminded her of when the Germans had ordered the Jews to gather a few years earlier for deportation to Auschwitz.[18]

In Stuttgart, on his own, Capesius hoped to return as quickly as possible to some semblance of a normal life. But that was not so simple since he was well aware that his SS background made that difficult in postwar Germany.[18] He realized that would not change until he went through the contentious and massive denazification proceedings begun by the Allies. That was a program meant to prevent former Nazi party and military officials from returning too easily to their prewar civilian careers.

Capesius knew that only a couple of months before the British had released him, the Allied Military Government Denazification Division had relinquished control to the Germans. The "Law for Liberation from National Socialism and Militarism" enacted that spring had created an enormous judicial bureaucracy to handle the huge backlog of cases. All Germans were now required to fill in a Meldebogen (application), a streamlined two-page questionnaire far less intrusive than the Fragebogen. More than 500 new tribunals, called Spruchkammer, employed more than 22,000 Germans. New government divisions, so-called Ministries for Political Liberation, were established in each German state. Freshly appointed public prosecutors, meanwhile, had to sift through hundreds of thousands of files and determine case by case which of five categories applied: *Major Offenders* could get the death sentences; *Offenders and Profiteers* were liable for 10-year jail terms; *Lesser Offenders* got probation and travel restrictions; *Followers* were fined and had some political rights curtailed, and; *Persons Exonerated* got no sanctions, but instead received an all-important Denazification Certificate that allowed them to return unencumbered to West German life.

It was regrettable, but unavoidable, that some of the Germans who ran the new tribunals had been officials in the Third Reich judiciary. The Allies had little choice since by early 1946 there were nearly a million cases backlogged. In order to expedite the handling of that colossal logjam, some former Nazis would stand in judgment on the denazification claims of their countrymen.

Laws were passed throughout the year in an effort to reduce the number of pending cases. First, everyone born after January 1, 1919 – no older than 26 at the end of the war – was automatically excused. Then the disabled were given amnesty. The final exemption was for anyone who had earned less than 3,600 RM a year during the Nazi era. Since Capesius did not fall into any of those groups he had no choice but to begin his formal denazification proceeding.

On June 4, 1946, only 10 days after the British freed him, Capesius filled in a Meldebogen. It was his first step toward obtaining a full hearing. He lied about three critical parts of his wartime resume. He said "no" when asked if he had been in the Waffen-SS or had participated in any Nazi organization. As for the time he was posted to Auschwitz he claimed instead to have served as a "military official" at Berlin's main medical headquarters.[19] According to an August 16, 1943 entry in his military pay book: "Now assigned as a replacement troop unit, garrisoned at the Zentralsanitätslager (central medic camp) for the Reich-SS medical staff and the police of Berlin-Lichtenberg." Although he did not have to provide any supporting documentation with the questionnaire, that was what he intended to offer if pressed about his wartime service.[20]

It is not surprising that Capesius lied. It was widespread knowledge that the denazification tribunals were overwhelmed. That meant, he thought, it was unlikely they had the resources to cross check and verify the accuracy of each answer. He also knew that he would have to eventually present his own case before a court. And while in British detention he had picked up a lot of useful information from the jailhouse lawyers. As prisoners came and went, they brought with them the latest news about what defenses were working best in order to be fully exonerated through denazification.

Armed with that knowledge, Capesius reached out to former colleagues asking them to provide letters he could attach as part of his ultimate defense. Such character letters that bolstered someone's reputation were so widespread in postwar Germany that a new word entered the dictionary to describe them: *Persilschein*. Named after a popular German washing powder, Persil, it literally translates as "Persil ticket," and was meant to convey how those letters might thoroughly wash someone's past of their Nazi affiliations. For his Persilscheins, Capesius wrote to everyone from his prewar Romanian pastor to some of his Farben/Bayer superiors.[21]

In fact, he knew there was a thriving black market in fake Persilscheins, underground brokers who sold glowing sworn statements priced according to the seriousness of the charges. There were even fake denazification certificates for those wanting to skip the Spruchkammer entirely and willing to take the risk that their documents ultimately would not be unmasked as forgeries. Capesius did not want to buy black market fakes. That might work for a low level technocrat or army private, someone looking to return to a blue collar job in a rural part of Germany. But he was a professional and wanted to revive his pharmaceutical business. He had always intended that the gold he had stolen from Auschwitz would allow him to buy his own pharmacy one day. That would never happen, he knew, unless he got a legitimate exoneration. Or at least he would never stop worrying that he was about to be exposed at any moment. That was not the way he wanted to live in Germany, especially since his ultimate goal was to reunite with his wife and three daughters.

The following month, in July, Capesius visited his friends, the Stoffels, in the Bavarian town of Bad Tölz, for the first time since the end of the war.[22] He complained bitterly about the restrictions on him because of his Waffen-SS service and condemned the Spruchkammer as time consuming and unnecessary. Capesius told the Stoffels he expected the denazification process to be so slow that he had applied to study electrical engineering at Stuttgart's Technical University.[23]

But his complaints about denazification unexpectedly took a back seat that summer. During a trip to Munich on August 21, a Polish survivor, Leon Czekalski, recognized him at the main train station, Hauptbahnhof.[24] Czekalski had been an early political prisoner at Auschwitz. As inmate 2955 he had arrived in August 1940 and worked mostly as a barber. As a result of being there so long, he was able to identify many of the camp's SS, even if he had no direct knowledge of what crimes they had committed. When he saw

Capesius, he ran across the road to get close enough to be sure he was not mistaken. Once certain, he notified the American military police (all of Southern Germany was in the American occupation zone).[25] The MPs detained Capesius that same day and reported it to the local U.S. Counter Intelligence Corps (CIC) office in Munich.[26] Although the British, in their sector of Germany, had decided that Waffen-SS membership was no longer a criminal offense per se, the Americans had not adopted that lenient policy.

Capesius was transferred to Dachau the next day. The U.S. Army had split the former Nazi concentration camp on the outskirts of Munich into a makeshift prison for Nazis and a resettlement center for refugees. It had been rechristened "Civilian Internment Camp Dachau." There he was registered and fingerprinted. Two CIC agents, Willard Zierold and Erich Zieger, who had earlier interviewed Czekalski and found him credible, were waiting to interrogate him.

More importantly they had obtained a copy of the questionnaire Capesius had completed only two months earlier to commence his denazification proceedings. Czekalski had identified Capesius by his Waffen-SS rank – Sturmbannführer (major) – as well as his position as the camp's chief pharmacist. The CIC agents noted immediately that Capesius had omitted any reference on his June questionnaire about the Waffen-SS or Auschwitz.

They ordered Capesius to strip to his waist. That revealed his SS blood-type tattoo, which they noted in their "CI Arrest Report," public here for the first time. It was the physical evidence confirming Czekalski's accusation that the man detained was at least an SS member.[27] In formally arresting Capesius, the agents noted the reason: "Falsification of Fragebogen."

At the end of a several hours interrogation, Capesius finally admitted his lies. Insisting Capesius put his admission in writing, the agents typed up a one-page document that he dictated in German. In that declaration, also published here for the first time, Capesius provided a sketchy but accurate wartime resume. He admitted that, "On August 1, 1943, I moved to the Waffen-SS central hospital camp in Berlin. . . . I was promoted to Hauptsturmführer (Captain) by the Waffen-SS. In November 1943, I was stationed at the Dachau hospital camp for 3 weeks and then returned once again to Berlin. In February 1944, I was named leader of the pharmacy of the Auschwitz concentration camp. I practiced at this job until 20 January 1945. In November 1944, I was promoted to the Waffen-SS rank of Sturmbannführer (Major)."

Sturmbannführer was a key admission. It was the minimum rank qualifying for automatic arrest by the British and Americans.

Capesius nevertheless tried minimizing his SS service by noting, "I stress that I was never a member of the SS death head units."

After summarizing how he had fallen into British custody in May of the previous year, he came to the all-important confession on which the CIC interrogators insisted.

"I admit that when filling out the Fragebogen, I concealed my membership in the Waffen-SS and my rank."[28]

Being caught in such a blatant lie about his wartime service was a humbling and worrisome moment. What the Americans would now do with that incriminating information was the great unknown.

Chapter 14

"WHAT CRIME HAVE I COMMITTED?"

Although Capesius was depressed at finding himself in American custody after having spent more than a year in British detention, he was by that time well aware that his fate was much better than that which had befallen many of the Third Reich's top echelon, as well as his former superiors and colleagues. Dr. Eduard Wirths, who had first welcomed him to the camp, had hanged himself in British custody (Before his death, Wirths wrote a letter to his wife, saying, "What crime have I committed? I really do not know!").[1] Enno Lolling, chief of the Medical Services and Camp Hygiene who had assigned Capesius to Auschwitz, had shot himself as he was about to be arrested. Commandant Rudolf Höss had been captured by the British the previous year and before he was hanged had given chilling testimony about the atrocities at the camp before the International Military War Crimes Tribunal. The British had hanged Josef Kramer, who had been in charge of Auschwitz's main killing center. Ernst Kaltenbrunner, chief of the Reich Security Head Office, and Hans Frank, the Governor General were scheduled to be hanged that October.

As for the doctors Capesius had served with, their fates were mixed. Josef Mengele and Wilhelm König were fugitives. Besides Fritz Klein, who had been hanged, Dr. Helmuth Vetter, who oversaw Farben/Bayer's experiments of untested drugs on prisoners, was also executed. Dr. Werner Röhde, who had done the Evipan experiment with Capesius's help, was set for execution the following month. Carl Clauberg, who had performed medical experiments and had bragged to Capesius that "his sterilization method was completely perfected," was in a Soviet prison awaiting trial.[2] Hans Münch was in a Polish prison pending his trial. Dentist Willi Frank and SS sergeant Josef Klehr were in an American jail awaiting a final decision as to whether or not there was enough evidence to prosecute them. SS guard Irma Grese, of whom Capesius said "may have been a perverse bitch," had been hanged by the British.

Not all the news about his colleagues was bad. His good friend, the dentist Willi Schatz, had been released by the British nine months earlier and had started a dental practice in Hanover. Otmar Freiherr von Verschuer, the German professor who ran Berlin's preeminent Kaiser Wilhelm Institute for Anthropology, Human Hereditary Teaching and Genetics and received many of the human specimens from Auschwitz, had been fined 600 Reichsmarks ($240) and returned to a prominent career as the dean of the Münster medical school and the chairman of the German Society of Anthropology. Capesius's Auschwitz friend, Roland Albert, had falsified his discharge papers and paid a bribe to a well-connected Austrian lawyer to make certain that his SS service file was "lost."[3] He slipped quietly away with his family to the picturesque town of Kufstein in the Tyrolean Alps, where he became a private religious studies tutor.

Capesius was not, of course, aware that behind the scenes the victors had been mired in a heated debate over how aggressively to pursue wide-ranging war crimes trials. The sincere intentions of the prosecutors and investigators tasked with developing criminal charges had run into political and logistical headwinds. Initially, Stalin wanted no trials and instead demanded shooting 50,000 top Nazis as a symbolic measure of justice. The Americans and British were adamant that any executions could only be the result of trials in which the defendants had an opportunity to defend themselves.

The British and Americans prevailed and a series of trials – with the main ones at Nuremberg in southern Germany – began in 1946. But even once the decision had been made to hold them, there was a fierce debate about whom to charge. Top SS and military leaders were obvious defendants but not everyone thought that German businessmen were criminally responsible. The compromise made in the main Nuremberg case was to include Hjalmar Schacht, the civilian finance wizard for the Third Reich.

Complicating this discussion about whom to charge with war crimes, the British and Americans were quickly locked in a new cold war. The Soviet Union had put much of Europe and eastern Germany behind an Iron Curtain and there was some opinion that a strong and quickly revitalized West Germany was critical to check Stalin's power. Those in America and Britain who argued against extensive war crimes trials contended that it was impossible to jail all of Germany's top businessmen and political leaders without hobbling the country's ability to rebuild itself and become a bulwark against Soviet aggression and expanding communism. While it was distasteful, undoubtedly there was strong sentiment that many of the businessmen, judges, and even some government bureaucrats who had thrived under the Third Reich, should eventually return to their former positions in a newly constituted German republic. And there was a growing resentment among ordinary Germans, and some sympathetic Americans and Brits, that denazification had gone too far and had turned into a form of collective punishment.

As for Allied intelligence, it was not concerned about bringing Nazis to justice for their crimes, but instead preferred to find those who might help fight the new Red menace. Operation Paperclip, for example, was a large American covert program that recruited more than 700 Nazi engineers and rocket scientists after the war. U.S. and British intelligence found themselves in a race against the Soviets, who had a similar program (Operation Osavakim), to recruit Nazis who were experts in chemical warfare, ballistics, medicine, science, and cryptography.[4] Some were brought back to the U.S. and Britain for interrogations. A few of those, like former V2-rocket inventor Werner von Braun and Dr. Hermann Becker-Freyseng, later convicted of war crimes, went to work for NASA. Others found covert jobs in Washington and London. And a handful were put into so-called ratlines and sent to freedom in South America and the Middle East.[5]

Capesius had no such value. No intelligence source had him on a short list for having important information that could be useful in the new Cold War. A pharmacist from Auschwitz had to fend for himself. There was no Allied intelligence "get out of jail free card" waiting for him.

At Dachau, Capesius was less interested in the broader implications of the political news than he was in the immediate question of his own fate. He later told his friends, the Stoffels, that the Americans had "posted his photograph everywhere with the words: 'Who knows the SS pharmacist Dr. Victor Capesius of Auschwitz, born in Romania, and who can testify about him?'"[6] He did not know, as the author has discovered in previously classified U.S. Army documents, that they had cross checked him through the U.S. "War Crimes Central Suspect List" and had assigned him an active file number.[7]

In September, the CIC distributed a "work sheet" seeking additional information about Capesius.[8] In the meantime, the Third Army Headquarters ordered him transferred 160 miles away to Flak-Kaserne Ludwigsburg, a former German military barracks that the U.S. had renamed Civilian Internment Enclosure No. 74. The barracks happened to be near Stuttgart, where Capesius had earlier rented an apartment, and also the jurisdiction in which he would have to fight his denazification before a German tribunal. For reasons not made clear in declassified U.S. Army files, Capesius was transferred back to Dachau just a month later, on October 14. Although he had been in American custody ever since his August detention in Munich, his return to Dachau was classified as a new "Automatic Arrest."[9] As a result, on October 17, he completed a new six-page, 131-question Fragebogen. It is revealed here for the first time.

In his handwritten answers, Capesius again admitted that he had lied about his Waffen-SS service and his rank, acknowledging that he was an SS Major (Sturmbannführer) and chief pharmacist at Auschwitz.[10] As for whether he had ever taken an oath of loyalty and sworn allegiance to an organization, he admitted, "Yes. Waffen-SS." On a section titled "Income and Assets" he noted that his 9,000RM he earned at the death camp was more than any prewar salary from Farben/Bayer.

When he signed and dated the last page, he wrote a caveat near his signature: "The details above are written down from memory and without written documents. . . . They are provided with this limitation to my best knowledge and conscience."[11]

His answers served him well. On November 8, First Lieutenant Erich Mahlgut, in the Headquarters of the Ninth Infantry Division responsible for the administration of Dachau, sent a two-page summary and recommendation to the Assistant Chief of the Headquarters for U.S. Forces in Europe. Under "Findings" Mahlgut drew the all-important conclusion: "Subject is not considered a security threat."[12] Capesius later told the Stoffels that although the Americans had tried hard to build a case against him, they were stymied because "there were no incriminating statements made by anyone."[13]

The Army transferred Capesius back to the Ludwigsburg camp near Christmas, 1946. There he was allowed to formally begin his denazification proceedings while he remained in custody. He had already begun accumulating copies of the Persilschein good character letters.

On Christmas Eve, 1946, he completed a second two-page Meldebogen (also revealed here for the first time). This one was not for his American captors, but instead he sent it directly to the German tribunal. It was meant to replace the one in June on which he had omitted his SS role. On the new questionnaire, however, he still modified a key part of what he had confessed just a few months earlier to the U.S. counterintelligence agents. Although he now listed his Waffen-SS service and his correct rank, he described his wartime role simply as 'pharmacist' but again left out "Auschwitz."[14]

Three days later, he completed a new detailed Fragebogen, his fourth questionnaire in a short time. This he also sent directly to the Germans. Again he listed his Waffen-SS service and rank. Yet, again, in response to question 29, he changed the truthful answer he had given recently to the Americans. He had written back in October that he was "Chief Pharmacist, Auschwitz, reporting to Dr. Wirths" throughout 1944. On this new form, he changed it to "Pharmacist, Central Station, Berlin, reporting to Sturmbannführer Wehle."[15]

It was a risky gamble. On the one hand, Capesius knew that the single word *Auschwitz* would be a red flag before any denazification court. Having been there, especially as a ranking SS officer, might on its own torpedo whatever chance he had to return to unrestricted civilian life. On the other hand, he knew there were simply too many POWs for the US authorities who ran the detention camp to read every piece of prisoner correspondence. They did, he knew, randomly check mail. If they read his new questionnaire, and compared it to the one he provided to the CIC in October, he could be charged once again for "falsifying his Fragebogen." A second such offense, especially brazenly done right under the nose of his captors, would undoubtedly keep him in custody for a much longer time. But he clearly thought the greater risk was putting *Auschwitz* before the German denazification tribunal.

On January 3, 1947, Capesius sent a handwritten 4-page letter to the Ludwigsburg public prosecutor. That letter, revealed here, set forth the heart of his defense that the denazification laws did not apply to him. He said that he had been forced to become "a foreign member of the Waffen-SS," emphasizing that his training was medical not military. As a Romanian, he contended, according to Nazi race laws it was impossible for him to be a full member of the SS. He pointed out that he did not have an SS number, had never joined the Nazi party, and that he had wanted as a pharmacist to "help suffering people, not to disobey the Hippocratic oath." Capesius also emphasized his role as a director of a Lutheran church group in Bucharest and that while the SS wanted him to leave the church, he had refused. He also played for sympathy by claiming that he had "lost everything" to Communists in Romania and that all his family – parents, wife, and daughters – were living in "a state of emergency" there.

"I am unlucky to be a prisoner of war," he concluded, stating that the Americans were holding him on the technicality of his Waffen-SS membership, a classification the British had long ago discontinued. He failed, of course, to mention that the U.S. was in fact holding him because an Auschwitz survivor had identified him and that after his detention the American interrogators realized he had lied on his earlier questionnaires about serving at the death camp.[16]

With his letter, he included a number of Persilscheins attesting to his good character and honest nature. He had the right to submit more before a final date was set for a formal hearing.[17] To bolster that he was really a good Romanian first and foremost, one of the Persilscheins was from Karl Heinz Schuleri, his childhood friend who had been the pastor in the Romanian army unit in which they both served. Reverend Schuleri said that Capesius "had not left the church when he went to the Waffen-SS." And moreover, Capesius "had stayed in regular contact" with the pastor and throughout the war had maintained a "Christian world view." Two of his former Farben/ Bayer colleagues attested to their "complete satisfaction" with his work, and noted that "every task he was assigned he took care of with great success, all through his hard work."[18]

He also, incredibly, had completed another long-form questionnaire, his second Fragebogen in less than a week, and sent that in with his January 3 letter. In that form, he gave the same answers as on his last. He was not certain whether it had to be part of the package that arrived with his own letter and supporting witness statements. So not wanting to take a chance of delaying his denazification hearing, he again took the risk of sending a questionnaire through the detention camp that not only omitted his time at Auschwitz but lied by putting him in a much more innocuous job at Berlin's medical headquarters.

Capesius was pleased at least that he had finally started the clock running on his denazification proceedings. The result was that on February 12, 1947, a hearing file was opened for him at the Ministry for Political Liberation in Württemberg-Baden. The Ludwigsburg prosecutor shared an 8-page summary of the case pending against Capesius with the U.S. Army. It basically reiterated the charges about his Waffen-SS service and rank. Nothing was mentioned about Auschwitz.

On May 2, the public prosecutor stunned Capesius by issuing a formal indictment (Klageschrift) charging him in the most serious category, Major Offender. It meant possibly even capital punishment. Although the charge had caught him by surprise, when he read the short summary of the prosecutor's case, he was somewhat relieved to discover that his placement into the Major Offender category was mostly automatic based simply on his SS membership and rank.[19] In fact, the indictment stated, "It is assumed his activities fit at least one of the categories [of the most serious charges] but this has not been proven."[20]

Capesius immediately realized what was necessary. He had stated the gist of it in his letter to the prosecutors four months earlier.

On May 12, only ten days after the indictment, he submitted a full-throttled defense set out in a four-page typed letter. It was a more robust and detailed version of his earlier letter. And it revealed how much he had learned about the law during his nearly two years in British and American detention. He sounded at times more an attorney than a pharmacist as he cited "that Article 39, paragraph 3 of the Denazification Law was exculpatory" since "it exempted anyone who was forcibly required to provide health services."

Capesius focused on the specific paragraphs of the law that defined war criminals and argued the law simply did not apply to him as an ethnic German Romanian. He emphasized that he had not volunteered but was drafted to the Waffen-SS. For the first time, he maintained the rather incredulous argument that because of the many restrictions on communications in his native Romania he did not know anything about the criminal nature of the SS at the time he became a member. And, he added – without any documentation – that he was "racially unfit" for serving in the SS-Totenkopfverbände, the elite Death's Head SS responsible for administering the death camps.[21]

Moreover, he argued that his November 1944 promotion to the rank of Sturmbannführer was not for his "zeal in service" but was an automatic advancement the Nazis had done for all Romanian ethnic Germans in the SS as compensation for having lost their property and savings when Romania had turned against the Third Reich earlier that year. That promotion was, he said, like a "tranquilizer pill" for having lost his family behind the communist front lines.

The Americans had investigated him at Dachau, he said, and had "exonerated" him of any crimes.

Capesius went out of his way to let the court know he had been raised in a multi-cultural environment and that as a result he understood and was sympathetic to peoples of all nationalities and ways of thinking. In a clumsy effort to underscore the point he gave a few examples of how he had studied or worked under Jews. In describing his time at the University of Vienna he noted the good doctoral evaluation he had received from his primary Professor, Dr. Richard Wasitzky. "Dr. Wasitzky is since 1938 a professor in America. At that time, he left Vienna because his wife was included in the 'Nuremberg Law.'" And "the apolitical nature of our work" at Farben could be attested to by Dr. Alexandro Bardeanu (formerly – Rotbart) and Moritz Scheerer, both of whom "had to leave the firm [in 1939] . . . because of the Nuremberg Law."[22] Capesius did not mention, of course, that he had no idea where Bardeanu and Scheerer were. As Romanian Jews it was likely they had been in the mass deportations to Auschwitz in 1944.

Still emphasizing his good character, Capesius said he was not only raised in the Lutheran church but remained in the faith throughout the war. He was still a member, he said, even if he did not go to weekly mass. He noted that his three daughters had all been baptized.

Despite all the details, what was missing was what he did while serving in the SS. It was clear he was a pharmacist, but he avoided saying where he was stationed. His strategy was not to address Auschwitz unless he was confronted by it.[23]

Once again Capesius submitted more Persilscheins. There was a letter from Dr. H. Koch who attested to his good character and described how Capesius was on very good terms with some former Jewish colleagues at Farben.[24]

Ten days after submitting his detailed defense, he appeared before a panel of five German judges. Capesius represented himself without an attorney. He stuck steadfastly to his story. And remarkably, no one asked him what he had done during 1944. That allowed him to say he had been assigned to "a central medical station."[25]

That same afternoon, the judges gave their verdict: not guilty. Capesius was ecstatic that they had accepted so completely his arguments.[26] He was a good Lutheran, they concluded, who had been forced by law to join the SS, and he had only provided medical services. That decision, he thought, meant he should soon be freed from detention and given a denazification certificate by which he could finally restart his life. It took five weeks, until June 30, for Captain John Austin to formally process for the U.S. Army the decision of the German tribunal.[27]

When, on August 2, 1947, he was set free from the Ludwigsburg detention camp, Capesius thought that the final chapter in his two-year odyssey with the Allies was over.[28] He was right, he would not again have to worry about the British or Americans. But that same day he was jolted by a directive from the Ministry for Political Liberation. That was a quasi-judicial German department created by the Allies to oversee and review denazification cases. The Ministry had the authority of a typical appellate panel to reverse the findings of the trial court.[29] And that is precisely what they did by overturning Capesius's acquittal. The new ruling questioned whether he was eligible for the exemption carved out for "the performance of medical services under certain circumstances of coercion." That defense was meant, said the court, "only when a physician, without being a member of a criminal organization, was ordered and forced to make medical examinations." The Ministry for Political Liberation thought it likely that Capesius "was not drafted into the Waffen-SS for the purpose of practicing medicine, but rather for the fulfillment of his military service."

His file was sent back for a hearing before a new court, which the Ministry urged to "demand exculpatory material concerning his political orientation. In the absence of which, by virtue of his successful promotion to Sturmbannführer, it is to be suspected that he fulfills the requirements of being a Major Offender."[30]

Even though he was a free man, it was an infuriating setback. He had been so close to closing the chapter on his wartime service. Now he had yet another contentious round still to go.

This rare prewar photo (circa 1928) of 21-year-old Victor Capesius (left) relaxing at the public pool in his Romanian hometown of Sighisoara with the Böhm family. Eight-year-old Ella (next to Capesius) called him her Pharmacist Uncle. Sixteen years later (May 1944) the Böhms, and nearly 2,000 of their neighbors, were rounded up by the Nazis and sent to Auschwitz. Upon arriving at the death camp, Gisela Böhm (far right), a pediatrician, and Ella, were stunned to recognize Capesius as one of the SS officers at the death camp's railhead. (*Auschwitz Trial Court Exhibit*)

Before joining the Waffen-SS in 1943, Capesius worked as a sales representative for I. G. Farben's Romanian pharmaceutical subsidiary. Frankfurt-based Farben was the world's fourth largest conglomerate and an integral partner of Hitler and the Third Reich. Many pharmacists like Capesius wanted to work for its Bayer brand. The company's science labs had produced a record four Nobel Prize winners in chemistry and medicine. In his Farben/Bayer job, Capesius traveled throughout Romania and counted many Jewish doctors, pharmacists and textile manufacturers among his clients. (*Bundesarchiv and Courtesy of Hessischer Rundfunk*)

Dr. VICTOR CAPESIUS

«Bayer»
SECTIA STIINTIFICA

Reprezentanta pentru România:
»ROMIGEFA« S. A. R.
Sucursala CLUJ, Cal. Motilor 18
Tel.: 37-22—Căsuta Post. 127

I. G. Farben's advanced technologies and patents for synthetic oil and rubber were critical to Hitler's dream of making Germany militarily self-sufficient. Adjacent to Auschwitz, Farben built a huge manufacturing plant. In 1941, SS chief Heinrich Himmler (2nd from left) met with Farben engineers at the construction site. The company initially named the facility Monowitz, after a nearby Polish town. Himmler renamed it Auschwitz III, an extended part of the Nazi's sprawling death camp. (*Yad Vashem*)

Auschwitz III cost Farben a record one billion Reichsmarks (about $55 billion in 2015). The sprawling facility was several square miles in size and required more electricity than Berlin. Of 300,000 forced laborers, about 25,000 were ultimately worked to death. (*Yad Vashem*)

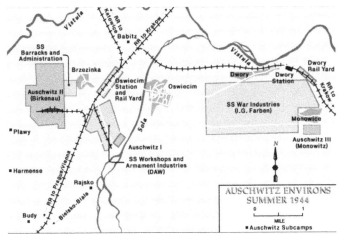

By the time Capesius arrived at Auschwitz it was a staggering 15-square-mile complex composed of three main camps. The original Auschwitz I was largely administrative but also included Block 10, the site of medical experiments. Auschwitz II (Birkenau) housed the most prisoners and was also the location of the gas chambers. Auschwitz III (Monowitz) was I. G. Farben's slave labor camp. (*US Holocaust Memorial Museum*)

At Auschwitz II-Birkenau, incoming trains packed with Jews from around Europe were met by SS doctors, including Capesius, who performed life and death selections at the railhead. Of the 1.5 million deported to Auschwitz, 1.1 million were sent immediately to the gas chambers. Others, judged able-bodied, were put to work, many at Farben's neighboring plant. In this rare photo, the SS have split the arriving prisoners into separate lines of men and women. (*Yad Vashem*)

Farben paid millions to the SS for a steady supply of camp inmates. It paid four Reichsmarks (then about $1.60, $20 in 2015) a day for skilled inmates, three for unskilled prisoners and one and a half (60 cents) for children. For that, the SS provided transportation to and from Auschwitz I, some four miles away. Above are female inmates gathering for work. (*US Holocaust Memorial Museum*)

One of the few pictures of prisoners marching from Auschwitz I to Monowitz (Auschwitz III). The Nazis demanded that every forced laborer who left the camp after a 4:00 AM roll call be accounted for at the evening one. Workers dragged along the corpses of co-workers who had died during that shift to assemble at their cellblock so that the Nazis could count the dead bodies. (*US Holocaust Memorial Museum*)

Jews deported to Auschwitz were each allowed to bring a maximum of 110 pounds of personal belongings. Believing they were being resettled to work camps in Nazi-occupied Eastern Europe, they took along their most valuable possessions, hoping to hide them from the Nazis. At the railhead, those goods were piled next to the trains. One of Capesius's duties was to search for medicines and medical instruments brought by arriving doctors. (*Yad Vashem*)

The personal belongings of the arriving Jews were taken to large warehouses in Birkenau and sorted by prisoners. Cash, diamonds and jewelry were often sewn into the linings of overcoats, dresses, and suits, hidden inside bottles of lotions and creams, and even in secret compartments cut into suitcases. The Nazis soon became proficient at knowing where the victims stashed their valuables. (*Yad Vashem*)

Left is a typical work room for Capesius and the other doctors in Auschwitz's autonomous network of hospitals and clinics. The first infirmary had been built in the camp in 1940 but by the time Capesius arrived there were wards for prisoners, outpatient clinics for the SS, a dental suite, as well as his dispensing pharmacy. Inmates nicknamed the hospital a "waiting room for the crematorium." (*Yad Vashem*)

As the chief pharmacist, Capesius was in charge of storing Zyklon B, a cyanide-

based pesticide originally used to fumigate prisoner barracks and clothing and later as the killing agent in the camp's gas chambers. Farben, Capesius's prewar employer, ran the firm that had a patent on Zyklon B and it produced stunning profits as demand for the pesticide soared at Auschwitz. (*Wikipedia Commons*)

Part of Capesius's responsibility was to distribute drugs and medications, including test compounds from Farben and Bayer, for medical experiments. The companies paid for prisoners that the SS doctors used as guinea pigs. Most of those inmates suffered horrific side effects or died. One of the deadliest series of tests were those for Bayer's B-1034 compound (right), an experimental typhus cure. (*Auschwitz-Birkenau Memorial Museum*)

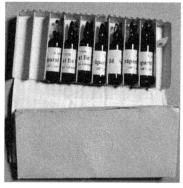

The camp's two dentists, Drs. Willi Frank and Willi Schatz, ran their clinic from a room inside the same building as Capesius's pharmaceutical dispensary. They were responsible for storing the gold extracted by inmate dentists assigned the grisly task of pulling the teeth of every corpse taken from the gas chambers. The dental gold was part of 65 to 75 pounds of the precious metal reaped daily at Auschwitz, everything from coins, watches, cigarette cases and jewelry. Before it was sent to Berlin to be smelted into coins, the teeth and fillings were stored with the dentists for safekeeping. (*US Holocaust Memorial Museum*)

The dental gold, kept in large suitcases in the attic of the dispensary, proved too great a temptation for Capesius and the dentists, who stole some and smuggled it to relatives outside the camp. One of Capesius's inmate pharmacists recalled "Capesius would walk up to the suitcases. Inside they were filled with teeth and pieces of jaw, gum, and bone still clung to them. Everything had begun to decompose. It stank terribly. It was a macabre sight. . . with his own hands [Capesius] began to dig around in this stinking mess. He pulled out a denture and tried to estimate its worth. And I ran away." (*Yad Vashem*)

Capesius spent many weekends socializing at the nearby homes of fellow ethnic Germans from Romania. One was Armin Rump, a fellow pharmacist, whose shop (left) was in the town of Oswiecim (Auschwitz in German). The Rump family home was so close to the camp, Capesius noted, that from their "balcony at night you could see the light of a huge fire burning . . . and everyone knew that human beings were being burned here, you could smell it too, when the wind was blowing in the wrong direction." (*Yad Vashem*)

Many of the SS assigned to Auschwitz took regular breaks at Solahütte, a little known resort along the Sola River 18 miles from the camp. In the summer of 1944, Obersturmführer Karl-Friedrich Höcker, the adjutant to the commandant, compiled a chilling photo album of SS personnel enjoying themselves in a myriad of social festivities that seemed a world apart from the death camp in which they served. (*US Holocaust Memorial Museum*)

On May 5, 1945, British troops detained Capesius in northern Germany but released him a year later without formal charges. Acting on a tip from an Auschwitz survivor, American forces arrested him in Munich in August 1946 but after failing to gather sufficient evidence also set him free after a year. Capesius had to submit to denazification proceedings in 1947, German tribunals that determined the culpability of those who had served the Third Reich. In a series of questionnaires designed by the British and Americans, and in handwritten letters to the tribunals, Capesius often lied about or omitted completely his service at Auschwitz. (*Bundesarchiv*)

The Americans freed Capesius in 1947, just as the trial began of 24 top executives of his prewar employer, I. G. Farben. Included among the defendants were three directors who ran the company that manufactured Zyklon B, the poison for the gas chambers that Capesius stored in his dispensary. Also on trial was a director who had approved payments for some of Auschwitz's medical experiments. Capesius and other SS colleagues were relieved when 10 of the Farben defendants were acquitted and the remainder given light sentences that were eventually commuted. (*US Holocaust Memorial Museum*)

Capesius stole enough of the gold teeth fillings from Auschwitz to enable him to open his own pharmacy (above) in 1950 in the small German town of Göppingen. In 1952 he had earned enough money from that pharmacy to open a successful cosmetic institute in a neighboring village. The institute's motto was 'Be Beautiful with Treatment by Capesius'. (*NDR, stills from the 1964 film "Bleiben die Mörder unter uns?"*)

By the 1950s, Capesius thought he had successfully avoided any punishment for his crimes at Auschwitz. He was unaware that two men were working to build war crimes cases against former Nazis, including him. Hermann Langbein (left) had been an inmate in the chief doctor's office in Auschwitz and after the war had formed the largest survivor's organization. He was relentless in tracking down witnesses, taking statements, and prodding German authorities to open files on Nazis living in plain sight in postwar Germany. (*Schindlerfoto Oberursel*)

Fritz Bauer (right) a jurist who had served time briefly in a German concentration camp, had become in 1956 the first Jewish chief prosecutor in the nation's history. Bauer had a passion for investigating war crimes. His goal was to locate enough high ranking SS officers who had served at Auschwitz to hold a showcase trial about the crimes of the Final Solution. (*Schindlerfoto Oberursel*)

Capesius was arrested by German detectives on December 4, 1959, outside his pharmacy in Göppingen. He was held in jail without bail until he, and nearly

two dozen of his SS colleagues from Auschwitz, went on trial on December 20, 1963. Charged with murder and conducting medical experiments, Capesius hired two highly acclaimed lawyers. Hans Laternser (left) had defended the Army High Command at the main Nuremberg war crimes trials. His ju-

nior partner, Fritz Steinacker (right), was a former Nazi party member who also represented the family of the fugitive SS doctor, Josef Mengele. (*Schindlerfoto Oberursel*)

Each defendant was assigned a number that was placed on a placard in front of them. This was designed to make it simpler for witnesses to identify the person about whom they were testifying. Capesius, number 18, was the only defendant who often wore dark glasses inside the courtroom. (*Courtesy of Elan Steinberg*)

The trial lasted 20 months and included testimony from 359 witnesses from 19 countries. One of the most emotional accounts was given by a Romanian physician, Mauritius Berner. Before the war he had bought Bayer medications from Capesius. In May 1944, Berner and his family were deported to Auschwitz. He recognized Capesius at the railhead and begged in vain for him to protect his family. (*Courtesy of Hessischer Rundfunk*)

Berner was with his wife and three daughters, two of whom were twins. "They will just have to go back to their group," Capesius told Berner. "Don't cry. Your wife and children are just going to take baths. You will see them again in an hour." Berner learned after that his family was gassed within an hour of their arrival. (*Courtesy of Hessischer Rundfunk*)

Capesius shocked many courtroom observers as the only defendant who often smiled or laughed, even at some of the most damning testimony against him. He grinned constantly to the other accused and to his family and friends in the courtroom. Late in the trial, he tried explaining the odd behavior by claiming to the court that his "smiling was unconscious." (*Courtesy of Hessischer Rundfunk*)

On August 19, 1965, Capesius was found guilty of the lesser charge of "accessory to murder" and sentenced to nine years in prison. However, after two and a half years, he was freed. He returned as a hero to his small German town. (*Schindlerfoto Oberursel*)

The year before Capesius was freed from jail, his chief accuser, Hermann Langbein (third from left) was recognized at Yad Vashem, Israel's Holocaust Memorial, as one of the "Righteous Among the Nations," an acknowledgement of non-Jews who risked their lives to save Jews during World War II. (*Yad Vashem*)

Chapter 15

NO ONE KNEW ANYTHING

While Capesius's travails with the Allies and the denazification proceedings were all consuming, only a few days after he was set free he had a stark reminder that his legal problems were slight in comparison to the top executives at his prewar employer. I. G. Farben. He had been released just in time to follow the sixth major war crimes trial at Nuremberg starting that same month. *The United States of America v. Carl Krauch, et al.*[1]

What to do about Farben had been the 900lb gorilla in much of the internal debates between the U.S., Britain and Russia. It was the world's fourth largest company and had almost singlehandedly supplied and profited from the Nazi war effort. Farben's defenders, of which there were many, contended that the company was simply a bastion of leading scientists and inventors and it was preposterous to hold them responsible for Nazi crimes. Some British and Americans were sympathetic. A vocal minority complicated matters by arguing that seeking justice in the early trials had given way by 1947 to Jewish "vindictiveness."[2] John Rankin, a Republican congressman from Mississippi, called the pending Farben trial "disgraceful" and said that while "every other country has now washed its hands and withdrawn from this saturnalia of persecution, a racial minority, two and half years after the war closed, are in Nuremberg not only hanging German soldiers but trying German businessmen in the name of the United States."[3]

Those who had investigated Farben's history and its pivotal World War II role, however, knew that to portray the company as anything but a fully-fledged and enthusiastic partner with Hitler was disingenuous at best and deceptive at worst. Brigadier General Telford Taylor, who had replaced Supreme Court Justice Robert Jackson as America's top war crimes prosecutor, was blunt: Farben's hierarchy had been "the magicians who made the nightmare of Mein Kampf come true."[4]

In fact, the previous year, a report commissioned by General Dwight Eisenhower determined that Farben had been so indispensable to the Nazis that any of its plants used for war production should be demolished and any remaining ones seized and divided among the victors. How to accomplish that was still under debate as the criminal trial got underway.

Twenty-four senior executives had been charged in a sixty-page indictment setting forth counts of "Waging Wars of Aggression," "Plunder and Spoliation," and "Slavery and Mass Murder."[5] The defendants included Farben's chairman, Carl Krauch, as well as Fritz ter Meer, Otto Ambros, Heinrich Bütefisch, Christian Schneider, and Walter Dürrfeld, all directors with some oversight of Monowitz. Also in the dock were Heinrich Hörlein, Wilhelm Mann and Dr. Carl Wurster, three chemists who had been directors of Degesch, the Zyklon B manufacturer (Mann was its wartime chairman).

The trial's first day was August 27, 1946. The second-floor courtroom was the same that had served as the dramatic setting for the main Nuremberg trial of top Nazis a year earlier. Carl Krauch, who had been awarded the Knight's Cross medal for distinguished service to the Third Reich by Hitler himself, was now in the chair that Hermann Göring had occupied. Three noted American justices sat in judgment.[6] The 300 spectator seats were packed and the press gallery was overflowing. The stakes could not have been higher: the defendants faced the death penalty.

Joshua DuBois, Jr., Telford Taylor's thirty-three-year-old deputy, acknowledged the dichotomy between the brilliant minds at Farben and the charges in the indictment: "This is the story of twenty-four geniuses who changed the face of the earth. The most brilliant men in Europe, they headed the industry known as I. G. Farben. . . . These I.G. Farben criminals, not the lunatic Nazi fanatics, are the main war criminals. If the guilt of these criminals is not brought to light and if they are not punished, they will represent a much greater threat to the future peace of the world than Hitler if he were still alive."[7]

DuBois had spent the war running the U.S. Treasury's efforts to track, block, and seize Nazi financial assets. In that role he had become an expert on Farben, including its myriad subsidiaries, ghost firms, and foreign trusts and partnerships. That influenced his decision to start his case with the charge that the company had conspired with Hitler to "wage an aggressive war." To prove that, DuBois relied on an enormous quantity of fairly obtuse documents, organizational charts, patent licenses, and intensely detailed corporate reports.

Many courtroom observers thought it was a mistaken strategy. There was even disagreement among his colleagues. Emanuel Minskoff, a junior prosecutor, argued that, "We should have started with Auschwitz."[8] But DuBois was not persuaded. It was too late to change course when after a few weeks, Judge James Morris said from the bench, "Mr. Prosecutor, this organization, so far as records show here, was simply a big chemical, commercial, and business concern, the like of which there are many throughout the world. . . . I am at complete loss to comprehend where documents of this kind are of the slightest materiality to the charges. This trial is being slowed down by a mass of contracts, minutes, and letters that seem to have such slight bearing on any possible concept of proof in this case."[9]

The Farben defendants were not that concerned about which charge the prosecutors first addressed because they had secretly adopted a strategy to avoid admitting anything incriminating. Even those responsible for I. G. Auschwitz would maintain that they saw nothing unusual. The crux of their argument would set the standard for an entire generation of Germans who later claimed they knew nothing about the extermination of the Jews.

As the trial progressed, it seemed at times as though each defendant tried outdoing the others when it came to how little they knew.

Otto Ambros, who had first located the site in Poland for Farben's Monowitz complex, swore that it never crossed his mind that the Nazis could supply slave laborers from the adjacent concentration camp.[10] In a memo he had sent to the Farben board describing one of his visits to Auschwitz, Ambros wrote, "The institution of a concentration camp is something horrible. It is torture for the inmates." DuBois introduced that memo to demonstrate that Ambros knew terrible things were happening in the camp. Nothing of the sort, maintained Ambros, who claimed he had simply an aversion "for the short-cropped hair [of the prisoners]. . . . That is the torture to which I referred."

Ambros also backpedaled from correspondence in which he boasted about a "promising new friendship with the SS," claiming he never knew about life and death selections of prisoners until the Nuremberg trials. As for the malnutrition that plagued Monowitz laborers, it must have been due to some "unjust distribution of the food after it had gone through the kitchen." What about the crematorium at the entrance he saw during one trip? "I was told that if anyone of these human beings should happen to die, he would be cremated there. That was all."

Prosecutors showed Ambros many reports about incidents of the SS brutalizing the workers who built Monowitz. Ambros claimed that was news to him, despite his eighteen visits there, he protested: "I am only a chemist . . . I think it isn't possible to expect the chemist to read every construction report." What about the many documents that listed Ambros as the project manager? "I was the business manager, but only an honorary one."

Fritz ter Meer, who was the Frankfurt-based director responsible for Monowitz's chemical plant, said he could "not recall" whether Ambros had ever mentioned neighboring Auschwitz and its ready supply of forced laborers.[11] As for an inspection visit he made to Auschwitz III in 1943 with Ambros (his third trip there), ter Meer claimed not to remember seeing any guard towers. He could not even give a description of the condition of the workers since "I was inside the camp in the afternoon at a time when these people [inmates] were not in the camp, for they were working at the time and there were not many people about."

Had he seen Auschwitz's main crematorium? Yes, ter Meer said, "I was told it served to cremate the corpses in the case [of] deaths."[12]

What about Auschwitz's enormous chimney? "I have no recollection of it."

Christian Schneider, Farben's personnel chief who was in charge of the synthetic fuel plant, testified at length about a construction conference he attended at Monowitz in January 1943. According to him all the inmates he saw "made a very proper appearance." At one stage, Schneider was brought to a large room where "the staff and the foreigners together took their noonday meal. I tasted the food. It was good." Schneider claimed he had not witnessed a single thing that was unusual from the many other German complexes Farben owned. "If something had not been quite in order, I would have remembered it," he testified.[13]

Heinrich Bütefisch, one of Farben's top synthetic fuel specialists, was responsible for the first formal request to Himmler for Auschwitz inmates to be used as forced laborers.[14] Besides his senior I. G. Auschwitz role, Bütefisch was also an SS Obersturmbannführer (Lt. Colonel). He echoed the testimony of his colleagues that on his many visits to Monowitz and its sub-camps, the workers always seemed fit, strong, and well fed. He could not remember memos addressed to him about the lack of washing facilities for thousands of workers and he dismissed the construction of a mortuary as something that was needed "for purely sanitary purposes." As for how many times he went to I. G. Auschwitz, he could not answer since his wartime travel records were supposedly missing.[15]

Three of the defendants, Heinrich Hörlein, Wilhelm Mann, and Dr. Carl Wurster, were Farben scientists who were also wartime directors of Degesch, the Zyklon B manufacturer. Their testimony was remarkably similar. They recalled "an insect plague in the East" and could not remember ever knowing that the eye irritant and warning labels had been removed from the poison canisters sold to the SS. As businessmen on the Degesch board they claimed not to pay attention to scientific details. This despite Mann being a pharmaceutical director, Hörlein a chief of Farben chemical research and former chief of Bayer's pharma labs, and Wurster the head of I. G. Auschwitz's chemical plant. They did not recall that in 1943 Zyklon B made up a remarkable 70% of Degesch's business and that 90% of all the Zyklon B sold went to Auschwitz.

To cast doubts on the accuracy of the prosecutor's case, defense attorneys submitted 386 affidavits, including some from convicted Nazis who had been posted to Auschwitz, purporting to show that the defendants had not known or approved of the worst of the crimes.[16] Two men already found guilty of war crimes over slave labor, Field Marshall Erhard Milch, and corporate titan, Friedrich Flick, testified that the Farben defendants had acted out of "legal necessity," since refusing to follow Nazi directives would have led to their arrest and imprisonment.[17]

Prosecutor DuBois summed up the heart of the Farben defense. "The Farben directors knew nothing of this [the Final Solution]. The two who picked the site [at Monowitz], and the one who headed the construction, knew nothing. The one who procured inmates from Himmler knew nothing even after he moved to Auschwitz. The director in charge of employee welfare at Auschwitz didn't know a thing. The fifth, the sixth, the seventh, and the eighth directors – who headed the firm of Degesch which shipped all the Zyklon B to Auschwitz and the institution which shipped the typhus vaccines and drugs – didn't know anything either."[18]

As the drama in the Farben trial played out, Capesius had meanwhile felt compelled to finally hire an attorney, Dr. Rudolf Pander, in Stuttgart.[19] Pander was a lawyer who had during the war been a Lt. Colonel in the Abwehr, German Intelligence, assigned to Bucharest from 1942-43.[20] He also had been detained by the Americans in 1945 and fully interrogated and debriefed before his release the following year. Pander had reopened a legal practice and quickly developed a reputation as a smart advocate who knew his way through the intricacies of the denazification process.

On October 7, 1947, Pander appeared before a new tribunal. He contended that as a matter of law Capesius should be acquitted and that the original court had reached the correct decision in acquitting him. According to Pander, the reversal was in error because the ministry had mistakenly thought that Capesius might have been a battlefield SS officer. Anyone conscripted to work in healthcare, he argued, had a broad exemption under Article 39, Section III, of the denazification statutes.[21]

Two days later, Capesius took the stand before five new judges. He knew his script well. He hit all the highlights from stressing his Lutheran faith and emphasizing that he never was a Nazi party member. As for his wartime service, Pander had counseled him that his intuition was correct to avoid mentioning Auschwitz unless it somehow became unavoidable from the questioning by the judges. When asked, Capesius said only that, "After training on September 1, 1943, I arrived at the central medical station in Berlin where I was appointed the pharmacist for dispensing drugs there." He stayed there, he said, until the end of the war in April 1945.

The court did not have a copy of the October 1946 questionnaire Capesius had given to the Americans where he admitted his Auschwitz service. Not one of the judges asked if he had ever been stationed in a concentration camp.[22]

The final chapter in Capesius's denazification came that same day, October 9, 1947, when the tribunal handed down his second acquittal. The verdict could not have been better if Pander himself had written it.

"The person in question" has "conclusively demonstrated" that he was "forcibly called up into the Waffen-SS," and therefore he "cannot be considered a member of a criminal organization." It even accepted his contention that he was not suitable for full SS membership since he was "racially a type III (Eastern type)." In accepting Capesius's lies wholesale, the court concluded that he was "not active in the SS, nor in the secret field police or border police." Instead his "only" work was the "health service," in the "Central Medical Clinic in Berlin," where he performed his duties, "the preparation of medications for the individual troop units."[23]

Capesius had maintained a low profile in Stuttgart since the Americans released him in August. Now, armed with his formal denazification card demonstrating that he was free to work without any restriction, he landed a job as an assistant pharmacist at Stuttgart's

Reitelsberg Apotheke.[24] It was a small, family-run pharmacy owned by a lady by the name of Monika Raff. She was pleased to see he had a formal clearance from the German courts, but she also was typical of most Germans in that she was not at all interested in learning about what her employees had done during the war.[25]

While Capesius was taking the initial steps to rebuild his life, the Farben trial came to an end on May 28, 1948. Over its 152 days there had been nearly 200 witnesses, 3,000 affidavits, and 6,000 court exhibits. The trial transcript was a daunting 16,000 pages. The backdrop against which the judges weighed the evidence were daily headlines over the escalating cold war with the Soviets. The Communists seized power in Czechoslovakia and the Soviets put in place a blockade on West Berlin the week the trial finished. It added to the feeling that prosecuting Nazi crimes three years after the end of the war was an unaffordable luxury, especially when West Germany had to morph from a punished enemy to a valuable ally.

It took two months for the judges to reach a verdict. That decision would determine whether the era for holding Germany's top industrialists responsible for the crimes of the Nazis was coming to an end.

Chief Judge Curtis Shake read the majority verdict from the bench.[26] Counts one and four were about waging aggressive war and conspiracy. All the defendants were acquitted of both. As for count two – crimes over plunder of property and assisting in deportations from occupied countries – fourteen of the twenty-three were acquitted. As for the most explosive charge, count three, slave labor and mass murder, although the court rejected the defense of "legal necessity," it found five defendants most directly involved with I. G. Auschwitz – Krauch, Ambros, Dürrfeld, Bütefisch, and ter Meer – guilty.[27]

Prosecutors were stunned that ten of the defendants escaped without so much as a word of reprimand. Included in that number were Dr. Wilhelm Mann, who had been the wartime chairman of Zyklon B manufacturer Degesch, and who had personally approved the Farben payments for Josef Mengele's Auschwitz medical experiments.

The prosecution was dealt a further setback when it came to sentencing. As DuBois thought it unlikely anyone would receive the death penalty, he had asked for terms ranging from 20 years to life. But the longest punishment to be handed down was eight years to Ambros and Dürrfeld. Five of those convicted for war crimes were given less than two years. And the court gave all the guilty another break by crediting them for time served while awaiting trial. DuBois and his team left the courtroom in a fury. "The sentences were light enough to please a chicken thief," he muttered.[28]

Chapter 16

A NEW BEGINNING

Capesius closely followed the sentencing of the Farben directors as he went about mapping out the next chapter in his life. In 1949 he moved from his tiny apartment to a 3-room condominium he bought for 50,000 DM ($205,000 in 2015) on Fruhlingstrasse, an upscale neighborhood of Göppingen, a tiny town about 30 miles outside Stuttgart. If anyone had been paying attention, it might have seemed surprising that Capesius – cut off from his family and any savings in Romania and only earning a minimum salary as a pharmacist assistant – had so much money. He had told his American and British captors and German denazification tribunals that he lost his net worth of some 20,000 Reichsmarks "through the occupation of Romania after the war."[1] Luckily for him, no one asked where he got the cash. German prosecutors later came to believe that a postwar reunion in Göppingen that Capesius had with Drs. Frank and Schatz, the two Auschwitz dentists, took place because the trio had managed to retrieve the gold they had stolen from the camp and had finally divided the loot.[2] He had always intended that gold to help him get a fresh start after the war. And now it did. In Göppingen, in 1950, he obtained an operating license as a druggist from the state of Baden-Württemberg and purchased a butcher shop for over 150,000 marks. Soon he set about converting it into a state-of-the-art pharmacy.[3] The Markt-Apotheke (Market Apothecary) opened for business on October 5 that year.[4]

Capesius was pleased at the speed of his private rehabilitation. But he marveled at the quick change in fortune for the top Farben executives. A couple of months after Capesius started Markt-Apotheke, the front-page news in Germany was that the company's wartime chairman, Carl Krauch, was freed less than two years into his eight-year sentence. All his co-defendants followed him to freedom shortly after when John McCloy, the American high commissioner, responded to German pleas for clemency and commuted the sentences of about 70% of convicted Nazis.[5] A horde of reporters greeted the jailed Farben directors as they walked out of Landsberg prison. Fritz ter Meer, referring sarcastically to the standoff in Asia between the U.S. and Communist China over the Korean peninsula, smiled and said: "Now that they have Korea on their hands, the Americans are a lot more friendly."[6]

Capesius admired the fact that despite being tried and convicted, the professional careers of these men had not been damaged in the new Germany. This despite the fact that the Allies had originally barred war criminals from returning to the same industry. Carl Krauch became a lavishly paid director at Chemische Werke Hüls AG, a former Farben subsidiary that had been a key part of the company's synthetic rubber production. Hermann Schmitz, former Farben CEO, became the chairman of Rheini Steel and a director of a Berlin-based bank. Heinrich Bütefisch landed a role as a director of Ruhr-Chemie. Fritz Gajewski, who had run Agfa for Farben during the war, became the chairman of three consecutive German chemical companies. Wilhelm Mann and Heinrich Hörlein, the former Degesch directors, joined Bayer's board of directors. Christian Schneider, head of the gasoline production at I. G. Auschwitz, became a highly paid consultant to several European chemical consortiums. Otto Ambros, who had chosen the site for I. G. Auschwitz, became a chairman of Chemie Grünenthal, and a director of half a dozen of Germany's most prestigious chemical firms. Max Ilgner, who ran Farben's foreign intelligence operatives, became a successful political lobbyist in Bonn.[7]

As for the conglomerate itself, Farben remained under Allied supervision through 1949 only to be formally dissolved in 1951.[8] Coincidentally that same year a Jewish survivor filed the first civil suit seeking reparations for slave labor that eventually resulted in payments to 5,855 victims of amounts ranging between $1,250 to $8,500 ($8,800 to $60,000 in 2015).

Four major companies emerged from Farben's dissolution.[9] Bayer, by its size, instantly became one of the world's top ten pharmaceutical companies; Agfa became the leading manufacturer of imaging products; BASF was spun off as the planet's largest chemical firm; and Hoechst, a chemical and science conglomerate, immediately became one of Germany's most profitable companies. And who better to run these companies than some of the senior Farben executives freed from their war crimes sentences? Fritz ter Meer, the only defendant to be convicted on two war crimes counts, became the all-powerful chairman of Bayer.[10] Carl Wurster became the chairman of BASF and the president of Germany's Chemical Industry Association. And Friedrich Jähne, Farben's chief engineer, was appointed the chairman of Hoechst.

For those who had tried to bring the Farben executives to justice, their return to power was bittersweet. DuBois later bemoaned how the American and British fear of the Soviet Union in the Cold War had led to the embrace of "those German industrialists who were the generals in gray suits in World War II."[11]

The return to power of the Farben directors emboldened Capesius and many SS colleagues to have a false sense of security that the worst was over when it came to the pursuit of justice for Nazi crimes. He stopped fretting daily over whether or not he might face charges over his Auschwitz service and instead concentrated solely on his business and bringing his family to Germany. That single-mindedness translated into great success. By 1952 he had earned enough money from the Markt-Apotheke to open the Institut für Cosmetologie (The Cosmetic Institute), a modern beauty spa in Reutlingen, a small town also near Stuttgart. The Institute's motto was *Be Beautiful with Treatment by Capesius*.[12]

When he wrote to Fritzi about his new accomplishments, it reaffirmed her faith that the ambitious man with whom she had first fallen in love had the talent and discipline to prosper in the new Germany. It would only be a matter of time, she predicted to friends, until he reunited the family in West Germany.[13] At least she hoped it would be quick since her children were starting to pay a price for having an infamous Nazi father; 17-year-old Melitta had been expelled for "political reasons" from a mechanical engineering school (Universitatea Politehnica Timisoara).[14]

Capesius seemed to everyone in Göppingen to be just another successful story of the economic boom that gripped Germany during the 1950s. The Wirtschaftswunder (Economic Miracle) of that decade saw the wages and purchasing power of the average German nearly double. As the nation rebuilt itself from the ravages of bombed out cities and demolished infrastructure, Capesius benefited from the one rule that all Germans instinctively followed: never ask what someone did during the war.

By the mid-1950s his pharmacy was turning over profits of 425,000 DM annually (over $100,000 then) and he had fifteen employees.[15] He indulged his love of hunting by leasing a game lodge in Austria and took expensive safaris to Africa. In Göppingen, his new friends considered him charming and he moved easily in the best social circles. Capesius was a member of the tennis, riding, hunting and even a glee club. It was at this time that he petitioned the Red Cross, citing humanitarian grounds, to help get his wife and children out of Romania. While the Red Cross was occasionally successful in reuniting families split by the Iron Curtain, Capesius took no chances. He therefore separately invested an unknown amount of money into what was dubbed the "family buyback" program, essentially a legal scheme of bribing cash-strapped Communist officials to allow people to emigrate to the West. He understood that this process could be drawn out, but he was confident that his family would ultimately rejoin him.

Capesius was also buoyed by shifting attitudes about World War II in West Germany. The public mood toward war crimes had changed considerably from the time the Allies had conducted trials that resulted in the execution of some of his Auschwitz colleagues. In the wake of those trials, there was widespread antipathy among ordinary Germans who considered the charges of war crimes as mere political vengeance by the victors.[16] The Americans and British had turned full control of the judiciary back to the Germans in May 1955. One of the first directives under the new jurisdiction was that Nazis convicted and serving sentences of less than three years were immediately released.[17] From that point forward, the sole responsibility for prosecuting Nazi crimes fell to West German courts and prosecutors. But many of the justices who had served under the Third Reich were back on the bench. Not a single judge from the notorious "people's courts" was even charged with a crime.

A year later, the German parliament (Bundestag) annulled the top two criminal categories – crimes against humanity and war crimes committed in furtherance of genocide – that the Allies had relied upon in their trials. The Bundestag ruled that those were post-facto laws invented by the Americans and British and that no one should be convicted of statutes not in existence when the crimes happened. The Bundestag also abolished capital punishment.[18] Germany's first postwar chancellor, Konrad Adenauer, thought it important to integrate ex-Nazis instead of excluding them from the new Germany. He included some prominent former NSDAP officials in his cabinet, most notably the ethnic cleanser Theodor Oberländer, who was forced from office in 1960 after an East German court sentenced him to life for war crimes.[19]

Not surprisingly, all of this translated into a sharp drop in the number of formal investigations into Nazi crimes. In the four years after the war, the Allies convicted 4,419 Nazis. In 1955, the first full year of German control, there were only 21 convictions. The open investigations dropped from nearly 2,000 in 1950 to fewer than 200 by the mid-1950s.[20] The problem was more than just a failure to start new investigations; in the instances in which charges were brought during the 1950s, the acquittal rate was about 80%.[21]

The more laissez-faire judicial attitude made Capesius feel ever more comfortable. However, he and other SS colleagues who had never been charged with a crime were unaware there were some dark clouds on the horizon.

In 1956, Fritz Bauer, a 52-year-old jurist who had briefly been in a German concentration camp during World War II before he safely reached exile in Sweden and Denmark, was transferred from the State Attorney's office in the town of Braunschweig to the city of

Frankfurt.[22] Bauer was appointed the first Jewish chief prosecutor in postwar Germany. Sweden's archbishop, Lars Lilje, knew Bauer well and had no doubt that he would quickly establish himself as "the first and foremost jurist . . . who took seriously the systematic pursuit and prosecution of Nazi murderers."[23]

Although Bauer downplayed his Jewishness, it was undeniable he had a passion for investigating wartime crimes. That was a matter of heated discussion inside the German judiciary. Bauer soon found himself embroiled in a brutal internal battle with colleagues who had dismissed his focus on Nazis as impetuous and unnecessary, and spread the rumor that he was a homosexual, something that was still then illegal in Germany.[24] Ladislas Farago, a prolific author on World War II, wrote about Bauer: "His work [would] earn for him the passionate hatred of former Nazis and neo-Nazis, the stricture of people who preferred to let bygones be bygones, and the hidden antagonism of certain members of his own staff. They regarded him as a do-gooder, an avenging Jew, a fire-eating old grouch who let his emotions run away with him when his head should have prevailed."[25]

Bauer knew that the fragmented, half-hearted and sometimes redundant local probes of Nazis were unlikely to result in significant charges. Some of the State's Attorneys' offices suffered from a personnel shortage that prevented them from thoroughly investigating complex cases. Others had no desire to pursue them, considering it a vestige of the past. An essential part of the cure, contended Bauer, was to collect evidence about those crimes in a single central office and then forward solid, well-developed cases to local prosecutors. That idea finally took hold on October 1, 1958, when the State Justice Ministers throughout West Germany finally agreed to create the Central Office of the State Justice Ministries for the Investigation of National Socialist Crimes of Violence in Ludwigsburg.[26]

It seemed an obscure bureaucratic change of little significance. And its effect was not immediate. But over the next few years, the number of investigations would multiply from 400 to more than 6,000. One of those was an ever-growing file with the name "Victor Capesius."

Chapter 17

"INNOCENCE BEFORE GOD"

Bauer was not the only person whose pursuit of wartime justice should have concerned Capesius and his former SS colleagues. Hermann Langbein, an inmate assistant in the chief doctor's office at Auschwitz, had made it his life's mission to bring the camp's perpetrators to justice. At the camp, Langbein had an unusual birds-eye view of the mass murder. As his office had overlooked the entrance to Crematorium I, he was able to watch as prisoners were packed into the gas chambers and their corpses later carried out by the Sonderkommando. In 1952 Langbein had co-founded the International Auschwitz Committee (IAC), then the largest group of survivors. He was relentless in tracking down witnesses in more than a dozen countries, taking their statements, and even sometimes playing amateur sleuth in hunting for Nazi fugitives. By the late 1950s he had compiled the world's largest private evidentiary archive of crimes committed at Auschwitz. The men he wanted indicted, he told German prosecutors, had blood on their hands. Capesius was only one of several dozen on Langbein's list.

A confluence of events in 1958 brought Langbein and prosecutors together. On March 1, an Auschwitz Kapo, Adolph Rögner, sent a letter to the Stuttgart prosecutor. He claimed that Wilhelm Boger, a sadistic SS officer who had invented an eponymously named device by which prisoners were savagely beaten at the camp, was living openly in Stuttgart and working as a supervisor at an airplane factory. Boger had last been seen when he escaped in 1945 from a train taking him to Poland to stand trial.

The prosecutors were skeptical. Rögner had a long arrest record, a history of making false charges about Nazi crimes, and was in prison for a perjury conviction when he sent his tip.[1] The information initially languished since the chief prosecutor not only thought

Rögner untrustworthy but that he was a "vengeful psychopath." Still, the police took Rögner's statement. Their conclusion: he got his detailed information about Auschwitz from a large collection of books in his apartment and he was simply an attention seeker. They were not certain if it was worth following up on two other Rögner leads, SS officers from Auschwitz he claimed were residing in Germany under their real names.

But Rögner had written not only to the Stuttgart prosecutor. He wisely had sent his original tip to Langbein and the IAC. When Langbein asked the prosecutors about the status of their Boger probe, they hurriedly authorized a more thorough investigation for fear that they might appear to Holocaust survivors as lackadaisical in chasing war criminals. Langbein was concerned not only that the prosecutors might drag their feet, but that Boger might somehow get tipped off and again flee.

Langbein tried speeding up the probe by providing nearly a dozen witness statements over the summer. Still, it took until October 8, 1958, before the police arrested Boger. Under German law, when someone is suspected of serious crimes and there is a risk they might flee, prosecutors can put a suspect into pre-trial custody. That investigative detention can last through to a criminal trial.[2]

"I have no guilty conscience or I would have fled," Boger said after his arrest. His wife told a German reporter that she had lived with her husband at Auschwitz. "I can't believe he did the things they say. How could he have killed children? He had children of his own."[3]

Meanwhile, a Frankfurt reporter had sent Fritz Bauer some documents a survivor had recovered. They listed the names of 37 SS men involved in executing attempted escapees from Auschwitz. Relying on those papers, Bauer started his own investigation. And he filed a motion with the Federal Court of Justice in Karlsruhe asking that his office have the exclusive right to prosecute all Auschwitz crimes, no matter where in Germany the defendant was arrested. The high court agreed and Boger's Stuttgart file was transferred to Bauer in Frankfurt.

In April 1959, Bauer ordered the arrest of three SS men who had served in Boger's Auschwitz Gestapo unit: Pery Broad, Klaus Dylewski, and Hans Stark. All were living in West Germany under their real names. Reexamining Nazi crimes picked up in June when a judge in Freiburg issued a murder indictment against the fugitive Josef Mengele.[4] Langbein had been relentless in pushing for those charges.

The following month Bauer was again on the move. On July 21 he arrested Oswald Kaduk, a non-commissioned officer that the German weekly *Der Spiegel* called "one of the cruelest, brutal, most vulgar" SS men at Auschwitz.[5] Kaduk had been sentenced by a Soviet military court in 1947 to 25 years at hard labor but had been released in 1956. When Bauer found him, he was a nurse at a West Berlin hospital. That same day, police arrested two other Nazis sought by Bauer, Franz Hofmann, the former head of Auschwitz's security guard, and Heinrich Bischoff, a Kapo.

The progress made by Langbein and Bauer encouraged many others to join the reenergized effort to bring perpetrators to justice. By late 1959, the World Jewish Congress appealed for all Auschwitz survivors to step forward. And Bauer published a letter in a dozen leading international newspapers seeking witnesses.[6] Survivors eager to provide their stories soon inundated both the prosecutors and the IAC.

The detention of the ex-Nazis was big news in Germany. Boger had lived and was arrested in Stuttgart, where Capesius had originally settled after the war. Göppingen, where Capesius had his pharmacy, was only a short drive away. None of this could have been comforting for Capesius. But far more alarming was that Bauer had tapped two young public prosecutors, Joachim Kügler and Georg Friedrich Vogel, to initiate a formal criminal investigation that April into Capesius. It was a probe, that Kügler later admitted, was "extremely difficult."[7]

The pharmacist of Auschwitz learned about that inquiry over the summer when the police sent notice that they wanted to question him.[8] Authorities thought Capesius seemed nonplussed. He was living in plain sight and had made no effort at running. That was because he was innocent, he insisted to anyone who asked. Even his friends did not think he was particularly concerned about the turn of events.[9]

Behind the scenes Capesius was far more anxious than he let on. He enlisted the help of Hanns Eisler, a friend of his brother-in-law, to track down some SS members who had served at the camp, and a few of his favored former inmate pharmacists, in the hope they might provide exculpatory declarations. Capesius thought it would be useful insurance. Eisler was sworn to secrecy and Capesius told him that if the effort became public he would deny any knowledge of it (he later did just that).[10] Capesius gave Eisler a hefty 50,000 DM budget (about $12,000, four times the average salary of a working family in the United States).

Eisler's first stop was not an auspicious one. He went to the home of Ferdinand Grosz who had not only been a Jewish prisoner pharmacist at Auschwitz, but had known Capesius during his Bayer drug sales. Before the war Grosz had worked in a drugstore in Târgu Mures, and he had told Langbein that Capesius "would spend hours in our pharmacy."[11] Maybe Grosz, who once described himself "as a protégé of Capesius," might at least credit him for his survival.[12] "I threw him [Eisler] out," Grosz later recalled. "Whether by accident or coincidence he [Capesius] had saved my life, one must not forget the gassing of those many thousands of human beings he had selected for extermination, a crime which can never be atoned for."[13]

Capesius suggested that Eisler stick to possibly friendlier people such as the Stoffels and the Rumps, his ethnic German friends on whose estates he spent his free time while at Auschwitz. Eisler did visit the Stoffels at their home and later took them on a hunting holiday at Capesius's Austrian game reserve. Eisler told them "to try and remember and get down in writing everything that happened."[14]

On December 4, 1959, Victor Capesius arrived at his pharmacy, as was his routine, a few minutes before 9:30 that morning. He did not at first pay attention to the two men who were waiting outside. They quickly blocked him and identified themselves as investigators working with Bauer's office. Before Capesius could utter a word they informed him he was under arrest for investigative detention.

Capesius was stunned. It is surprising that the arrest of six other SS officers who had served with him at Auschwitz had never made him fear that his own detention was imminent. His denial about his own conduct at the camp was so great that it had allowed him to think that he was immune from what had happened to Boger and the others.

The two investigators escorted Capesius to the local courthouse in Göppingen. A senior judge, Dr. A. Trukenmüller, and the public prosecutor, Joachim Kügler, were waiting. The judge informed him of the general charges in the arrest warrant. They included that he had "carried out and monitored, along with the SS doctor Mengele, selections on the ramp, made selections in the camp, and managed and delivered the killing agent Zyklon B and phenol." Also, the inquiry was looking into whether he participated in deadly medical experiments.[15]

Capesius had a right to remain silent at this arraignment. Kügler asked if he would answer questions for a sworn statement. Capesius was without a lawyer but was cocky enough to agree. But it was more than simply hubris that made him say *yes*. Although it would mark the first time he publicly discussed his time at Auschwitz, for many years he had carefully thought about what he would say on such a day. He knew that what he said would, with some variations and elaborations, become the cornerstone of his defense moving forward. And it was all carefully choreographed to diminish his role and authority in the death camp, relieve him of any personal responsibility, and to mix his answers with a combination of flat denials in some instances and in others to question the credibility of his accusers.

Kügler began the questioning about Capesius's background, from his education to his civilian job before the war at Farben/Bayer, to his postwar detention by the Americans and British. It was calculated to put Capesius at ease and he seemed relaxed. When talking about his induction into the Waffen-SS, he made a point of replaying what he had raised successfully in his denazification proceedings 12 years earlier: "it was not of my own volition." He passed off his six weeks of SS training as focused innocuously on "pharmaceutical work designed for administration." He also downplayed his brief initial assignment to Dachau, claiming he had "nothing to do with the camp," but only supplied medicines to Waffen-SS fighting units "when ordered to so."[16]

As for Auschwitz, he said that in February 1944 he had become the chief pharmacist after the death of his predecessor, Adolf Krömer, which occurred about two months after he had arrived there, but had left by Christmas 1944.[17]

Kügler asked Capesius to explain what he did at the camp. In laying out his duties, Capesius emphasized his responsibility as the pharmacist to "supply all medicines for the SS personnel and inmates." That meant he "often had to fetch the medicines with an ambulance from the Birkenau ramp . . . where a pile of suitcases and instruments was already lying ready. There, a uniformed man would hand the things over."[18] Sometimes, he claimed, he skipped the ramp pickup and assigned it to two junior officers.

Whenever possible he put in a good aside: "I did my best for the inmates I employed in the pharmacy. I managed to supply them with extra food and their meals were cooked secretly in the attic."[19] At another point he related a self-serving tale of dubious authenticity. He was, he boasted, the SS officer primarily responsible for eliminating the scourge of typhus from Auschwitz. That was because Dr. Wirths, the chief physician, had dispatched him in the spring of 1944 to Berlin to visit his friend, Dr. Josef Becker, at the Central Military Hospital. Wirths, claimed Capesius, had "ordered me to get 70 ampules to treat typhus." He and Becker added three zeroes to Wirths' order so Capesius returned with 70,000 ampules. "In four years typhus had made the camp unbearable," testified Capesius. "The epidemic had again broken out among the inmates. The ampules were distributed between the camps as necessitated . . . after two months there was no typhus anymore."[20]

Capesius knew his account was impossible to disprove. Wirths was dead, as was Becker, and most of the records of Berlin's Central

Military Hospital had been destroyed in the Allied carpet bombing at the end of the war. For the most part, however, Capesius avoided too much detail. From his denazification hearings he knew that the more precise his information, the easier it was for the prosecutors to later find contradictions or mistakes.

Kügler was not so easily about to let Capesius control the tone and temperament of the hearing. He had brought a large stack of papers and file folders. He pulled out a thin book titled *I Was A Doctor in Auschwitz*, written by Gisella Perl, a Jewish inmate physician who had worked for Dr. Mengele. Perl had written her 189-page book, detailing the horrors of Mengele's medical experiments in Auschwitz, in 1948. She had been a pediatrician in Sighet, Romania, before the war, and had mentioned Capesius several times in her published account. She had met Capesius in 1943 when he was a Farben/Bayer rep and he had made a sales call on her. When she and her family were sent in cattle cars to Auschwitz in the spring of 1944, she had recognized Capesius on the ramp. She did not know the SS officer next to him, but later learned it was Mengele, for whom she was assigned to work. Both Capesius and Mengele stood at the front of the long line of newly arrived inmates. They sent Perl and her brother to the right. Her father was sent to the left and the gas chambers.[21]

Kügler read from the book. "'Jewish physicians step out of the lines!' Dr. Mengele, chief physician of the camp ordered. "We are going to establish a hospital.'

"Along with a few others I stepped forward and came face to face with Dr. Kapezius, standing beside the chief physician. I had just recovered from an unsuccessful attempt at suicide. My head was shaved and the dirty rags that covered my body did not hide my pitifully weakened condition. For one second, I could not believe my eyes. In a flash I saw my home, my son holding the violin under his chin, my husband and our guest (Capesius) listening to him with rapt attention. The scene revolved in front of my eyes while his face smiled mirthlessly, then darkness settled over everything. When I came to, I was lying on the floor of my block and was ordered to report to Dr. Kapezius immediately.

He looked me over from head to foot and smiled again. When he spoke, his voice was cold and jeering and my loathing was so strong that at first I could scarcely understand his words. His voice, however, succeeded soon in reaching my consciousness.

'You are going to be the camp gynecologist' he barked. 'Don't worry about instruments . . . you won't have any. Your medical kit belongs to me now, and also that unusual wristwatch I admired . . . I also have your papers, but you won't need those. You can go.'

I never saw him again."[22]

It was obvious that the Perl excerpt caught Capesius by surprise.

"I cannot recall a woman, Dr. Gisella Perl," he said slowly, after a short silence. "But I do not want to state that I did not know her." [Much later, Capesius would try and sully Perl's reputation by telling a journalist that "Mengele needed embryos for [research] . . . So Perl did a lot of abortions, until they could get a living, viable embryo."[23] In fact, when Perl had "learned that they (mother and newborn) were all taken to the research block to be used as guinea pigs, and then two lives would be thrown into the crematorium, I decided that never again would there be a pregnant woman in Auschwitz. . . . In the night, on a dirty floor, using only my dirty hands. . . . Hundreds of times I had premature deliveries, no one will ever know what it meant to me to destroy those babies, but if I had not done it, both mother and child would have been cruelly murdered."[24]]

Capesius fell silent again, trying to regain his composure. Having sworn a moment earlier he did not know Perl, he suddenly denied "ever taking anything away from her. I know for sure I never took away from an inmate anything that belonged to them, especially not a wristwatch, for my personal use."

He was in full denial mode.

"I never did a selection of inmates on the ramp in Birkenau," he declared. "It did happen that prisoners were standing about on the ramp, as I said before, while we were fetching the medicines. I was also there sometimes when the inmates were selected. The command 'right' and 'left' was heard from far away. But I never took part in it."[25]

Capesius then laid out what would be one of the keystones of his defense, his assertion that he strongly resisted the effort by Auschwitz's chief doctor to assign him to selection duty at Birkenau.

"It happened that the camp physician Dr. Wirths told me that I must also take part in the selections, and this was, as I remember, still in the summer or late summer 1944. As I remember the reason he gave for that was that it was a peak work time and everybody was needed [it was when hundreds of thousands of Hungarian Jews were arriving]. When I explained to Dr. Wirths that I did not want to do that and it was not my assignment, he became angry and said that he was the highest judge there and if I refused he could shoot me without any legal procedure. I did not persist in my refusal because I was afraid he would shoot me. Our relations were not good, also because I did not take part in the drinking banquets of the other SS officers. I drove then to Birkenau but I always managed to get away from them later. I occupied myself only with the medicines."[26]

"Dr. Capesius, your statement seems to be hard to believe," Kügler told him. "Before you stated that the sorted out packages containing the medicines were handed to you by a uniformed man. Also, considering that the arriving mass transports designed for gassing needed your help at the ramp, it is hard to believe that you managed to avoid the duty of the other doctors. How can you explain that?"

"There is no contradiction here," he rejoined. "Among the doctors there were a few who under the depressing work of these selections had started drinking and they would do anything for a bottle of Schnapps. Therefore, I could bribe them with Schnapps bottles that I purchased."

"Who were those doctors?"

"I cannot remember the name of even one of them. Possibly, Dr. Röhde or Dr. Mengele. One of them had a broad chest and was a big man, a real giant. (In one of his more obvious contradictions, Capesius later described Mengele as 5' 4", four inches shorter than his height, and certainly no "real giant)."

"How often did you do it," Kügler persisted.

"Dr. Wirths told me only once that I had to take part in the selections. The doctors often got Schnapps from me. On that single case I did it [gave the liquor] in order to buy myself out of the selection. On that occasion I said something to the doctor implying that I was unable to do it and he should do it for me, and would get a bottle of Schnapps in return."

Kügler switched topics.

"Have you had anything to do with Zyklon B?"

"No." Capesius did not miss a beat.

Kügler pulled out some more papers. Next was an account from Ignacy Golik, an early political inmate at Auschwitz. Golik was operating as a Kapo in the SS medical clinic by the time Capesius was posted to the camp. According to Golik, Capesius was responsible for the Zyklon B kept in the dispensary's storage room, and he often helped the SS take the poison canisters by ambulance to the gas chambers.

It was as if he had practiced his answer many times for the moment when the question of the deadly insecticide might be raised. "I had nothing to do with Zyklon B. Nor did I work with Zyklon B for other purposes, like the disinfestation of barracks. As I heard, the poison gas was kept in a bunker. From hearsay, I learned later on during my stay in Auschwitz that the Zyklon B was used for the gassing of inmates. . . . I can only repeat that when I was in 1944 in Auschwitz I had nothing to do with Zyklon B."[27]

What of a sworn statement, Kügler asked, by one of Capesius's top inmate pharmacists, Fritz Peter Strauch? Strauch also said that the poison gas was stored under the control of the dispensary through October 1944.

"If Strauch says that, until October 1944, then he is mistaken."

Maybe the witnesses were confused, he said, with "Schweinfurt green," a salt, copper and arsenic mixture also known as "Paris Green." It was used as a paint in the 19th century, before its highly toxic compounds transformed it into a widely used pesticide in the 20th century. That was deployed at the camp under the control of other SS officers "to fight insects."[28] It was possible, suggested Capesius that

Schweinfurt green shared the dispensary storage bunker, but he was not certain.

Kügler next switched to the charges that Capesius had provided drugs to doctors who used them in deadly experiments. In his statement, Golik had charged that Capesius provided phenol, mostly to Josef Klehr, chief of Auschwitz's euphemistically named Disinfection Unit, and that phenol was used to kill inmates with injections to the heart. Capesius claimed he had only learned of Klehr's name from recent news accounts and that "during my service in Camp Auschwitz I did not know that inmates were injected. Today I heard for the first time from the investigator, that the injections in Camp Auschwitz were used with Phenol."

Stanislaw Klodzinski, a Polish inmate doctor, described how Capesius had provided Evipan that Dr. Werner Röhde used in a botched experiment that killed four inmates. This time Capesius admitted that Röhde asked for morphine, Evipan and a liter of coffee.

"He [Röhde] told me that he wanted to conduct experiments," said Capesius, "that will enable, for instance, a spy to be inconspicuously served a cup of coffee with the addition of a sleep inducing substance, and quickly cocked out with the aid of Evipan, and for a longer period with the help of morphine so that the suspect could be carried away without resistance."

Capesius acknowledged that "It was clear to me that Dr. Röhde carried out these experiments on inmates."

He claimed, however, he was "not concerned at the time" because he had not given Röhde large quantities of morphine or Evipan and that the "coffee and the narcotics were not mixed in the pharmacy." Only later he learned that a Greek inmate had died of a heart attack from the mixture that he had provided. "But it could not be established what caused the heart attack," he claimed.[29]

Besides the drugs that Capesius might have dispensed for experiments, what about the charge that he withheld medications from sick prisoners? Kügler started reading from the statement of Ludwig Wörl, a German political dissident who was one of Auschwitz's early inmates. Wörl worked in the chief doctor's office and said it was widely known that Capesius was interested only in what he could find as valuables in the personal belongings of the prisoners who arrived at the camp. Capesius, charged Wörl, withheld any medications he found and refused to "waste" them on prisoners. They were saved only for the SS.

Capesius feigned surprise.

"It is incorrect. These medicines were not used for the sick SS men in Auschwitz but were distributed only to camp inmates." As if that was not enough to stretch credulity, he added, "Even the good medicines that I collected were kept away from the SS."[30]

As the long hearing drew near a close, the judge asked Capesius if he had anything to add. He took the opportunity to once again address Zyklon B.

"In my defense, I wish to add the following: In a proceeding before the military court in Nuremberg, as far as I can remember now, the main defendant was Dr. [Karl] Brandt. The way in which the Zyklon B was used for the gassing and how it was supplied to the camps was outlined. From that, it is clear that the SS pharmacist in Auschwitz, and especially me, in the year 1944, had nothing to do with it. I ask you urgently to look into these files."[31]

The result of the several hours of questions and answers resulted in a remarkable 14-page single-spaced "Public Prosecutor's Interrogation" that Capesius signed.[32]

The following day, December 5, two detectives accompanied Capesius on an express train for the short ride from Göppingen to Frankfurt's Hammelsgasse prison. He was locked into a cell with three foreigners. "The older one knew all the ins and outs of the penal code and always committed only those thefts that got him the least time in jail," recalled Capesius. He talked to that man and the other two "gangsters because I wanted to prove my innocence . . . that I could walk away free."[33]

Capesius had little time to persuade his jail mates that he had been wrongly accused. Two days after his arrival at Hammelsgasse he was brought to another judicial hearing, once again in the presence of the public prosecutor, Joachim Kügler.

Capesius began the hearing by informing the judge that the 14-page declaration he had signed a few days earlier had been "twice read to me by Prosecutor Kügler and also by the magistrate in Göppingen who questioned me. My statements made there are correct."[34]

Again he agreed to answer questions. He took this opportunity to elaborate on his earlier statement. At times he was more than simply cooperative, he was sometimes defiant. Again he denied direct culpability in all the counts that were the subject of Bauer's probe. As for performing the railhead life and death selections of the incoming prisoners, Capesius repeated his claim that he had no choice as Dr. Wirths had threatened to possibly even shoot him if he refused. But this time he changed the part of his story about how he had bribed some unnamed doctors with bottles of liquor in order for them to stand in for him on the selection ramp. In his original testimony, when Kügler asked which doctors he had bribed, Capesius claimed, "I cannot remember the name of even one of them. Possibly, Dr. Röhde or Dr. Mengele."

For some reason, in the intervening 72 hours his memory had greatly improved. Without equivocation he now claimed only one physician, his Hungarian friend and SS colleague, Dr. Fritz Klein, "took my place in the selections."[35] Klein had been executed for war crimes in December 1945. Whatever Capesius said about Klein could not be corroborated. Had Capesius remembered during the few days between his first court appearance and his new one what he had been told in 1946 by several ethnic Germans who had been on trial with Klein? It was they who had shared a secret with him when they were interred in the same British detention camp: that while Klein was "facing his death calmly," he was "happy" that "by his intercession in Auschwitz, he was able to shield [Capesius] from guilt." Capesius believed that to mean that Klein was willing to be his alibi for the railhead selections.

What about eyewitnesses who placed him at the ramp? All of that, said Capesius, was "not true." [36]

When pressed again about Zyklon B, he stuck to his claim that the "canisters were . . . never my responsibility, nor was giving them out."[37] When the judge asked if Zyklon B was stored in the same bunker as where Capesius kept his pharmacy supplies, he dodged a direct answer. Instead he offered only that his medical provisions took "perhaps only half of the entire bunker." [38]

The judge seemed skeptical that Capesius did not know what was stored in the other half of that single room.

"According to your own admission you were 8 to 9 months there as a camp pharmacist at Auschwitz. It seems to me hardly believable that you would not even be interested in all that time, or have found out in some other way, what was in the remaining part of the bunker sharing the space with your supplies?"

"I really do not know what was stored there," Capesius replied unconvincingly.

When the topic got around to Capesius's dispensing of the drug Evipan that Dr. Röhde used in a deadly experiment, he adhered closely to his story that he had given only a "non-lethal dose." The only change from what he said a few days earlier was that he claimed a "Greek inmate of Dr. Röhde . . . had died of a stroke," whereas the earlier account had him dead from a heart attack.[39]

In closing, Capesius took the opportunity to put a general denial on the record: "I deny having made in any way any offense while I was the camp pharmacist at Auschwitz."

Although he seemed calm and collected at the hearing, Capesius later wrote that he was in "shock" during those first days after his arrest. He was put in a private cell and placed on suicide watch. He described those early weeks as "solitary confinement, solitary walks in the yard, or with snitches and spies." Over time, incarceration he said "ruins your nerves."[40]

From his prison cell, Capesius wrote to Eisler pleading with him to "write letters as gushy or as sober as you like" since "one's innocence before God is totally irrelevant to the courts."[41]

Chapter 18

"THE BANALITY OF EVIL"

Capesius was despondent to spend New Year's Eve of 1960 in jail. His melancholy was tempered, however, by his hope that the case against him would fail to materialize, just as it had done 14 years earlier when he had been detained by American forces. One of the reasons for his confidence was that he had hired Fritz Steinacker and Hans Laternser, attorneys with great reputations when it came to fighting war crimes charges. The forty-year-old Steinacker had been a Nazi party member who served as a German bomber pilot. He was the firm's junior partner. Laternser was a legendary attorney who had defended the Army High Command and Wehrmacht General Staff at the main Nuremberg trials. He had also been Max Ilgner's chief defense counsel at the Farben trial and had represented General Albert Kesselring for ordering the massacre of partisans in Rome. Capesius was not their most controversial client. The Mengele family had also retained the pair to contest the 1959 indictment against the fugitive doctor.

Capesius was the only one of the defendants detained to date who could afford a private legal team. No one, not even his attorneys, knew the source of their retainer was the valuables and gold he had stolen from Auschwitz. Steinacker and Laternser assured Capesius they were prepared to aggressively contest the case against him at every step of the way. But Bauer was in no rush to cobble together a prosecution that fell short of obtaining a conviction. By 1960, only seven SS men from Auschwitz had ever faced a German court. The prosecutors had not had much to boast about in those cases. That year, for instance, Dr. Johann Kremer, who had kept a diary while in Auschwitz, was found guilty by a Munster court. However, Kremer had spent ten years imprisoned in Poland and the German judge freed him immediately after his conviction for "time served." And in one of the most highly anticipated prosecutions, that of Dr. Carl Clauberg – with whom Capesius had been friendly at Auschwitz – the case moved along at such a glacial pace that Clauberg died in jail before the trial even began.

Bauer wanted to accomplish much more with his investigation than simply bringing charges against several defendants. He knew that some 7,000 to 8,000 SS officers had directed the administration at Auschwitz. And he realized it was only possible to prosecute a tiny fraction of these. But the overall impact might be enormous. Bauer envisioned that if he could find and indict enough Nazis and combine all their cases into a single trial, that such a proceeding might be the country's great cathartic confrontation of its dark past. He wanted not only to expose the camp's low ranking murderers but also to put on trial the SS hierarchy that created the "Auschwitz complex." His ambitious goal was a reckoning of the crimes of the Holocaust presented in a German court, by German prosecutors, and ruled on by German judges.[1]

Capesius and his legal team banked on the widespread sentiment in Germany to forget about the past. The lack of public support, hoped Capesius, might mean that Bauer's investigations would eventually stall without ever getting to trial. To Capesius's great dismay, however, a stunning development that spring reignited widespread public interest in the crimes of the Nazis and the fate of the unpunished perpetrators. An Israeli commando team executed a covert operation straight from the pages of a bestselling spy novel. On May 11, 1960, Adolf Eichmann – the SS officer responsible for deporting millions of Jews to the death camps – had finished his shift at a local Mercedes-Benz plant in a suburb of Buenos Aires, Argentina. He had boarded a bus to his modest house on Garibaldi Street. When he got off that bus, he did not notice a nearby stalled car at which two men were working on the engine. And he paid no attention to another car with three men inside, parked near the bus stop. As he strolled past the first vehicle, the rear doors swung open and four men tackled him and shoved him inside. The snatch took less than a minute. Before he was bound and gagged, he managed to say only, "I am resigned to my fate."[2]

The covert squad transported Eichmann with high secrecy to Israel, where the Jewish state announced it intended to try him for genocide and war crimes. It was an electrifying moment that motivated private Nazi hunters –notably Vienna's Simon Wiesenthal and Paris's Serge and Beatte Klarsfeld – to accelerate their quests to find missing fugitives such as Mengele and the Treblinka commandant, Franz Stangl. Suddenly the crimes of the Final Solution were front and center once again.

No one then knew that Fritz Bauer had played a key behind-the-scenes role in putting Eichmann into Israeli hands. As far back as September 1957, Bauer had sent a secret cable to Isser Harel, the chief of Israeli intelligence, sharing information suggesting Eichmann was hiding in Argentina.

"Bauer told me that no one else knew," said Harel. "He said that he didn't trust the [German] foreign office and he didn't trust his embassy in Buenos Aires. He said we were the only people who could be relied upon to do anything with the information."[3]

Bauer's breakthrough came from a German Jew, Lothar Hermann, who lived in the remote Argentine town of Coronel Suarez. A young German from Buenos Aires, Nicholas Eichmann, had been pursuing Hermann's eighteen-year-old daughter. Based on some of what Nicholas had said to his daughter, Lothar wrote a letter to Bauer laying out his suspicions.

The Israelis, however, were not persuaded that the tip was accurate. It was not until December 1959 – the same month Capesius was arrested – that Bauer flew to Jerusalem to complain to Israel's attorney general. He revealed that an SS informant had recently divulged that Eichmann's alias was *Ricardo Klement.* Bauer also provided schematics and a key to his Frankfurt office to the Mossad could secretly obtain access in order to copy the Eichmann file. Five months later Eichmann was captured.[4]

Although the Eichmann case had reenergized the hunt for Nazi criminals, there were still prominent German voices opposing

Bauer's plans for a showcase trial. Notable among these was Helmut Kohl, later Germany's chancellor, then a 31-year-old up-and-coming state representative from Mainz. He expounded a popular view that the collapse of the Third Reich was so historically fresh that it was impossible to impartially judge individual actions free of emotion and anger.

Bauer had expected resistance from Germany's political leaders. What caught him by surprise was a significant new legal hurdle. In 1960, the same year Israeli commandos captured Eichmann, the Bundestag repealed all the remaining legal decrees the Allies had issued. That made it more difficult to prosecute Nazi crimes other than cases in which it was possible to prove *deliberate murder*.[5] The change in the law meant that so long as a defendant was following orders, he could only be held responsible for a lesser crime of an accomplice to murder. In the new Germany, that translated into a maximum ten-year sentence. And when that law was applied in the trial of a KGB assassin who had killed several western intelligence agents in West Germany, the court ruled that in a totalitarian government only those top officials who issued orders could be held guilty of murder. Since the KGB killer had followed orders from Moscow, the German court convicted him only as an accomplice to the homicides. This precedent made it clear that when applied to the crimes of the Third Reich, only a handful of the Nazi elite could be held accountable directly for murder.[6]

To circumvent that ruling Bauer knew he would need to establish that those he charged had killed someone at Auschwitz of their own volition, acting separately and beyond the scope of their orders. Otherwise they could only be indicted as accomplices.

Through 1960 Bauer and his team worked tirelessly to develop a short list of defendants who would represent a cross-section of the Auschwitz murder machine. The high profile perpetrators that Bauer would have preferred were no longer alive or were fugitives. Commandants Rudolf Höss and Arthur Liebehenschel had been convicted and hanged in Poland in 1947. Still, Bauer was pleased that

April when he located and nabbed Stefan Baretzki, a brutal SS block leader.

Capesius and his SS colleagues who had already been arrested were well aware that Bauer wanted marquee names before moving forward with his case. In an eight-page handwritten June 1960 letter to Gerhard Gerber, briefly Auschwitz's number two pharmacist, Capesius addressed this and other prosecution problems. Gerber was still free and had reunited with his family after the war before returning to work at a drugstore.

"They are trying to set this up as an Auschwitz show trial," Capesius warned Gerber. "And so they are trying to find 950 people according to the list. If anyone is suspected of having done anything, they will be brought to Frankfurt. Till now they have found twenty-six people in two years; so it appears the investigations may take a very long time. I am the only arrested officer of [such a high] rank from Auschwitz; the other arrestees are of lower rank. Unterscharführer Pery Broad, who back then was in charge of interrogations, is the only arrestee here sending you his greetings, since you were acquainted with him."[7]

Capesius wrote – sometimes erroneously – some of the most prominent Auschwitz doctors who were "still living, but with unknown addresses." In fact, Mengele was still on the run in South America and Dr. Bruno Weber was then living covertly in East Germany. Capesius also cited Horst Fischer and Werner Röhde but in fact Röhde had been executed by the British in 1946 and Weber – who had been tried and acquitted after the war – had died in 1956 of natural causes.

"Forty people [who had served] in Auschwitz [have already been] hanged: doctors, commandants, and Oberscharführers," Capesius told Gerber. He assured him, however, that "the dentists are at liberty," even letting him know that he had "spoken with Dr. Schatz and Dr. Frank." A glimmer of good news was that Dr. Münch, "from the hygiene department is living near Munich, and, having been acquitted, is free to practice."

Then Capesius got around to discussing the fate of the SS men who had worked with Gerber and him at Auschwitz, those who would have direct knowledge of what they had done at the camp. "Walter Berliner, [Fritz Peter] Strauch, and [Paul] Reichel are dead. Wirths hanged himself. Dr. Lolling took poison." Capesius added, "Unteroffizier Frymann and Rottenführer Dobrzanski have not been found."

SS Gruppenführer Carl Blumenreuter was alive, said Capesius. Like them, Blumenreuter was trained as a pharmacist and in the Waffen-SS. Blumenreuter had been the chief of the Berlin Medical Office, responsible for all pharmacological services at the concentration camps. In that capacity he had been in regular contact with Capesius at Auschwitz. When the British released Blumenreuter after the war he moved to Grömitz near the Baltic Sea where he became the director of a hospital pharmacy. Given the new life he had created for himself and his family in postwar Germany, it was not surprising that Capesius wrote that "he will not testify in our favor because of 'lack of knowledge.'"[8]

But the purpose of this extraordinary letter was more than simply to inform a former Auschwitz colleague about the fate of others who had served at the camp. Steinacker and Laternser had warned Capesius that prison authorities read all incoming and outgoing mail. With that knowledge, Capesius used it as an opportunity to set out his defense. In so doing, he not only reinforced his claims of innocence to the prosecutors, but also passed along to Gerber what he had told authorities. In that way, when Gerber was eventually questioned, he could stick to the same storyline.

As for the charge that he had stored and distributed Zyklon B, Capesius lamented that it was only an issue because his trusted inmate assistant, the late Fritz Peter Strauch, had testified in a 1949 trial against Guntrum Pflaum, an SS officer in charge of Pest Control at Auschwitz. Capesius wrote that Strauch had "said that the dispensary had been using Zyklon B without safety warning elements. After Strauch's death, it [his testimony] came back to haunt me."

Then Capesius signaled to Gerber what was the best defense.

"I have stated that Zyklon B was not stored in the dispensary, nor was it administered or handed out by us. Nor were any of us ever . . .

to get Zyklon B. . . . I have disputed [all of it], since nothing we had was ever stored there. I ask you also to answer to this point."

Capesius suggested to Gerber that when he was eventually questioned, he might be better off concentrating on the time they spent away from Auschwitz as opposed to what happened there.

"What I have said about you and me is that when we were off duty we spent time at the home of Armin Rump, the town druggist of Auschwitz, the one who moved from the Bucovina, from Dorna Watra. And that I also had spent weekends with Dr. Schatz visiting the Stoffel Csechischowa farm; the family now lives in Munich."

He boasted in his note that he had steadfastly refused to admit that he ever performed any of the railhead selections. And when the prosecutors said they had witnesses to prove otherwise, "that would mean that they were just lying. I said that my witnesses will refute that statement easily."

Capesius did not let his self-serving letter go by without the chance for some self-pity. He bemoaned that prosecutor Kügler "reproaches me, saying it is pointless for me to keep presenting myself as a helpful and decent human being, like when I say that I helped the inmates in every possible way – he says that is not the question here and it won't do me any good." And Capesius was upset that when Kügler learned about his postwar reunion with the camp's two dentists, Drs. Frank and Schatz, Kügler zeroed in on the fact that Capesius had failed to mention that in his first interrogation. "He probably suspects I am hiding something," Capesius wrote, "perhaps that we had divided up the gold from the teeth among us."

In concluding, Capesius made certain he got Gerber's full attention. He revealed that prosecutors had asked about Gerber in "my first interrogation." And he added, "The only incriminating thing here is the time period July 1 to October 15, 1944, the period of the Hungarian transports, as Hermann Langbein says he saw a table of duty assignments, in which we are supposedly listed."

There was a purpose to passing along this information. He hoped to undermine Langbein's credibility. Capesius told Gerber that he believed Langbein, "an old-line Communist," had "taken his own people off the lists of people to be killed by injections in the infirmaries . . . and replaced them with Jews."

Then he asked for help.

"If you know anything about this, a short incriminating statement would be important, nothing much can happen to them, since manslaughter has been under the statute of limitations since June 20, 1960. Still, in Frankfurt they would have less credibility as incriminating witnesses."

Capesius's letter had indeed sparked Bauer's team to add Gerber to their investigation, but in 1960, Gerber was far down their priority list. The prosecutors were still hoping to find a single high-ranking officer that could galvanize the public's interest. In November, Bauer's office made a breakthrough when it arrested Robert Mulka, the former Obersturmführer who had served for over a year as the right-hand assistant to Rudolf Höss, Auschwitz's notorious commandant. Bauer had located Mulka by luck only a few months earlier. In early September, a junior public prosecutor had read in a Frankfurt newspaper that the bronze medal winner on the West German rowing team at the Olympic games in Rome was Rolf Mulka. *Mulka* is an unusual German surname so the prosecutor checked Rolf's family. His father turned out to be the ex-SS official, operating his own import-export company in Hamburg (two years later, Rolf Mulka gave up his professional career to aide his father in his defense).[9]

Mulka was the biggest name to date. But there was no question that the plum defendant would be the highest ranking SS man still missing from Auschwitz, its last commandant, Sturmbannführer Richard Baer. He would be forty-nine if still alive. But he had disappeared after the war and no one had picked up his trail. It was not until late 1960 – after pictures of Baer had been published widely in the German press as part of the hunt for him – that Bauer's office got a break. A forester on the grand estate of Otto von Bismarck, grandson of the legendary political leader who had unified Germany in the 19th century, thought a co-worker might be Baer. The man was living as Karl Neumann. He kept mostly to himself. Whenever discussions came up about the war, Neumann said only that he had been a cook for Luftwaffe chief Hermann Göring.

In December, Joachim Kügler, the public prosecutor, drove to the tiny town of Dassendorf, adjacent to the Bismarck estate and arrested Neumann deep in the woods. It was only after several hours of insisting they had the wrong man that he finally admitted he was the long missing Auschwitz commandant.[10]

Baer's arrest was a triumph for the prosecution as it was a prominent name that gave new momentum to the push for a grand trial. It coincidentally marked the one-year anniversary of Capesius's arrest. His original cockiness about an early release was long gone. The prediction that he would be home by the close of the year and the case against him dismissed had proved terribly wrong.

By the start of 1961, Bauer's office had arrested thirteen ex-Auschwitz SS officers. Seven were free on bail, but Capesius was one of the incarcerated who was not going anywhere. That spring, Bauer began preparing a detailed preliminary investigation (Voruntersuchung), a necessary step in Germany prior to any formal indictment. In papers he filed that July he listed 24 possible suspects including Capesius.[11] During this time Bauer's office would have to determine whether it had sufficient evidence to bring all of them to trial. In the meantime, police and investigators continued searching for SS who had served at the camp in the hope of adding more defendants.

On April 11, Bauer and his team were transfixed, as were many Germans, when Adolf Eichmann's trial finally got underway in a Jerusalem district court. Charged with crimes against humanity, war crimes, and membership in a criminal organization, Eichmann sat in a specially constructed bulletproof glass booth. When he took the stand in his own defense, in remarkably dry and emotionless testimony, he explained how his efficient bureaucracy of trains had carried millions to their deaths. German born writer and philosopher, Hannah Arendt, who covered the trial for *The New Yorker* and later wrote an acclaimed book about it, dubbed Eichmann's cool, technocratic demeanor "the banality of evil."[12] Nazi hunter Simon Wiesenthal said, "The world now understands the concept of 'desk murderer.'"

Two days after the start of that trial, Capesius appeared in a Frankfurt District Court, accompanied by his attorney, Fritz Steinacker. At that April 13 hearing, prosecutor Kügler sought some clarifications from Capesius.

First up was Zyklon B, which Capesius had claimed within a couple of days of his December 1959 arrest to have never stored or distributed. Capesius began by reiterating his overall theme that no Zyklon was stored in "my pharmacy or in all ancillary rooms under my supervision. . . . If the witnesses say otherwise, they are wrong."[13] As for new evidence that he might have signed for upwards of twenty boxes of the poison, he claimed out of the blue that it was for a Red Cross Commission visit to Auschwitz and that the content of these boxes was an Ovaltine replacement product.[14]

When Kügler next moved to the selections, Capesius knew the prosecutor had statements from an ever-growing number of survivors who had known him from his Bayer drug sales before seeing him again at the Auschwitz railhead. He began by repeating his standard line that "I have not selected on the ramp in a single case." Then he added a new wrinkle that revealed Steinacker's careful coaching about how to cast his actions in a more innocent light. He claimed that sometimes when he got to the railhead, "the prisoners' goods were already removed from the ramp. . . . On such occasions, we were left waiting before we could take this luggage. On such occasions I have sometimes spoken with these doctors that recognized me. I knew namely about 3,000 Jewish doctors in Romania through my work at IG Farben."

In a somewhat rambling monologue, Capesius again described how the camp's chief physician had assigned him against his will to the selections and supposedly how his friend, the late Dr. Fritz Klein, had assumed his ramp duty in exchange for extra liquor provisions.

When Kügler moved to the charges that Capesius had knowingly supplied Evipan for the deadly experiments conducted by Dr. Röhde, the defense preparation was also evident. Capesius now claimed that

Röhde had only brought coffee beans to the pharmacy and discussed "a medical recipe." But he strongly denied knowing that "any drugs would be used on a prisoner."[15] After his 1959 arrest he had sworn to the opposite, "He [Röhde] told me that he wanted to conduct experiments. . . . It was clear to me that Dr. Röhde carried out these experiments on inmates." [16]

The hearing closed with Steinacker making a failed motion for bail of 100,000 DM ($25,000) to end his client's pretrial detention. It was a motion Capesius hoped might free him from jail after nearly 18 months. He later confided to his family that he was "crushed" that the judge denied it, ruling Capesius too much of flight risk.

Back in his cell, Capesius glumly followed the progress of the Eichmann trial. Germany's press had saturation coverage. A key component centered around Eichmann's responsibility for the massive deportations of Hungarian Jews to Auschwitz in the spring of 1944. It was sworn statements from survivors of those very deportations that were now proving so problematic for Capesius and his defense team.

The Eichmann defense and prosecution rested on August 14, 1961. That same month, Bauer succeeded in getting Heinz Düx – a justice with an impeccable reputation – appointed as the examining magistrate. This marked the second phase of Bauer's Auschwitz investigation. Under German law, once the prosecutors believed they had compiled enough evidence to proceed they were required to turn over their files to an independent judge.[17] It was Düx's daunting job to essentially run his own investigation, free of the police and prosecutor's office. It required him to review more than 50 thick binders already assembled, complete with witness statements and documentary evidence. Before he would finish his work, Düx would conduct hundreds of his own witness interviews.[18]

But before he got very far into his new assignment, two fellow justices on the Frankfurt court called on him. He recounted what happened next: "They thought it would ease my workload if I were to reject the jurisdiction of the Frankfurt Regional Court for at least some of the accused, given that there were so many. Should I follow this advice, I could count on the court administration to cover my back. It was easy to see through their proposal, which was not directed at my workload, but instead was aimed at preventing proceedings that would at long last record the structures of a German extermination camp, over 15 years after the end of the Second World War."[19]

Düx politely but firmly said no. And when he proved particularly energetic in his new role, a defense lawyer tried unsuccessfully to remove him for "impartiality." At other times, the Minister of Justice refused to assist him in obtaining witness statements from behind the Iron Curtain.[20]

The year 1961 closed on an ominous note for Capesius and his fellow SS colleagues who were the target of Bauer's huge probe. On December 12, three judges in a Jerusalem court found Eichmann guilty of war crimes and crimes against humanity. They ruled that he had gone far beyond simply following orders and that he had been a major architect of the genocide. Three days later at a hearing, Eichmann was the first person in the short thirteen-year history of the new Israel to be sentenced to death. Although there was no capital punishment in Germany, the news of Eichmann's fate still sent a chill through the imprisoned Auschwitz defendants.

Even Josef Mengele, hiding in a Paraguayan rain forest some 6,500 miles from Frankfurt, was anguished over the nonstop Eichmann coverage. Writing in a journal he kept while on the run, the fugitive Mengele suspected that somehow the Jews must be behind the resurgence in legal interest about Nazi crimes: "It is unbelievable what is allowed to be slanderously written in German magazines. The magazines are the illustrated proof of the lack of character and lack of proper attitude of the current German government that tolerates such self-defilement. The political lie triumphs and time and history have been warped and bowed. It drips of 'humanitarianism and Christianity,' and 'in this God' is the most often quoted. Behind all this stands only one thing: that is all the Old Testament hate toward everything in the German consciousness, heroic and truly superior."[21]

Chapter 19

"I HAD NO POWER TO CHANGE IT"

apesius's mood was low as 1962 got underway. Only a month earlier he had marked his two-year anniversary in jail. His legal bills continued mounting and none of his attorneys could give him a realistic estimate of when Bauer might finally file a formal indictment or announce the evidence had fallen short and release him. Steinacker and Laternser were realists, however, and told Capesius that the odds of a dismissal were slim. The prosecutor and his team had put too much time and effort into the case and the eyes of the world, particularly in the wake of the Eichmann trial, were on them. It was likely, counseled Steinacker, that Capesius would face trial.

Starting January 10, Capesius at least had the feeling his case was making incremental progress. Accompanied by Steinacker, he was transported in a police van to the Frankfurt courthouse. Under German law, each defendant is questioned in separate proceedings, by the prosecutor and another time by the examining magistrate. This time it was Judge Heinz Düx's turn.

Before the hearing got underway there was a moment of high drama during which Capesius unexpectedly came face to face in the courthouse with Josef Glück, one of his survivor accusers.[1] Glück was the Romanian textile manufacturer who was a prime Capesius prewar Farben customer. Capesius had selected him at the Auschwitz railhead in June 1944. On that Wednesday morning in the courthouse, the victim and the perpetrator saw each other for the first time in 18 years as one left the interview room and the other entered. Those present later recounted in a court filing that Glück became extremely agitated, showing "significant signs of excitement." He proclaimed,

"That's Capesius! He looks still the same as before! He has not lost any weight. I recognize him with absolute certainty!"

Then Glück was so overcome with emotion that he had trouble speaking. He was so distraught that he misinterpreted a smirk by Capesius as a scar on his mouth. As Capesius was ushered out of the hallway, Glück was "so awestruck . . . that he burst into tears."[2]

Capesius, meanwhile, seemed totally unfazed by the encounter and was instead eager to start his hearing. That was the consequence of Capesius's pent-up frustration at his long pretrial incarceration and his misplaced belief that he could still somehow talk himself out of the charges.

As it came to each accusation against him, Capesius initially repeated what he had said before and occasionally elaborated with some fresh details. He often spoke in absolutes. "I never became a selector on the ramp."[3]

When Judge Düx asked about specific witnesses who identified him performing the life and death railhead selections, Capesius was suddenly afflicted with a poor memory. As for some eyewitnesses, he claimed "I do not know him." For others it was "I cannot remember." Sometimes he flatly "denied" the incident. And he offered a new explanation for why so many people who knew him before the war recognized him at the railhead: "I suppose that all of these witnesses confused me with Dr. Klein. Dr. Klein was Hungarian. He spoke Hungarian even better than me."[4]

The careful preparation by Steinacker was evident as Capesius expanded on what he said was his initial resistance to Eduard Wirths ordering him to perform the selections. Capesius now contended that Wirths brokered no compromise because "I was an unmilitary type. Also my education in Romania in the military was limited to basic training of one month. Incidentally, I was active only as a pharmacist. I suppose that Wirths therefore believed me not to be an energetic SS officer."[5]

He added a new twist to his tale to illustrate how distraught he supposedly was at the order to perform the selections. When he returned to his dispensary, he claimed that he told the inmate pharmacist Jurasek that he was contemplating deserting.[6] What stopped him from doing that was later the same day when he said Dr. Fritz Klein felt sorry enough for his plight to assume his selection duty. Maybe it was Steinacker who convinced Capesius that his earlier testimony that Klein had done the grisly extra duty for just a single bottle of Schnapps seemed unlikely. So this time Capesius made it sound as if he offered Klein a bigger payout by giving him all his Marketenderware (special ration coupons), including prized ones for alcohol, cigarettes and occasionally hard-to-get foods.[7]

Judge Düx noted that Capesius's testimony contradicted his previous sworn declarations. In his first statement after his arrest he had not even mentioned Klein. In fact, when he had been asked then about which doctors purportedly took over his selection duty, he had said: "I cannot remember the name of even one of them."[8] And he also provided two differing scenarios of how and when he supposedly approached Klein and beseeched him to take over his railhead duties.

Steinacker was a savvy enough attorney to know that the judge and prosecutor would jump on any inconsistencies. As a result, he had carefully prepared his client to explain them away. Without missing a beat, Capesius claimed that no attention should be given to his earlier statements since that was at a time when "I was under the shock of the sudden arrest. I did not express myself properly." Moreover, he told the judge that Kügler had fooled him into signing a sworn statement whose contents he did not understand "since I cannot read the shorthand." He had signed the incriminating December 4, 1959 statement, he insisted improbably, because he thought he was merely signing "what Kügler himself had said."[9]

"I didn't mention Dr. Klein in my first interrogation," Capesius later told a journalist, "because I was afraid of incriminating his daughters in Romania. I only brought Dr. Klein back into play after I was told that it would not matter if I named him."[10]

About charges that he had profited by stealing valuables from the personal belongings of those sent to the gas chambers, he again said it was all a slander. He admitted taking 1,500 suitcases from the railhead to his dispensary, but claimed incredulously that the only personal item he had ever taken for his own use was "some good coffee beans."[11] Every account that said he stole valuables was "incorrect" or he "disputed the accuracy."

And again Capesius denied knowing that the phenol he stored in his dispensary was used by SS doctors to kill inmates. He only learned about this, he said, from what he had read after the war.[12] And in any case, he told Judge Düx, the phenol was under the control of one of his inmate pharmacists, Fritz Peter Strauch. Strauch, of course, was dead. Capesius now used the same excuse regarding another experiment in which he claimed no knowledge: the Evipan used by Dr. Röhde to kill several inmates. That concoction "was [also] prepared by Strauch. . . . Strauch was responsible."[13]

Capesius thought he had pulled off a virtuoso performance of obfuscation, distortion, strategic lapses of memory, and a concerted effort to shift responsibility for any wrongdoing to either his inmate assistants or some SS colleagues who were conveniently dead. Steinacker was not as pleased. He thought that Capesius had still failed to adequately set forth the concept that all he did at the camp was to follow orders.

The conversations between attorney and client resulted in them returning to see Judge Düx just two weeks later on January 24. Capesius shocked the court:

"I found myself in a bad physical and mental condition for my last appearance [January 11] because during the recess I had particularly lost track of each summary of Prosecutor Kügler's allegations. My explanations were therefore not issued in my right mind or intentionally. After I had continued to resist . . . I was no longer in a position to clarify some important points or to further defend myself. I therefore retract the statement that I signed on January 11, 1962."[14]

In this new hearing, besides repeating many of his now rehearsed defenses about everything from Zyklon B to the selections to medical experiments, Capesius put into the record information that his defense team would later cite as evidence that he believed whatever he was doing at Auschwitz was simply following legitimate orders from his superiors. Because he grew up in a household in which "my father had constantly declared that Germany was the model of order and the rule of law. Given this attitude, I assumed that what was going on in Auschwitz was legal, although it seemed cruel to me."[15]

What about the selections for the gas chambers, asked Düx?

"I have never believed that in Germany such a thing is possible without a law," he repeated. Steinacker had clearly drilled into his client the concept that in order to avoid a life sentence for wanton murder, he had to emphasize that at the very worst he was simply a cog in the larger machine of mass murder. "Incidentally, I want to mention that I was never hostile to the Jews there. On the contrary, in the opinion of [some of] the witnesses . . . I treated the Jews too good in relation to the Poles."[16]

Düx tried one more time to shake Capesius from his script.

"Was what happened at Auschwitz compatible with the existing law as you knew it?"

"Inwardly, I reject any concentration camp in the style of Auschwitz. But I had no power to change it. Incidentally, I really tried to get away from Auschwitz. Moreover, I have taken a position against it when I was assigned to do the selection, as I have already described."

Beyond setting the basis for a "simply following orders" defense, Capesius used his latest appearance before Düx to also muddy some of the record of his camp service. For instance, he moved his posting to Auschwitz to April 12, 1944. He claimed to have recalled the "correct date" when he was recently reminded that he had spent Holy Week of 1944 with his mother and sister while he was still assigned to Dachau. It was a bold attempt by Capesius to shave nearly four months off his Auschwitz tour. If successful, he would automatically eliminate any of the damning eyewitness testimony about him before that date.

Joachim Kügler did not then challenge him, although court documents listed his service from "late 1943."[17] There would be more than enough opportunity to later reveal Capesius's change of dates as false. In fact, in his private letters written from prison, Capesius revealed that he had no precise recollection of what was his first day at the camp. "It would be good, too, to find out the death date for pharmacist Krömer," he wrote, "my predecessor at Auschwitz, because everyone gives a different date, and some put his death as early as the fall of 1943. Were we one month in Warsaw or six weeks? Where were we for Christmas 1943?"[18]

The January 24 hearing finished with Capesius listing a few of the people he expected to call for his defense. Among them were the Stoffels, the couple with whom he spent many weekends when away from Auschwitz. Also included was Armin Rump, the ethnic German pharmacist in Oswiecim, and Lotte Lill, an Auschwitz nurse with whom he had been briefly on leave in 1944. And he listed Victoria Ley, a fellow Transylvanian who had never been to Auschwitz, but was married to another SS officer, the late Josef Becker, and could testify evidently about physical similarities between Capesius and Fritz Klein.[19]

Following that January court appearance Capesius returned to his prison cell. While the prosecutors continued methodically building the case against him, he felt increasingly isolated. His contact with the outside world was mostly through visits from his legal team and there had still been no progress on his efforts to bring his wife and three daughters to Germany.

On May 31, Capesius and the other defendants detained by Bauer were in a somber mood. Israel's high court had rejected Adolf Eichmann's final appeals. A few minutes before midnight, Eichmann was hanged in Ramle prison (his ashes were later dropped into the sea, beyond Israel's territorial waters, so it would be impossible for neo-Nazis to make his burial site a shrine).

A few days later more pressing problems took Capesius's mind off Eichmann. Fritz Steinacker called Joachim Kügler. He reported that Adolph Rögner was trying to extort money from Capesius in return for locating exculpatory witnesses. Rögner was the Auschwitz Kapo with a long arrest record and a perjury conviction who had been responsible for the tip that led to the arrest of SS officer, Wilhelm Boger. Prosecutors had no doubt that Rögner was driven by a combination of vengeance, notoriety and money. Now Kügler was alarmed that Rögner might approach survivors he knew and use the perpetrator-victim dynamic that had worked so well for him as an Auschwitz Kapo, this time to pressure them into giving statements that he could sell to Capesius and other defendants. Kügler lost no time in calling Rögner and informing him bluntly he would be arrested if he did not immediately stop. That was the last time Rögner interfered with Capesius.[20]

The remainder of 1962 was quiet but frustrating for Capesius. He was growing ever more impatient at his long incarceration without formal charges. Not surprisingly, he kept bombarding his attorneys with a steady volume of inquiries about the case and exhortations to speed the process. And he sent a series of letters to acquaintances, sometimes seemingly careless about whether or not prison authorities monitored his mail. He told his brother-in-law that "my innocence has been proved . . . I no longer have anything to do with it. But please keep this information strictly to yourself."[21] In a letter to the Stoffels, he was surprisingly blunt in suggesting precisely what they should say when they were called to provide a statement. Referring to himself in the third person, he wrote: "Dr. Capesius always stressed how the whole atmosphere of Auschwitz depressed him, as he would sometimes glimpse an arriving train when he went down to the so-called ramp to pick up doctors' valises, and he would make occasional despondent comments about this."[22]

He urged the Stoffels to say how often they had visited him at the SS dispensary and "often chatted" with his inmate assistants. "We always got the impression that they were all happy with their boss. Strauch in particular would sing his praises. Everyone gave the impression of being well-nourished, everybody was always treated kindly. He was good to the prisoners."

It was no coincidence that Capesius suggested they highlight Strauch. He was not only conveniently dead and therefore could not refute anything said about him, and he was also the one whose testimony at an earlier war crimes trial had tied Capesius to Zyklon B. Capesius reminded the Stoffels they should not forget to talk about his "gregarious nature" or that "we owe Dr. C. a debt of gratitude" for urging them to leave the Auschwitz area before the Russian troops arrived.

When the Stoffels were eventually called by the prosecutors to give their statements, they stuck largely to the shameless self-serving script Capesius had written.[23]

The only good news for him as 1962 closed was something quite separate from his own legal problems. The money he had paid into the "family buyback" program in Romania was finally working. His youngest daughter, Christa, was the first to get permission to emigrate to West Germany. Although his wife and two other daughters, Melitta and Ingrid, were still on the waiting list, the processing of their applications were now only a matter of time. He was also pleased that his middle daughter, Ingrid, had received a degree in biology at the University of Cluj. That would open the door for her to many opportunities in West Germany. Capesius was frustrated, though, that after so many years the first meeting with one of his daughters would be in a prison cell. Still, he held fast to the hope that when he one day walked free, his entire family would be there to greet him.

Chapter 20

"PERPETRATORS RESPONSIBLE FOR MURDER"

Judge Heinz Düx started off 1963 by reporting that his near two-year investigation was complete. During his independent probe he had taken thousands of pages of sworn statements from hundreds of survivors in the U.S., Russia, Israel, Brazil, and across Europe. It was one of the largest files ever accumulated by an investigating magistrate. And it marked the judicial green light for Bauer to finally file official charges. Bauer was anxious to do so since Germany was in the midst of a heated debate over whether or not to extend its statute of limitations for murder. The existing limit of 20 years meant it would be impossible after 1965 to charge the Auschwitz defendants unless the Bundestag changed the law. The prosecutor's office did not want to rely on an uncertain political outcome with such high legal stakes.[1]

On April 4, Fritz Bauer's office issued its much-anticipated indictment. Some judicial pundits had predicted that the multiyear delay from the first arrests might make the formal charges anti-climactic. However, the sweeping range of crimes against twenty-four defendants set forth in the 698-page document sent shockwaves through Germany. In the first 195 pages, the prosecutors relied largely on a handful of esteemed Third Reich historians to set forth a thorough history of Auschwitz. It established the foundation for proving that the crimes of the defendants were an integral part of the camp's murderous bureaucracy. Testimony from more than 200 witnesses filled the details about the charges against each of the accused. The prosecutors' portrait of them was unequivocal: they were willing perpetrators who far exceeded their simple orders in zealously carrying out the Final Solution.

Bauer hoped the indictment would frame the public discussion. It included some of the most shocking accounts assembled during the five-year probe. The horror of the gas chambers, for instance, was brought to life in a statement by Richard Böck, a Waffen-SS officer in the Auschwitz motor pool: "I simply cannot describe how these people screamed. That lasted about eight or ten minutes and then everything was quiet. A shorter while later, some inmates opened the door and you could still see a blue fog hanging over the giant tangle of corpses. The corpses were cramped together in such a way that you could not tell to whom the individual appendages and body parts belonged. For example, I noticed that one of the victims had stuck his index finger several centimeters into the eye sockets of another. This gives you a sense of how indescribably terrible the death throes of this person must have been. I felt so ill that I almost vomited."[2]

Other stomach wrenching accounts, coupled with the breadth and specificity of all the charges, had undoubtedly captured the public's attention.

Besides Capesius, the defendants represented a wide cross-section of the camp. The last commandant, Richard Baer, was the highest profile officer. The others included one of Baer's adjutants, Karl Höcker, and Robert Mulka, the adjutant to Rudolf Höss. There was the chief of the protective guard (Captain Franz Hofmann) and two key men in his command (Oswald Kaduk and Stefan Baretzki), an SS doctor (Franz Lucas), the two SS dentists and Capesius's friends (Willi Frank and Willi Schatz), SS officers from the Gestapo/Political Department (Wilhelm Boger, Klaus Dylewski, Pery Broad, Johann Schoberth, and Hans Stark), block leaders and wardens (Heinrich Bischoff and Bruno Schlage), medical orderlies (Josef Klehr, Emil Hantl, Herbert Scherpe, Gerhard Neubert and Hans Nierzwicki), manager of the inmate belongings (Arthur Breitwieser), and one inmate Kapo (Emil Bednarek).

A few had surprisingly been tried and found guilty in earlier cases.

Arthur Breitwieser, for instance, was convicted and sentenced to death in the large 1946 Auschwitz trial in Poland. His sentence was commuted to life in 1948, but after 11 years in prison, the Poles deported him to West Germany. He had resumed civilian life as an accountant before Fritz Bauer detained him in 1961.

But for most of those charged, until the Frankfurt prosecutors had come along, they had simply returned to their prewar careers under their real names. Typical was Adjutant Karl Höcker, who had moved back to his hometown of Eingershausen and reestablished his banking business. Capesius's friends, camp dentists Willi Frank and Willi Schatz, had opened respectively successful Stuttgart and Hannover dental practices. Dr. Franz Lucas, a gynecologist, had restarted as a medical assistant at a hospital in Elmshorn, then became the assistant medical director, before finally being promoted to the chief of the gynecology department. The hospital asked for his resignation after 1963 newspaper accounts of his Auschwitz service, but he set up a prosperous private practice before Bauer finally arrested him. The most egregious example might have been Emil Bednarek who had incredibly managed to get a reparations payment as a camp victim before being unmasked as a sadistic Kapo.

The defendants were all charged with the most serious counts as "perpetrators responsible for murder." Some were generalized charges since the prosecutors could not pinpoint an individual victim. Those crimes were committed as part of Auschwitz's overall genocidal character. For instance, camp adjutant Robert Mulka was accused of being "exclusively responsible for preparation and execution of the extermination measures," although there were no eyewitness accounts of him carrying out his duties. Bauer knew that under German law the generic charges would be difficult to prove. And defense counsel instantly attacked those counts of the indictment. Mulka's attorney, for instance, noted there was no concept in Germany of "functional culpability" and said that "if one strips the indictment bare of all its general, sometimes polemical, comments . . . there is not a single concrete action which the evidence proves against him."[3]

In other instances, however, the indictment identified the names of those killed and tied the murders to a specific defendant. Oswald Kaduk, for example, was charged with "beat[ing] inmates in Block

8 and then strangling them to death by laying a walking stick over their throats and standing on it; in this way he killed, among others, the diamond dealer Moritz Polakewitz, the former secretary of the Antwerp Jewish Council."[4]

On June 17 the prosecutors suffered a blow when the most notable defendant, Richard Baer, died unexpectedly of a heart attack in jail. Historian Devin Pendas wrote that Baer's death "represented more than simply a loss of publicity for the Frankfurt prosecution; it also meant that the plan to hold a trial of the entire Auschwitz hierarchy would have to proceed without the head of that hierarchy."[5] Baer's unexpected death was a gift to the defense counsel. They realized it allowed them to muddy the issues regarding the chain of command and questions of individual responsibility versus simply following orders. This was critical since Germany's legal code only allowed a conviction of someone carrying out an illegal order *if* that person knew the order to be illegal. Otherwise, the responsibility lay only with the commanding officer who issued the order.[6]

The prosecutors suffered another blow before the start of the trial. In Germany, an indictment is only a suggestion to a court of the appropriate charges. The Third Criminal Division of the Frankfurt District Court was not persuaded that all should stand trial under the most serious charges as perpetrators of murder. In early summer, the District Court reduced the counts against half the defendants to accessories to murder. That meant they were facing maximum terms of ten years.[7]

Defense counsel greeted the news from the District Court with jubilation. Capesius and his highly paid legal team did not celebrate however. The charge against him remained "perpetrator responsible for murder." He was now one of only seven facing life in prison. Compounding his problem, he was the only defendant also charged as a willing participant in deadly medical experiments.[8]

When a journalist asked Fritz Bauer the legal culpability of the accused, the chief prosecutor did not hesitate: "I personally believe that the question can be answered only if we ask it this way: Were those who were present at Auschwitz there because they were committed

Nazis or not? By and large, especially for those at Auschwitz, one has to answer this in the affirmative . . . . This was no strange or foreign crime, the perpetrators were largely people who were at that time convinced they were doing the right thing, namely pursuing their National Socialist worldview to victory. In my eyes, those men are simply perpetrators, together with Hitler, committed with Hitler to the 'Final Solution of the Jewish Question,' that they believed to be right."[9]

Although Bauer was not shy to express his opinions, and was the driving force behind the multi-year probe, he removed himself from having any direct role at the trial. He instead appointed four of his office's best and youngest prosecutors, Hans Großmann as lead attorney, accompanied by Joachim Kügler, Gerhard Wiese, and Georg Friedrich Vogel. All had begun their legal careers after 1945, thereby eliminating any possible charge they were influenced or biased by their Third Reich experience.

On December 20, 1963, more than five years after the investigation had commenced, the Auschwitz trial got underway. Capesius's wife, Fritzi, and their second daughter, Ingrid, had been allowed to emigrate from Romania to West Germany only a couple of months earlier. They had arrived just in time to see Capesius on trial for his life.[10]

Chapter 21

UNINSPIRED BUREAUCRATS

The trial was expected to last 20 months. The Germans had constructed a special courtroom, the Bürgerhaus Gallus in Frankfurt, capable of holding all the defendants, their lawyers, the prosecutors, the court staff and judges, and what was expected to be an overflow of spectators and reporters. Since the Bürgerhaus was not complete when the proceedings began, the court convened in the city hall, the only government building capable of holding such a large assembly.

Three judges oversaw the trial. Hans Hofmeyer, a 59-year-old with a solid reputation as an extremely able, no-nonsense justice, was appointed chief judge. That was after another jurist, Hans Forester, had stepped aside over questions of whether he had a conflict of interest since the Nazis had persecuted some of his family. No one strenuously objected to Hofmeyer, however, having not only served as a German intelligence officer but also having been a staff judge for the Nazi's military courts. Because of the ages of all senior judges who were eligible to oversee such an important trial, it was impossible to avoid selecting one whose professional career had not developed during the Third Reich. Hofmeyer tried minimizing his wartime role by noting that the Nazi courts exercised little independence. "The NSDAP and its organizations had the power in their hands to bend the courts to their will."[1] A few legal observers thought it was ironic, at the very least, that the chief judge was justifying his past with a defense – following orders – that would be at the heart of the upcoming trial.

Hofmeyer's Third Reich history, though, was front and center in the East German press. *Neues Deutschland*, the official Communist Party newspaper, repeatedly referred to him as that "Nazi Military Field Judge" and charged he had been selected because he would "not go digging in the trial."[2] The East German media also railed about the absence of any I. G. Farben executives since the trial purported to be a definitive one about Auschwitz. The coverage was particularly vitriolic when an expert witness later submitted an East German sponsored study about the role of Farben and Hofmeyer refused to allow it into evidence, ruling it irrelevant.[3]

The other two justices were District Court Judge Josef Perseke and County Court Judge Walter Hotz (there were also two alternates in case one of the three main judges became ill or incapacitated). In sharp contrast to criminal trials in the U.S. and the U.K, in Germany, the cross-examination and interrogation of witnesses is not the exclusive domain of the prosecution and defense attorneys but in fact is dominated by the judges.

There was also a six-person jury, composed of three housewives, an office worker, a laborer and a coal dealer. And there were three alternates, all housewives. It had been difficult to find professionals willing to sit for such a long case. In Germany, jurors deliberate with the judges. They decide matters of law and fact and are only excluded from weighing in on questions about admitting evidence or the scope of witness testimony.[4] In a deferential society, in which nuances of complicated law were critical, most observers expected the judges would dominate the proceedings and deliberations and relegate the jurors to a minor role.

The Auschwitz trial took place against the backdrop of intense Cold War anxiety between the Soviet Union and its Eastern European satellites and the U.S. and its western allies. Germany was ground zero. It was only in 1961 that East Germany had built a wall dividing Berlin. The year before the trial began, a record number (22) of East Germans had been shot dead while trying to escape to West Berlin. Tensions in the early to mid-1960s were always high between the two Germanys, with both sides preparing for possible military invasion by the other. Adding to the pressure at the Auschwitz trial was that German law allowed civil plaintiffs with interests in the criminal prosecution to be represented by their own attorneys. Lawyers for those plaintiffs were permitted to conduct cross-examination and to submit evidence.

The trial was not yet underway when its first crisis was the application by a flamboyant East Germany attorney, Friedrich Karl Kaul, who demanded a civil seat on behalf of a group of nine East Germans who had lost relatives in Auschwitz. Kaul, who had been dismissed as a lawyer by the Nazis because his mother was Jewish, was a well-known attorney in the East with a hit TV show and a series of bestselling detective novels. He would undoubtedly push at every opportunity the intertwining of the Nazi's mass extermination goals with the financial interests of capitalist monolith Farben and the SS in the operation of Auschwitz.

Defense counsel adamantly objected to Kaul's admission, noting that his plaintiffs could not demonstrate their relatives had died at the hands of any of the 22 accused. Still, after much legal wrangling, the judges reluctantly allowed him to have a role less they be accused of unfairness.[5] All in West Germany braced themselves for the inevitable wave of propaganda he would generate.

The court set a trial schedule of Monday, Wednesday and Friday, with the other days for legal motions and procedural work. On the first day there were 22 accused. Two had been excused for poor health. Six were considered the main defendants, charged with the top count as perpetrators of intentional and willful murder. Capesius was one of them.

That morning, as would happen for every court day of the remainder of the trial, at 8:00 AM a convoy of three VW vans, with police cars in the lead and at the rear, transported the defendants from Hammelsgasse. After they were dropped off, police escorted them into the courthouse. Some sported sunglasses for that short walk. A few covered their face with a folded copy of the morning's newspaper. Capesius wore his dark glasses even in the courtroom.

On the advice of their attorneys, all dressed in conservative dark suits, white shirts and dark ties. None of the suits was stylish or looked expensive. No one sported a high-priced watch. Their shoes were highly polished but seemed more typical of a postman or store clerk than a stylized brogue of a business executive. Nothing about their appearance gave the impression of wealth or status or conveyed the remotest sense of entitlement. Quite the opposite, they appeared very much the ordinary clerks they hoped to mimic, bland men one could pass on the street and not give a second glance.

The defense lawyers understood that so long as their clients looked like uninspired bureaucrats, it bolstered the argument that they simply had not had the backbone to do anything other than follow the orders sent down the chain of command. Maybe it would be possible, some of the attorneys thought, to make their clients appear as quasi-victims, men who had wanted to do the right thing by serving their country but had been hijacked by top Nazis into a murderous machine over which they had no control and could not object. Certainly, went the thinking, it was a concept that a jury of ordinary Germans might embrace. In so doing, they could send a message to an entire generation of wartime Germans that only a handful of demented men were responsible for the horrors of the Holocaust and that the rest of the nation had simply been commandeered against its will.

Once inside, the accused sat on wooden benches normally occupied by local councilmen. A policeman sat to the right of each. All defendants were assigned a number prominently displayed on a placard placed in front of each. That was so it was easier for the witnesses to identify by number which of the defendants was the subject of their testimony. Behind them, displayed in front of tall windows, were two large boards with detailed sketches of Auschwitz I and Birkenau.

Television cameras were let in for fifteen minutes only on that first day. While the cameras ran, Capesius kept his head downcast and put his hand over the side facing the camera. His ex-colleagues who saw him on television, such as Roland Albert, were surprised that he looked heavy, fatter even than he had been during the war. His hair was grayer but he still wore it greased back.

There was one oddity that first day. Seats had been reserved for family members of the accused, and a large section was for the press.

Sixty seats had also been reserved for an expected throng of curious spectators. In fact, the police had expected to turn people away. They had setup a rope divider extending for nearly 100 feet in order to accommodate what everyone thought would be Germans interested in finding out more about the dark chapter in their history. But many of the courtroom seats were empty. That prompted headlines the next day in U.S. newspapers: "21 On Trial for Murder of Millions," with the subheading "Little Interest is Shown as Frankfurt Court Seats Go Unfilled."[6] The defense lawyers were not surprised. Ninety-percent of the mail they received was against the trial, considering it punitive and coming much too late after the crimes.[7] The scant interest and the German public ambivalence did not change as the trial progressed.

What followed was one of the longest legal cases in modern German history. It did not end until April 1965. By then, the court had heard from 359 witnesses from 19 countries. Most, 211, were camp survivors, although 85 were former SS. It was particularly difficult for many survivors, who had to relive horrific events and frequently had their credibility and recollection challenged by aggressive defense lawyers. Moreover, they had to travel to Germany. For some it was their first visit to the nation responsible for Hitler and the Final Solution. They had not seen their tormentors in 20 years and the trial was in German, the language of the executioners.

The 85 SS witnesses, in sharp contrast, had no such difficulty. They had known nothing, seen nothing or had forgotten everything. They had no shame, showed no guilt, and did not once indicate any second thoughts about their gruesome wartime service. To avoid any possibility of incriminating themselves, they emphasized that what had happened at Auschwitz might seem horrible in 1964 Germany, but it was legal pursuant to Nazi laws, rulings and decrees. At times, the SS witnesses seemed so cavalier that even the defendants began resenting that they were free and had never been charged.[8]

Chapter 22

"NO CAUSE FOR LAUGHTER"

The first couple of weeks were taken with the introduction into evidence of all the interrogations of the defendants. It was the public's chance to learn what those charged had said in sworn declarations to the prosecutor and investigating magistrate. On February 7, 1964, the fifteenth day, a German professor became the first witness. He explained the structure of the SS.[1] A week later, Dr. Otto Walken, was the first eyewitness. He was a Viennese physician who spent eighteen months at the camp and had kept a journal, an account that survived the war.

But it was the second eyewitness, Herman Langbein, whom many courtroom observers expected to set the tone for all who followed. And Langbein did not disappoint.

On Friday, March 6, the fifty-one-year-old Langbein took the witness stand. He was tall, thin, and sat slightly hunched forward, his hands clasped tightly in front of him. The court was spellbound by Langbein's deliberate and detailed account of the camp's horrific conditions, all of which he witnessed from his role as an inmate secretary to the chief SS physician.

At one point, the prosecutor interrupted and asked whether Langbein could identify any of the defendants. The judge gave him permission to walk through the rows of the accused to get a closer look. All were ordered to stand. A hush fell over the courtroom as Langbein strolled toward them. Some lowered their heads and averted their eyes. That did not dissuade Langbein from seizing full advantage of the moment. The trial was a personal culmination of his eighteen years of tireless work in tracking down Nazis and finding witnesses and accumulating evidence.

He stopped in front of Oswald Kaduk, the 6' 3" SS sergeant with a notorious reputation for cruelty.

"Fancy seeing you again," Langbein said to Kaduk, who clenched his jaw. "And here, of all places!"

"You know me," Kaduk shouted as he snapped to attention. "That's true. But that's trash what you've been saying about me here!"

"Don't you wish it were so," Langbein said calmly as he continued his slow inspection.

Next he stopped in front of Capesius. The judge ordered the ex-pharmacist to remove his sunglasses. He was perspiring profusely, his forehead glistening with sweat.

"And here's the good Dr. Capesius. How are you, doctor?"

"I never took part in selecting prisoners for the gas chambers as you testified."

In contrast to Kaduk, Capesius's voice trembled slightly.

"You certainly did and you know it."

The only sounds in the enormous courtroom were of Langbein's shoes scraping across the wood floor and the brief exchanges between him and the accused. Over fifteen minutes he identified eight defendants, saying they all "kept the murder factory that was Auschwitz functioning."[2]

While Langbein's powerful confrontation was cathartic for him and many fellow survivors, it sparked only defiance from the defendants. In fact, during the remaining 15 months of the trial, the one constant was that their SS loyalty to each other remained intact, not one spoke against another, and other than when asked to enter their pleas or answer questions directed by the judge, not one took the stand in his own defense.

The defendants instead turned over their fates to their attorneys. And none was more aggressive than Capesius's lawyer, Hans Laternser. Fritz Bauer thought it no coincidence that the only defendants who could afford the highly acclaimed and very expensive Laternser were Capesius and his two dentist friends, Willi Frank and Willi Schatz. That was the same trio Bauer suspected of having stolen dental gold from Auschwitz and then having rendezvoused in 1947 to divide their gruesome loot (Laternser's junior partner, Fritz Steinacker, represented Broad and Dylewski).

Laternser, who some commentators thought was a "right-wing Nazi sympathizer," certainly lived up to a reputation as an advocate who would do anything for his clients.[3] Outspoken and colorful, he had a grander strategy than simply mustering a defense of "following orders." He led the effort to shake the witnesses by suggesting they were exaggerating or that their memories were not reliable because of trauma and the passage of time. Laternser challenged the most damaging testimony by insinuating it was colored by a passion for revenge.[4] And he dismissed as useless all damning accounts of eyewitnesses from communist countries, contending they were part of an insidious Red plot to embarrass West Germany.[5]

No surprise that Ella Böhm, who had been selected at the railhead by Capesius, and many of her fellow survivors, took tranquilizers to calm their nerves before taking the witness stand. Dr. Ella Lingens had nightmares for weeks before and after her testimony.[6]

"It was very difficult for us to be among the people of the enemy's land," recalled Böhm. "Every stone made us weep, every word hurt. We were badly burned children."[7] Laternser's questioning of her was harsh. "My interrogation in the courtroom lasted over an hour. Laternser treated us in a very derogatory fashion. He bombarded us with misleading, confusing questions. When he asked me about my tattoo number and I said I no longer knew it by heart, he gave me a look of scornful disgust. And on top of that, the next morning the *Frankfurter Allgemeine* reported that I had been theatrical."[8] In so harshly attacking the survivors, many courtroom observers thought Laternser victimized the victims once again.

Compounding the problem was that the defendants each did their best to demonstrate they were unfazed by whatever witnesses said. Typical was an instance in which Oswald Kaduk played indifferently with his fountain pen at his courtroom seat while a former inmate described in chilling detail how Kaduk had beat and then executed prisoners each with a single shot from his pistol.[9]

The only sign that they were paying any attention was when one of them sometimes glared at a witness. "I saw that when I looked at the face of Boger or Kaduk, but also Capesius and Klehr," recalled

Henry Ormond, a civil attorney who represented some survivors' families. "Particularly during incriminating witness testimony, I could not escape the feeling that they wanted to say: "It was a mistake to have left you alive. We obviously forgot to gas you. Now that's coming back to haunt us.' Certainly, there was no trace, absolutely no trace of remorse."[10]

Capesius, meanwhile, was unrivaled when it came to appearing mostly undisturbed. What set him apart from the others was that he was the only one who often smiled or laughed. He grinned constantly to other defendants and to his family and friends who came to support him (the last of his daughters, 29-year-old Melitta, had arrived in the middle of the trial in October 1964). Capesius's smiling, which even a few friends thought inappropriate, was most pronounced when the testimony against him was particularly incriminating. And during the times when one of the judges asked him a question, he often seemed distracted, as if somehow he had to force himself to focus on the moment in court. He occasionally had difficulty giving an articulate answer, was forgetful other times, and was often fidgety.

No one was quite certain what was behind the strange behavior. Was the smiling his way of showing he was an innocent man who had few worries about the proceedings? Or could his grin and occasional fits of laughter be his way of denigrating as comical the evidence against him? Some thought it was all an act designed to make him appear a bumbling fool in the hope that might erase the damming prosecutorial portrait of a murderous SS officer.

Even the German press eventually described Capesius's behavior as "odd" and "out of place." When Judge Hofmeyer questioned him once about the charge that he had provided the phenolic acid used to kill prisoners by injections to the heart, Capesius took the opportunity to try and explain away his questionable comportment: "Your honor, last Monday morning, I was under great tension. That made me a little confused later on, and people have criticized me for smiling, quite unconsciously, the whole time. I certainly did not feel there was anything to smile about, and can only explain this by saying that I was in solitary confinement for over four years. This, plus all these people here, and all these electric lights, distracted me, and so I mostly couldn't concentrate on what I was saying."[11]

But few were sympathetic. By then a steady stream of eyewitnesses had taken the stand against him and mostly stood unbowed before his attorney's attack on their credibility.

Among them, Ella Böhm told of her arrival at Auschwitz and how she recognized Capesius on the ramp. Her mother, a pediatrician, was on the same train and confirmed he sent the new inmates to the left or right. Dr. Mauritius Berner, who had recognized Capesius from having done business with him before the war, described the heartrending story of how he beseeched Capesius in vain to spare his twin daughters.

Much of the testimony against Capesius was different from that given against any other defendant. None of the others had been identified by survivors as someone they knew from before the war. But with Capesius that testimony piled on. There was Josef Glück, who had been a key Farben/Bayer customer in Romania. He not only testified to Capesius selecting him at Auschwitz, but also described several occasions inside the camp when Capesius and Mengele selected prisoners to be gassed. "While they were doing it, they were laughing," he recalled. "They probably thought it was funny, seeing the boys cry for their mothers."[12]

One after another they took the stand and related their stories of how they had come to know Capesius when he worked for Farben/ Bayer and then the moment they recognized him at the ramp at Auschwitz. Among them was Paul Pajor, the Jewish pharmacist; Adrienne Krausz, whose mother he sent to the gas chambers; Sarah Nebel whose family lived in the same prewar Bucharest building; Dr. Lajos Schlinger, whose wife Capesius dispatched to her death; Albert Ehrenfeld, another Farben customer whose family he sent to the gas chambers.

Prosecutor Joachim Kügler explained to the court why these extraordinary accounts were so particularly damning. "The unique and monstrous part of this situation for Capesius was that it wasn't just about the nameless masses, but that all of a sudden he was confronted with people whom he had earlier known personally or professionally, people who were completely unsuspecting, who thought that by seeing him it was a lucky sign. They trusted him. What kind of a human being must this Dr. Capesius be, who – knowing that those he directed to the left with a wave of his hand had only one or two more hours to live – with a friendly smile and a few calming, reassuring words, sent the families of his old friends and business colleagues, their wives and children, to their deaths?

"How much emotional brutality, what devilish sadism, what merciless cynicism must it take to act in the way that this monster acted. And to think it would only have cost him, this Hauptsturmführer of the SS, literally a word, only a gesture, to give these few people their lives, these few who hardly mattered against that great mass of people."[13]

Not everyone who testified against Capesius had met him before the war. For many, they saw him for the first time at Auschwitz. Erich Kulka, a Czech Jew who worked as a locksmith in Birkenau's maintenance crew, witnessed many of the arriving trains crammed with prisoners. When asked to identify which of the defendants he had seen perform the life and death selections, he listed Boger, Baretzki, Broad, Kaduk, and Mulka. Then he extended his right arm and pointed across the court. "That gentlemen behind number 18."

"Do you know his name?"

"No."

The man behind the placard with number 18 was Capesius. He sat frozen in his chair.

"It is very important for the court to know," said Judge Hofmeyer, "whether you are sure you recognize Number 18 with certainty as one of the people who selected on the ramp."

"I saw Number 18 often. The men and women filed past him. He decided to which side they had to go. His face hasn't changed much. I definitely recognize him."[14]

Besides testimony from prisoners like Kulka, there were also the inmate pharmacists, men upon whom Capesius had relied in running his dispensary. They were the ones with the most incriminating accounts. Wilhelm Prokop and Jan Sikorski, his two most trusted assistants, conclusively tied Capesius to both the oversight of Zyklon B and the wholesale theft of personal belongings, including the dental gold, from the dead. As with the rest of his eccentric courtroom behavior, Capesius's response to what they said was often perplexing. When Prokop, for instance, testified that Capesius was "in charge of the keys" to the room where Zyklon B was stored, Capesius laughed out loud. Prokop went on to describe the scene in which he had chanced upon Capesius rummaging through suitcases of teeth and how the chief pharmacist had threatened his life should he tell anyone. That caused Capesius to again break out in laughter.

"Dr. Capesius," said Judge Hofmeyer, in his sternest tone, "this is really no cause for laughter. This was a death threat."[15]

Not only did Capesius seem completely nonplussed by whatever was said about him in court, but he also sometimes responded in the same cavalier manner when it came to what transpired with his fellow defendants. Once, for instance, a former prisoner testified that Oswald Kaduk had savagely beat him because the top of his jacket was unbuttoned. When Hofmeyer asked Kaduk if he recognized the witness, Kaduk said: "Your Honor, the witness looks familiar to me. But there were seventeen thousand prisoners in Auschwitz and we had to keep them in line." He admitted he occasionally had struck some. "But some fell down if I merely raised my hand; they only pretended." That caused Capesius to laugh uncontrollably.[16]

One thing he evidently did not find amusing was when sensational testimony about him made the front pages of the next day's newspapers. The most shocking stories were the ones that sold the most papers and attracted the largest television news ratings. Little wonder in Germany, that most of those who followed the trial got their information from tabloids such as *Bild-Zeitung*. There was a frenzy of media coverage, for instance, when on the 118th day, a gruesome Auschwitz photo album was entered into evidence. It was a collection of pictures by SS Sergeant Bernhard Walter, who indulged a sadistic passion for capturing on film the camp's misery and death.

Some commentators dubbed the salacious reporting "the pornography of horror," and one scholar concluded it "contributed to a general collective public detachment from the defendants at the trial."[17] Often lost was what Fritz Bauer had hoped the trial might offer: a chance to be educational about the Final Solution for a new generation of Germans while at the same time sparking introspection and reevaluation by the wartime generation.

When the inmate nurse, Ludwig Wörl, testified in April that a Capesius friend suggested there might be 50,000 DM for any witness who could give evidence that Zyklon B was not the responsibility of the chief pharmacist, the next day's headline was "Bribe Allegation at Auschwitz Trial!"[18] In June, Jan Sikorski's testimony led to "Auschwitz Druggist Tagged As Jekyll-Hyde Character."[19] And that same month after Wilhelm Prokop's gruesome recounting of Capesius hunting for gold by sorting through rotting dentures, the lead stories were "Chemist Stored Gold Teeth" and "Horror Loot of a Nazi Camp Told."[20]

"Auschwitz Story Written in Blood" was the headline in August 1964 when Josef Glück broke down in tears as he pulled a photograph from his pocket of his dead sixteen-year-old nephew. "Children slit open their arms and wrote their names in blood."[21] That same month, when Dr. Berner told how Capesius had dispatched his wife and daughter to the gas chambers, the front page coverage was: "Doctor Testifies Nazi He Aided Killed Family."[22] And a week after Berner had been on the stand, Magda Szabó recounted Capesius screaming at an inmate, "I am Capesius from Transylvania. In me you will get to know the devil."[23] "Nazi Called Self The Devil!" was the following morning's banner headline.[24]

In each instance, when Judge Hofmeyer asked if he wanted to say anything about the damning testimony against him, Capesius seemed oddly incapable of mustering much more than a conspiracy theory to try to explain it away. In the case of Magda Szabó, for instance, he picked up the theme established by his lawyer that all Eastern Bloc witnesses were part of a Communist plot. She had lied and colluded with other witnesses to frame him, charged Capesius. That prompted a stern warning from Hofmeyer that he "objected most energetically" to any insinuation that an eyewitness was part of some unproven, nebulous cabal.[25] That did not dissuade Capesius. When Sarah Nebel testified she knew Capesius from the 1930s when they both lived in the same Bucharest apartment building, and that he selected her at the Auschwitz railhead, he declared, "The fact that my countrymen say so over and over again is no proof. A plot has been concocted about that in Romania."

Hofmeyer blew apart Capesius's communist-inspired scheme, "The witness comes from Israel."[26]

Capesius looked around as if trying to determine if somehow he had been tricked. Laternser, his attorney, grimaced.

Another time, the pharmacist Paul Pajor testified that he not only knew Capesius from his Farben/Bayer days, but that Capesius had selected him at Auschwitz, "Dr. Capesius was standing about twelve to fifteen feet from me, addressed me in Hungarian, and selected me. That he did select is one hundred percent certain; one can't forget such a thing."

Hofmeyer addressed Capesius. "What we want to know from you above all is whether you selected new arrivals on the ramp or not. What the witness said, in short, all sounds very plausible."

"It only sounds that way," retorted Capesius. He then launched into a diatribe about how Communist Romania had framed him as early as 1946 when he was convicted in absentia.[27]

When yet another witness produced a holiday card he said Capesius had given him before the war, Hofmeyer asked if the handwriting was his. Capesius said yes. Then, a few days later, seemingly remembering his claim that all the Romanians were lying, he changed his mind and contested the handwriting.

In other instances, Capesius's standard response – denying he recalled meeting any of the witnesses before the war and that they must have confused him with Dr. Fritz Klein at the Auschwitz ramp – sounded stale and increasingly preposterous the more he repeated it. When a witness testified that behind his back they called Capesius *Mopsel* (pug-face or tubby), he took the opportunity to say that he was not pug-faced but that the description fit Dr. Klein. That prompted one of the civil attorneys, Henry Ormond, to say that he had met Klein during the Bergen-Belsen trial and that "it is hard to imagine someone bearing as little resemblance to Dr. Klein as you do."[28] Ella Lingens, one of Mengele's inmate physicians, said: "Dr. Klein was then (1944) the same age as Dr. Capesius is today (1964). Their faces bear absolutely no resemblance to each other. . . . Dr. Klein spoke accent-free High German. I did not know that he was from Romania. The language of the two was not similar. Dr. Klein spoke more without accent; Dr. Klein spoke like someone whose mother spoke German. He may even have spoken a little Swabian dialect. He spoke Transylvanian the same way I speak Viennese. But for me, Dr. Capesius sounds like someone who had one parent that spoke Romanian. Dr. Capesius speaks German like a Romanian, more like a foreigner."[29] (One of Capesius's character witnesses, a childhood friend, Viktoria Ley, later tried boosting the Klein-as-alibi defense by testifying that she met Klein one time in 1944 and he confided to her that he "took over all the unpleasant assignments from Capesius." Under questioning by Hofmeyer she admitted that key elements of her testimony came from newspaper accounts she had read).[30]

At other times, Capesius failed to offer any satisfactory explanation for why someone of his rank would have gone to the ramp to collect luggage and medical supplies instead of assigning it to a junior officer, especially if he found the railhead as upsetting as he claimed. And once, when the prosecutor showed him a picture of a selection underway, Capesius refused to admit that he recognized it. The judges seemed puzzled by his convoluted effort at dodging the question. When pushed, he threw up his arms in desperation. "I have no precise idea how it is supposed to have looked there!"[31]

Although he liked pretending that not much presented in the court got under his skin, his lawyers knew he was particularly irked that the press had consistently portrayed one of his co-defendants, Dr. Franz Lucas, as the "good German." Lucas claimed that in the five months in 1944 when he was at Auschwitz, he had "never violated orders, but I did what I could to circumvent them."[32] Capesius thought that he deserved some good press for claiming that he tried to get out of selection duty. He was miffed that Lucas was seemingly the media darling. A greater humiliation was that Fritz Bauer's team had chosen Capesius as the poster boy for making the case that the Nazis stole from the dead.

At one stage the prosecutor argued: "Capesius systematically and ruthlessly took advantage of the situation in Auschwitz, and he purposefully pursued his own material interests. The evidence will show how he was guilty, not of robbery or of extortion – for the people whose property he appropriated were already dead – but rather how he perpetrated this particularly hideous form of looting the dead. The evidence will prove that the accused, Capesius, had a highly personal stake in remaining at Auschwitz and in the continuation of the murderous events there, a fact that legally is highly significant, and reveals the true intentions of the accused. [It was a] widespread custom in Auschwitz with respect to the valuables confiscated from prisoners on their delivery to the camp: some SS would set them aside as a kind of old-age insurance for themselves. But according to what we have heard, none of the accused persons indulged in this practice to such an extent, with such businesslike efficiency, and as unscrupulously as did Capesius."[33]

It was one thing to be accused of murdering Jews who were considered less than human by the Third Reich, thought Capesius, but it was insulting to be marked publicly as no better than a grave robber.

However, much as Capesius seethed over those charges, he tried hard to show he was never flustered. The effort to conceal his rage and embarrassment led to some cringe-worthy moments. In June 1964, the inmate pharmacist, Wilhelm Prokop, stunned the court in describing how Capesius had "bent over and started picking through the jawbones" of the dead in his search for gold. That caused Capesius to laugh uproariously until Hofmeyer ordered him to "stop it!"

When Prokop finished testifying, Hofmeyer asked Capesius if he wished to say anything. No longer smiling, he stood to attention at the defendants' table: "I never broke gold from the teeth. Only once did I examine the teeth – and the gold was already gone."[34]

Even Laternser seemed puzzled by his client.

As the trial played out, Capesius seemed in his own world, spending much of his time in jail reading about Auschwitz, making notes, suggesting strategies for his attorneys, and generally feeling sorry for himself. Letters he wrote in prison reveal that instead of the trial prompting his own soul searching for what he had done at the camp, he griped incessantly about everything from loneliness to the poor quality of jail food to his perceived sexual deprivation.

At Hammelsgasse, he whined that "they only allow you one five-kilo package at Christmas if you are in pretrial detention. Sentenced prisoners doing time here, on the other hand, are allowed half a chicken and a cake when their family comes on monthly visits; we in detention are given at most a bottle of Coke from the soda machine here, and that's supposed to keep us from escaping?" Capesius said that "my [Auschwitz] inmates were better nourished." The bad food had caused him at one stage to shed 40 pounds, which he said had left him "practically impotent, and with no desire for intercourse. There is no sex with a wife or a girlfriend, and everyone has to deal with this somehow. But you can only keep up this regimen for so long, given the nervous tension you feel all the time. This then leads to sexual torment, or at least need. . . . Even in Auschwitz, setting up a bordello was just a stopgap measure."[35]

Capesius was also aggravated by what he called "all sorts of privations for someone in solitary confinement. . . . You have no company, no one to talk to." At other times, he complained about the "alienation" from his family and that "back at home there are people who need taking care of." His wife, he noted, was newly arrived in West Germany and "my children still have no father, all three are still in school, because their studies are not accredited here, or only partially. Those are all problems that they could have dealt with differently if they had had a father who was free, instead of a father in prison. What is it to have a father who will be free . . . because they haven't got any evidence on him?"

What about the eyewitnesses and evidence of his guilt? "Of course, a peaceful conscience is a great comfort, but when you find out how the accusations are exaggerated with lies, you just don't understand the world anymore. The witness can be presented as unreliable, but he still gets featured in all the books and in the theater, even if his testimony was rejected in the first verdict: the accusation that you sent 1,200 children to the gas chamber sticks, because 'scripta manent'" (a Latin proverb "spoken words fly away, written words remain").[36]

Although Capesius had nothing but praise for his legal team, he noted "Wealth and property are gone. Debts are piling up." Eventually, he spent about 100,000 DM on his defense.

Capesius was pleased as the trial reached its concluding phases. An unusual event outside the courtroom gave him some hope that modern Germans were becoming ever more forgiving about wartime crimes. Heinrich Bütefisch, the chemist and Farben director who had been sentenced to seven years at the Farben trial, had successfully returned to the corporate boardrooms of some major German chemical companies. In that way, he was similar to his fellow convicted directors, all of whom had regained their positions at the top of German industry. The difference in late 1964 was that the President of Germany gave Bütefisch the country's highest civilian award for public service, The Grand Cross of Merit. The idea that a convicted war criminal could receive the Grand Cross kicked off a firestorm. And while Bütefisch much later returned it, as the Auschwitz trial neared its conclusion, it seemed merely another indicator to Capesius that good fortune might be breaking his way.

Chapter 23

THE VERDICT

Closing arguments began on May 7, 1965. In his full denial, Capesius thought that meant he was one step closer to an acquittal. By that time, two of the defendants, Heinrich Bischoff and Gerhard Neubert, had their cases separated because of poor health. It took three months for the prosecutors, lawyers for the civil plaintiffs, and attorneys for each of the remaining twenty defendants to finish. The prosecutors made a strong closing, not only restating how Auschwitz was the main killing center in the Final Solution, but highlighting the chief evidence against each of the defendants. As far as Fritz Bauer was concerned, the core of the prosecution plea was a common sense one: "The be all and the end all of this trial to say, 'You should have said no.'"[1]

In the summation by the attorneys for the civil clients, Henry Ormand dubbed Capesius "one of the biggest ghouls."[2]

In June, Hans Laternser gave his highly anticipated summation for Capesius and his other clients. The *Frankfurter Allgemeine Zeitung* described his argument as "ironic, insulting, but very logical and smart." Laternser disparaged all the eyewitnesses as unreliable since it was "beyond human capabilities" to accurately recall such terrible events twenty years after they happened. Plus, he said, the mixed motivations of revenge and political propaganda from Communist-bloc witnesses, cast further doubts on their reliability.[3] And he played to his long running theme of witness tampering by noting that since more than half the witnesses were from foreign countries, they could not be prosecuted in Germany.

But what grabbed the public's attention was Laternser's perverted argument that the selections were not a crime but rather an act of mercy. Since Auschwitz was a death camp, survivors owed their lives to the SS officers who had chosen them at the ramp. In Laternser's singular view of the world, selection sabotaged the Third Reich's directive to liquidate all of Europe's Jews. Selection, he contended, was an obstruction of murder, not an aid to it; the defendants had chosen life, not death, by serving at the ramp at Auschwitz. "You can say those who participated in the selections played the saviors of those selected, and thus subverted Hitler's plan," he contended.[4]

Laternser's partner, Fritz Steinacker, followed with a broadside that the entire trial was flawed since it was nothing more than a political farce. He argued strenuously that no matter how objectionable everyone found it, the Final Solution had been legally ordered by the architects of the Third Reich. His clients were simply ordinary men who had followed their duty to the state.

On August 6, 1965, the 180th day of proceedings, the defendants entered their formal pleas (Under German law, they come at the end of the trial, not the beginning). Capesius managed to avoid his trademark stumbling and forgetfulness. He had obviously practiced his statement many times. He said that it was only an "unfortunate circumstance" that allowed him, "a Romanian officer, and a Romanian citizen married to a half-Jewess . . . to be the chief pharmacist of Auschwitz, of whose existence I had previously not even known."

A few spectators and reporters behind him frowned at his use of *Jewess*, a term that had become one of the Third Reich's derogatory ways of referring to Jewish women.

"Your Honor! I did no harm to anyone in Auschwitz. I was polite, friendly and helpful to everyone whenever I could be. I was on the ramp at various times to pick up the doctors' luggage for the camp pharmacies. I never selected, and I must stress that emphatically. In my capacity as pharmacist I did my job as best I could as the circumstances permitted . . . I am guilty of no crimes in Auschwitz. I beg for you to acquit me."[5]

Although the many independent witness accounts of him performing the selections at the ramp seemed conclusive, he knew he had to deny doing any. Admitting even one would be as damning for his legal fate as if he had performed dozens.

All the defendants were remanded in custody as the trial drew to a close that same day (two, Willi Schatz and Pery Broad had been free on bail until then). It was time for the judges and jury to deliberate. Any vote would have to be carried by a majority of 5 since there were three judges and six jurors.

In the early discussions, a few jurors thought that too much time had passed for the witnesses to be credible and that a judgment could not be based on their testimony alone. But there were documents that backed the witnesses, as the judges pointed out. And most important, a visit late in the trial (December 14-16, 1964) to Auschwitz by the judges, jurors, and lawyers, had corroborated much of the eyewitness testimony. After ten days they finally began voting on the charges against each defendant. By the court rules, the jurors voted before the judges, with the youngest going first.

Thursday, August 19, 1965 was the verdict day. Legal observers were surprised it had taken only 12 days for judgments to be reached on so many charges for all defendants. The courtroom was packed. Not only had the world press returned, spectators filled every available seat. Although surveys showed that more than half of all Germans had not followed the trial in any media, it seemed suddenly that everyone wanted to be there for a moment of history.[6]

At 8:30 the defendants began entering the court. Höcker and Baretzki joined Capesius in hiding behind large sunglasses. The three judges entered a few minutes before 9:00 AM. Judge Hofmeyer announced, as he had every day for the past twenty months, "The case of Mulka and others is being heard." All the defendants rose for the last time.

Hofmeyer announced he would read a summary verdict from the bench. It was in fact an "oral justification" for the full decision, which he noted, was 457-pages and "includes specific reasoning and evidence for the verdict issued in the case of each defendant."[7] Even the oral summary and verdicts took two days.

The judge began by explaining that the court had decided it was not obligated to reach a verdict that carried any historical significance about Auschwitz. "Although the trial has attracted attention beyond the borders of this country and been given the name 'Auschwitz Trial,' as far as the court is concerned, it is the proceedings against Mulka and others. That is to say, as far as the court is concerned, the only consideration was the guilt of the accused men. The court was not convened to master the past; it also did not have to decide whether this trial served that purpose or not. The court could not conduct a political trial, let alone a show trial."[8]

Then Hofmeyer pointedly rejected the prosecution contention that everyone who worked at Auschwitz was automatically an accomplice to the crimes there. The chief judge said that if the defendants were to be found guilty based just on their SS membership and service at the death camp, then the trial would have "been over within hours" and the West German court would be "no better than the rule of law as practiced at Auschwitz."[9]

However, Hofmeyer made clear that the defendants would not benefit by being "little people,' since "they were just as vital to the execution of the extermination plan as those who drew up this plan at their desks."

In reaching the verdicts Hofmeyer noted the difficulty with eyewitness accounts given so many years after the events. "The court has carefully and soberly checked the testimony of every witness," he said, "and as a result has not been able to arrive at verdicts of guilty on every one of the points in the indictment." The court's ability to crosscheck the accuracy of the witnesses was limited, he noted, since the Nazis had "wiped out all traces" of the crimes, "documents which might have been of great help to the court have been destroyed," and the defendants themselves "have not furnished any clues to help in the search for the truth, have kept silent on many points, and have largely failed to tell the truth."

Then he proceeded to the judgments for each of the twenty defendants in the numerical order in which they sat during the trial. That meant Capesius had to listen to seventeen verdicts before he knew his own fate. In those seventeen, fifteen were found guilty of either the top charge of murder as a perpetrator or the lesser count of aiding and abetting murder. Capesius's friend, Dr. Willi Schatz, was acquitted. It must have given some hope to Capesius that his defense had also convinced the court of his innocence.

Capesius stood to attention when Hofmeyer turned to him. The chief judge began by dismissing Capesius's claim that since he lived in Romania he had not fully appreciated that what happened at Auschwitz was a universal crime. And Hofmeyer described his conduct at the camp as "cruel" and "malicious." Capesius would later tell a friend that he could not believe the words from the bench were about him. The court concluded he had performed the railhead selections and in so doing had been responsible for sending "at least 8,000 of his Romanian fellow citizens to death on the ramp." In fact, his persistent refusal to admit his role on the ramp, the court ruled, was evidence "he knew very well that he was facilitating the extermination program and contributing to the death of victims" through the selections.[10] Capesius was also responsible, said Hofmeyer, for the murders "inasmuch as he also supervised the insertion of Zyklon B."

A small bit of good news was that Capesius was not accountable for distributing the phenol used to kill inmates, since the court determined that those experiments had ended before he became the chief pharmacist. And it did not hold him responsible for inflicting beatings and performing selections in the women's camp, discounting the eyewitness testimony that had put him there.

Hofmeyer's conclusion, however, was particularly damning. The court found it "despicable that the defendant had enriched himself with the property of the murdered victims."[11]

To some observers it seemed as if all the air was let out of Capesius. His shoulders slumped, he cast his head downward, and he braced himself with his hands against the edge of the defendant's table. When the judge stopped talking, his attorney had to tell him it was time to sit again.

That morning seemed a surreal nightmare for Capesius. He had trouble fully comprehending that twenty years after the end of the war, a German court was insisting that he be held legally responsible for the murders at Auschwitz. Over the intervening decades he had become fully invested in his own denial, completely believing he was simply a victim of fate and bad luck. Criminal liability had not seemed a real risk to him, even after his 1959 arrest. But now, hearing the rush of words from Hofmeyer, he could not understand that the court had failed to appreciate his plight. The guilty verdict was not a revelatory moment that suddenly made Capesius realize his past had finally caught up to him. Instead he felt sorry for himself. As the Nazis had 'victimized' him by drafting him into the Waffen-SS, he thought now a West German court was again making him the victim, to pay for crimes beyond his control.[12]

Capesius's attention was brought back to the courtroom when Laternser tugged on his jacket. Judge Hofmeyer had finished reading the verdicts. Seventeen of the defendants had been found guilty of at least some of the charges. Three were acquitted on all counts (Breitwieser, Schatz, and Schobert). Although Capesius was glum, Laternser was pleased. His client was the only one of the seven defendants indicted for "intentional murder as a perpetrator" who had been found guilty of the lesser charge of "accessory to murder."

Hofmeyer next moved to the sentences. The six found guilty of deliberate murder got the maximum of life in prison (Boger, Kaduk, Klehr, Hofmann, Baretzki and Bednarek). The rest, convicted of aiding and abetting, got reduced sentences. They ranged from 3 years for Dr. Franz Lucas to 14 for Mulka. Capesius got 9 years. He turned to look at Laternser as if seeking a confirmation that he had heard the number correctly.[13]

"Thus this trial before the Frankfurt court has come to an end," Judge Hofmeyer declared. "During the twenty months of this trial the court had to relive the suffering and tortures which the people were subjected to and which will forever be coupled with the name Auschwitz. There will be some among us who for a long time to come will not be able to look into the happy, trusting eyes of a child without seeing the hollow, questioning, uncomprehending, fear-filled eyes of the children who went their last way there in Auschwitz."[14]

Hofmeyer thanked the jurors, both the prosecution and defense attorneys, and then ordered all those found guilty remanded to custody.

He then brought his attention back to the men on whom he had just passed judgment. "Will all the defendants please rise. You have heard the verdict. It is my duty to give you some legal advice. You may appeal the verdict but only on the basis that the verdict violates the law, not on the contention that the findings of the court are not founded on fact. An appeal must be filed within a week."

He slammed the gavel for the final time.

"This court is now closed."

Fritz Bauer was terribly disappointed by the verdict. He thought it was another example of Germany's unwillingness to confront its wartime past. The convictions for the lesser counts of aiding and abetting was the court's way, he said, of feeding a "residual wishful fantasy that there were only a few people with responsibility in the totalitarian state of the Nazi period and the rest were merely terrorized, violated hangers-on or depersonalized, dehumanized characters who were compelled to do things that were completely contrary to their nature. Germany was not, as it were, a society supporting Nazism, but a country occupied by the enemy. But this had little to do with historical reality. They [the 'small fry'] were virulent nationalists, imperialists, anti-Semites and Jew-haters. Without them, Hitler was unthinkable."[15]

Bauer thought an underlying failure in the judicial system was the German refusal to retroactively apply the country's 1954 laws banning genocide and mass murder to the Nazis. "There was an order to liquidate the Jews in Nazi-controlled Europe; the instruments of murder were Auschwitz, Treblinka, and so forth. Whoever operated this murder machinery is guilty of participation in murder . . . [just as if someone] is a member of a band of robbers, then he is guilty of murder, regardless of whether he issued the murder order as the boss at the desk, distributed the revolvers, or did the shooting with his own hand."[16]

In under a week all the defendants had filed appeals seeking reversals of their convictions. Under German law, the prosecutors were also allowed to appeal. They asked for a reversal of Willi Schatz's acquittal and new trials for Capesius, Mulka, Höcker, Dylewski,

Broad, Stark and Schlage.[17] All, the motion argued, had gotten off too lightly and life sentences were the appropriate punishment for each.

The prosecutors were not the only ones crestfallen. Hermann Langbein, now the secretary general of another survivor's group, the Comité International de Camps in Brussels, had mixed feelings at best. While he was pleased that 17 defendants were found guilty, he thought the court was far too lenient in its sentencing. Langbein was perplexed that the camp's two adjutants, Höcker and Mulka, had not gotten maximum sentences. And what had Langbein and other survivors steaming was that Capesius had been convicted only as an accomplice and not as a willing perpetrator. "Anyone who did not shy away from profiting from mass murder clearly wanted and willed it," Langbein told a reporter.[18]

Langbein was not alone. Newspapers in Zurich, Paris and London criticized the sentences and highlighted Capesius and Mulka as the two who had gotten off too lightly.[19] East Germany's *Neues Deutschland* said "the judgment is an insult to the dead of Auschwitz."[20] The following year, when playwright Peter Weiss opened his four-hour drama, *The Investigation*, it was based almost entirely on the trial testimony. Capesius, once again, was portrayed as someone who had gotten off with a slap on the wrist.

"The respect of the world is gone," Capesius wrote to his family. "I am branded by the press, and then that little theater piece of Weiss's, where he quoted me, but it was really [Dr. Fritz] Klein: 'You'll see each other again in an hour.' They were speaking lines on stage . . . books about the trial, and the mention of Auschwitz in every article, even when it has nothing to do with the subject; but in many countries, this witch-hunting promotes sales."[21]

For Capesius, all the notoriety had at least an unexpected upside. Between the merely curious and those who wanted to show him some support, business at his Markt-Apotheke pharmacy in Göppingen was booming.[22]

Chapter 24

"IT WAS ALL JUST A BAD DREAM"

The formal end of the trial did not stop the activism of survivors like Langbein. He contacted Vienna University in September, 1964, requesting it revoke Capesius's pharmacy doctorate. The university did not know Langbein and assumed he would go away if they simply said no. Once he got rejected, he did what he had done so many times before when facing apparently immovable bureaucratic resistance and inertia. He adeptly built a strong coalition to demand the revocation. It included the Simon Wiesenthal Center, Hungarian and Romanian professional immigrants' associations, a few prominent survivor doctors living in Israel, and even the Israeli ambassador to Austria. By November, much to Capesius's anger, Vienna University stripped him of his professional degree.[1] (Langbein also successfully got medical degrees annulled for the dentist Willi Frank and the physician, Franz Lucas).

Besides further motivating Langbein and other survivors, the trial had some other good, unintended consequences. Some of the trial testimony led to the unmasking of Dr. Horst Fischer, an Auschwitz colleague of Capesius, who had been practicing medicine in East Germany. After his arrest, a court there found him guilty, and Fischer was the last person in Germany to be executed in 1966 by guillotine.

The Frankfurt trial also gave Fritz Bauer the momentum to complete several related investigations in his office. From 1966 through 1971, Bauer brought three smaller Auschwitz trials. In those, he got a series of convictions against some of the chief Kapos at both Auschwitz and Farben/Monowitz. The highest profile accused was Dr. Horst Schumann, who had performed gruesome sterilization experiments at the women's hospital at Auschwitz. Schumann had been a fugitive in Ghana until November 1966, when he was finally extradited to Germany (Six months into his trial he was released from prison due to 'poor health;' he lived another 11 years a free man).

The Auschwitz trial had also reenergized the debate, which had scandalously dragged on for years, over whether or not there should be a statute of limitations for Nazi crimes. In West Germany after 1945, the original limit for charging someone with murder was twenty years. When it was set to expire in 1965, the limit had been temporarily extended to cover all of Bauer's cases. But he and others used the sweeping historical record from the trial with Capesius and his 21 SS colleagues to argue forcefully that there should be no limit at all on murder committed during the Nazi era. (It would take until 1979 for that to become law).

As for Capesius, he remained in jail and pursued his appeal. His wife and daughters visited him regularly, in addition to some old friends, like the Stoffels. As it was during the trial, his most frequent callers though were his attorneys. Capesius spent his days trying to help them by reviewing the case that had been presented against him and to look for reasons why his verdict should be vacated.

On January 24, 1968, less than two and a half years into his nine-year sentence, the German High Court stunned almost everyone by freeing Capesius from prison while his appeal was pending. The court, noting that he had well-established business and family ties in Germany, did not think he was a flight risk. And it accepted his attorney's humanitarian argument that there should be some consideration for the four and a half years he was in custody from the time of his arrest to the sentencing.[2] Weeks before his 61st birthday, Capesius walked out of jail while his appeal moved forward. It caused a firestorm of outrage from Bauer's office, survivors, and much of the press.

But for Capesius it was a moment of victory. His attorney, Hans Laternser, correctly predicted that he would never again return to jail. Capesius would have preferred that an appellate court had overturned his conviction and declared him an innocent man. But short of that, serving less than three years of his nine-year sentence, was undoubtedly some consolation.

After his release, Capesius's first public appearance in Göppingen was with his family one evening at a classical concert. As he walked into the music hall the audience broke spontaneously into enthusiastic applause.[3]

Fritzi, who never felt particularly at home in Germany, initially suggested they might be better off starting a new life abroad. She was longing to return to their native Transylvania but that was not an option since the 1946 death sentence against him was still in full force and effect. More importantly, he did not want to leave Germany. It was his new home and he had given up too much, he said, by being tried and convicted to simply pack up and move. The warm reception from his neighbors, coupled with the unexpected news that summer that Fritz Bauer had died at sixty-four of a heart attack, had in part reinforced his confidence that the right decision was to stay.

Most important, however, was that he did not want to leave his children after having been separated from them for so many years. It was clear they were establishing permanent roots in the west. His eldest, Melitta, was studying engineering at Stuttgart's Technical University, the same school he had applied to after the war (when she graduated with a degree in mechanical engineering the following year she moved to nearby Ludwigsburg and went to work for the manufacturing firm Mann + Hummel). While he was in prison, Ingrid, his middle daughter, had received her doctorate in Biology and Natural Sciences from one of Germany's oldest and most acclaimed schools, the Eberhard Karls University in Tübingen. As he adjusted to life as a free man, she pursued postdoctoral studies (the year after his release she joined the teaching staff in the Biology Department of the University of Heidelberg). And Christa, his youngest, had decided to follow in her father's footsteps by finishing her degree as a pharmacist (she joined an Apotheke in Schwäbisch Hall, an hour north of her parents).

His daughters wanted him to stay also. As adults they had only seen him either in prison or at his trial. His freedom meant they had an opportunity to get to know their father at last.*

For the next seventeen years – until his death of natural causes on March 20, 1985, at the age of 78 – Capesius and his wife lived alone in the same Göppingen house he had purchased in the early 1950s (Fritzi stayed there on her own until her death in 1998). The couple returned to owning and managing the pharmacy and beauty store businesses although, since he was stripped of his pharmaceutical degree, he could no longer fill the prescriptions himself.

Over the years, however, many visitors to the couple thought they seemed burdened by her homesickness and his constant need to justify his wartime service. Although a free man, friends found him still very much a captive to the narrative of his time at Auschwitz.

The Romanian poet Dieter Schlesak, whose family had known Capesius before the war, visited the couple in 1978 for research he was conducting on a novel based on Capesius. Schlesak was surprised at how they seemed confused about names and places and wrong often about their recall of events.

He later wrote: "The most irritating thing about Capesius that one could not ignore: that soft, strained, yet casual-sounding voice in a Transylvanian accent. I am convinced that in the camp he had had a commanding voice, but then had undergone a personality change in his fall from commander to prisoner, such that he now sounded like a befuddled, whining old man. When my mother heard his voice on

---

* Melitta Capesius retired from Mann + Hummel in 1992 and later became a county chairwoman in Germany's largest Transylvanian Saxon Association, a cultural organization for ethnic Germans from Romania. It was a group in which her mother, Friederike, had been active. Melitta died in 2013. Ingrid Essigmann-Capesius became a full professor of biology at the University of Heidelberg in 1980, a post she held for twenty years. Her scientific papers were published widely. And Christa Eißer – the only daughter to drop her maiden Capesius after marriage – retired as a pharmacist in 2014. The author located Ingrid and Christa but neither agreed to an interview or to assist in any way. In declining, however, Ingrid made a few telling comments, noting that "in the past what was said had been turned to lies." In Cluj, where she and her sisters were raised, she said "there was harmony between the different ethnic groups." She claimed that "He would have preferred not to be there [Auschwitz]. He tried to help people." One of her father's most trusted inmate assistants, whose name she could not recall (in fact, Fritz Peter Strauch), was Jewish, she said, and would have testified favorably but died before the trial.

tape, she said, surprised, 'Vic was an educated guy, just listen to how he sounds now, he's definitely gone soft in the head.'"[4]

To Schlesak, and other friends and acquaintances willing to listen, Capesius carried on for hours on end about how his conviction was a miscarriage of justice. What about the many eyewitnesses who put him at the center of the railhead selections and supervising Zyklon B?

"They were foreigners, they had been bought off, it was a conspiracy. They had to slander me, to make Communist propaganda . . . a Communist plot against me . . . I was handed over to them, and they finished me off!"[5]

At times he got teary eyed, working himself into a tsunami of self-pity. Fritzi wanted desperately to believe that the man with whom she had fallen in love while both were medical students in Vienna was incapable of doing the crimes with which he had been charged. In many instances she enabled his denial. She claimed that since his trial he had "been severely depressed." And she often argued that he would have been exonerated had he not "often been confused . . . [those] four years in solitary confinement, and then all those people and lights, he was befuddled and distracted . . . his lack of concentration . . . he was smiling absentmindedly."[6]

What about the railhead selections?

"Because you have to do everything that you are ordered to do, without protest, just like back home," Capesius said.

"Yes, because you resisted doing 'selections,'" Fritzi added.

"Right," confirmed Capesius. [7]

What about Auschwitz itself? If he disliked his posting there as much as he claimed, why had he not asked for a transfer to the Eastern Front?

"I could not volunteer for the front; I was too old."

Did he ever try?

"No. They said we couldn't do that, that we were not needed there, that we could only be used behind the lines."

Once, it was pointed out to Capesius that his friend, Roland Albert, had requested and gotten a transfer to the front.

"He was reassigned in November 1944, by then everything was all over." Of course, if Capesius had asked for a reassignment at that same time it would have spared him the last three months in Auschwitz.

"All the horror," said Fritzi, "Victor has sometimes said it was all just a bad dream. Not dreamed by him, but by somebody else."

Ultimately, Capesius excused himself and justified what he had done by reverting to the standard defense that he had no choice.

"Could you run away? No! No desertion! You would have been caught right away! You would have been hung from the nearest pole. The individual could do nothing to resist. . . . You couldn't go against the system. Discipline was the highest value. It was war."

Henry Ormond, one of the attorneys for some civil plaintiffs in the Auschwitz trial had demonstrated this defense to be a complete lie.

"This leads me to make a few remarks about a myth – the myth of Befehlsnotstand, or the requirement of compulsory obedience to orders from a superior – which over the past few years has become an outright falsification of history. When the Central Office for the Investigation of Nazi Crimes was set up in Ludwigsburg in 1958, it began to investigate this matter more thoroughly, and to take a closer look at those witnesses who were handed on from one proceeding to another, and to check their statements somewhat more intensively. And note: it turned out that not a single instance could be substantiated – *I repeat, not a single instance* – where someone could have been brought before an SS or police court, let alone, as they like to portray it, been summarily shot, hanged, or gassed. Simply put, someone who declared his inability to participate in criminal killings could expect not to be punished!"[8]

That was only how it appears, claimed Capesius.

"In the trial, everything was different from the way things were in Auschwitz."

EPILOGUE

For many decades, the 1963-1965 Auschwitz Trial seemed a footnote in German legal history. It had little effect on how historians viewed the Holocaust and it did not prompt much soul searching among ordinary Germans. That was mostly because the record of the trial itself was missing for a long time and no one could study it. It was the last major case before verbatim transcripts were kept. Instead, the testimony of each witness was tape-recorded, intended for the judges and jury to use during deliberations. Following a verdict, the plan was to destroy all the files and tapes. For reasons still not clear, Judge Hofmeyer did not destroy them but instead sealed them under protective custody for thirty years, until 1995. The tapes were stored in the basement of the public prosecutor's office in Frankfurt, where a local radio station discovered them disintegrating in 1993. That kicked off a two-year project to transfer the recordings to digital files.

Since the material became public in 1995, the Fritz Bauer Institute, a Holocaust-themed documentation center named after the former prosecutor, began the arduous task of transcribing the more than 500 hours of courtroom testimony. The availability of the trial materials made it possible for history professors Devin Pendas and Rebecca Wittmann to complete acclaimed scholarly reviews of the trial and its aftermath in 2006 and 2012.[1]

In 2011, a German court meted out a five-year jail sentence to John Demjanjuk for his role in killing 28,000 inmates while he was a sadistic guard at the Sobibor death camp. That was a high-profile case since Demjanjuk was a former autoworker from Ohio and had fought extradition for years from the U.S. to Germany. But legal scholars knew the case potentially had far greater impact than the single conviction of yet another Nazi criminal. As the Frankfurt Auschwitz trial had demonstrated, it was not possible to obtain a murder conviction unless the evidence established convincingly that the defendant was linked to specific killings. But in the Demjanjuk case, the Munich prosecutor had convinced the trial judge that it was impossible for anyone who served at Sobibor not to have played an integral part in mass murder.

That decision gave prosecutors around Germany the chance to open dozens of investigations against camp guards, cases that had been closed because it had been impossible to prove individual acts of murder. *The New York Times* dubbed the new prosecutors "the grandchildren generation," and noted they "bring a less conflicted view of culpability to crimes committed during the war."[2]

Within six months of the Demjanjuk verdict, the Central Office for the Investigation of Nazi Crimes in Ludwigsburg had obtained a list of 50 ex-Auschwitz guards from the camp's museum. It also had identified seven additional suspects living outside Germany, scattered in the U.S., Austria, Brazil, Croatia and Poland. By September 2013, the Ludwigsburg office had sent cases against 30 former Auschwitz guards, ranging in age from 86 to 97, to local prosecutors.

"My personal opinion is that in view of the monstrosity of these crimes, one owes it to the survivors and the victims not to simply say 'a certain time has passed, it should be swept under the carpet,'" said Kurt Schrimm, who since 2000 has held the same chief prosecutor role for Nazi-era crimes as had Fritz Bauer.[3] "We take the view that this job, regardless of what they can be individually accused of, makes them guilty of complicity in murder."[4]

Schrimm made it clear that the old Nazis from Auschwitz were the first targets but not his only ones. He promised to widen the search for ex-guards to five other death camps – Belzec, Chelmno, Majdanek, Sobibor and Treblinka – as well as the SS who served in mobile killing squads, the Einsatzgruppen.

The aggressive steps to prosecute the last Nazis were widely hailed. Typical was Efraim Zuroff, the Simon Wiesenthal Center's top Nazi hunter. "This is really an important milestone in the efforts to bring Nazis to justice. There has never been anything like this in recent years."[5]

Many thought the renewed prosecutorial vigor was a way to demonstrate that the same German legal system that had grappled for decades with how to make ex-Nazis answer for their crimes was finally capable of bringing the surviving perpetrators to justice.

"It is better late than never," concluded Lawrence Douglas, an Amherst College legal scholar who has studied Nazi crimes. [6]

The first trial from all the new investigations was the 2015 case of 95-year-old Oskar Groening, a bookkeeper at Auschwitz, who was convicted and sentenced to four years as an accessory to the murder of 300,000 people. During the past two years, three other trials were scheduled. One defendant, a 93-year-old Storm Trooper who had served at Auschwitz for two years, died just before the start of his April 2016 trial. The case of another, an Auschwitz medic, was suspended when a doctor ruled he was too ill. But one dramatic case that got to trial was the 2016 case of 94-year-old Reinhold Hanning, an SS guard.[7] Hanning was charged as an accessory to murder in the deaths of 170,000 people during the 18-months he was at the death camp.

For the first couple of months of his trial, Hanning said nothing. Then on April 29, 2016, he broke his silence. Sitting in a wheelchair, his voice weak, he addressed the court.

"I want to say that it disturbs me deeply that I was part of such a criminal organization. I am ashamed that I saw injustice was being done and I did nothing to stop it. I apologize for my actions. I am very, very sorry."[8]

For many survivors that apology was not enough. A better measure of justice was delivered in July when the court found him guilty and sentenced him to five years in prison. Hanning, who said that he had "spent my whole life to forget about this time [since]Auschwitz was a nightmare," seemed to expect to spend the rest of his life in prison. "I deeply regret having listened to a criminal organization that is responsible for the deaths of many innocent people," he said, "for the destruction of countless families, for the misery, distress and suffering on the part of victims and their relatives."[9]

Hanning's acknowledgement that simply by working in a death factory he had facilitated many murders was the first time any SS soldier had ever apologized or accepted any blame for what had happened at Auschwitz. It was precisely the honest reckoning that Victor Capesius, unburdened by a guilty conscience, always avoided. Capesius preferred instead going to his grave protesting his innocence. By so doing, he marked himself not only as a convicted murderer and grave robber, but as a man without enough moral character to accept any responsibility for his actions at Auschwitz. Capesius was very much the ordinary man that he liked to portray to the public. But he was capable, as were many other Nazis like him, of extraordinary crimes. Ultimately, he chose the coward's path, preferring to live and die in denial. That is to his eternal shame.

ACKNOWLEDGEMENTS

Writing about a man who spent more than half his life resolved to burying his past through distortions and lies was no easy task. This book is the result of two years of research. During that time, I have gathered a large documentary archive on Victor Capesius and also on I. G. Farben, his prewar employer. I am satisfied that I have conducted a thorough investigation, and I take full responsibility for the accuracy of the information and the soundness of the judgments.

Much of my research would not have been possible if not for the help of many people and organizations. In the development of documentation I was aided by Paul B. Brown in the Reference Branch, Larry Shockley, Archives Specialist, and Rick Peuser, Chief of the Reference Sections, National Archives and Records Service, Washington, D.C.; Rosmarie Lerchl, Archivist, State Archives, Munich; Christiane Kleemann, Diploma Archivist, Hessian State Archives, Wiesbaden, Germany; Archivists Michael Conen, Berit Walter and Sven Devantier, Federal Archives, Koblenz, Germany; Dr. Peter Gohle, Federal Archives Branch Department at Ludwigsburg, Germany; Dr. Liviu-Daniel Grigorescu, Chief Archivist, and Laura Dumitru, Publications and Scientific Publications, National Archives, Bucharest, Romania; Sigrid Bratzke, Provincial Archives, Baden-Württemberg, Germany; Mihai Cuibus, Cluj County National Archives, Cluj-Napoca, Romania; Dr. Ioan Dragan, Director of Archives at the Ministry of the Interior, Bucharest, Romania; Vincent Slatt, United States Holocaust Memorial Museum, Washington D.C.; and Emmanuelle Moscovitz, Yad Vashem, Jerusalem.

I am also appreciative for the fast and very helpful information in response to many queries from Peter Stroh and Roland Klostermann, DPA Picture-Alliance, Frankfurt, and Carol A. Leadenham, Hoover Institution Archives, Stanford University. I am grateful to the special guidance of Dr. Werner Renz, Fritz Bauer Institute, Archive and Documentation, Frankfurt.

Professor Tudor Parfitt gave assistance far beyond his obligation. Tina Hampson spent days in the National Archives in Kew, England, searching for files that still remain elusive about Capesius and his time after the war in British custody. Her diligence in searching through the vast records there is greatly appreciated.

Rabbi Abraham Cooper, the Associate Dean of the Simon Wiesenthal Center, encouraged me early on to pursue this project.

I also owe a special acknowledgment to David Marwell, a friend and historian whose specialty is World War II and the Third Reich. He was kind to patiently field my many questions, suggest others who were helpful when it came to archival documents, and also offered some good critiques of some early drafts. And David was kind enough to recommend Ilona Moradof, who helped us with interview requests in Germany.

The photos in this book were made possible by the generosity of several people who worked to provide pictures at an affordable licensing fee. In this regard I am most grateful to Christine Scherrer of Studio Hamburg Distribution and Marketing and the images she cleared for Norddeutscher Rundfunk (NDR) and the 1964 film Bleiben die Marder unter uns? And also a special thanks is due to Gaby Schindler of Schindlerfoto Oberusel.

I am most indebted to the great generosity of Michael Hofmann, the Head of Program Sales at the Frankfurt-based HR Media (Hessischer Rundfunk). He allowed the use at no cost of a number of important pictures that helped illustrate the story of Capesius, especially after the war. None of the HR Media photos would have been possible without the pioneering work from which those still images are taken: the documentary Auschwitz vor Gericht by filmmakers Rolf Bickell and Dietrich Wagner.

The many historical documents in German, Romanian, Hungarian and Hebrew, required a group of translators that worked long hours, often on decades-old files of poor legibility. Their diligent translations were crucial to the story of Capesius. Special thanks are due to Ruth Winter, Israel; Alex Ringleb, Thomas Just, and Oren Nizri, Miami. I am indebted to good friends, Christopher Petersen and Ann Froehlich, for their review of the manuscript. They took time from their own busy schedules to meticulously review the manuscript and their constructive criticism was instrumental in making it a better book. Ellen Durkin was a conscientious copyeditor who fine-tuned the manuscript.

In the pursuit of this project, a special acknowledgment to my publisher, Christopher Lascelles. He had an unfailing receptiveness to my proposal of a biography about Victor Capesius. His enthusiasm, editing, and savvy involvement at every stage of this book is rare nowadays in publishing and I am greatly in his debt.

And finally I want to thank my husband, Gerald Posner. He has always encouraged me to write this book. His belief in my ability to do so gave me the confidence to successfully complete this project. In every way in life we are bound together inextricably as equal partners. This was certainly the case in uncovering the story of Victor Capesius. Gerald is an indefatigable researcher and his editing eye kept me focused always on the narrative. There would be no book without him.

SELECTED BIBLIOGRAPHY

Books

Arendt, Hannah. *Eichmann in Jerusalem: A Report on the Banality of Evil.* New York: Viking, 1964.

Bonhoeffer, Emmi. *Auschwitz Trials; Letters from an Eyewitness.* Translated by Ursula Stechow. Richmond, VA: John Knox Press, 1967.

Borkin, Joseph, *The Crime and Punishment of I. G. Farben.* New York: The Free Press, 1978.

Browning, Christopher. O*rdinary Men: Reserve Police Battalion 101 and the Final Solution in Poland.* New York: HarperCollins, 1992.

DuBois, Josiah E. Jr. *The Devil's Chemist: 24 Conspirators of the International Farben Cartel Who Manufacture Wars.* Boston: The Beacon Press, 1952.

Ferencz, Benjamin B. *Less Than Slaves: Jewish Forced Labor and the Quest for Compensation.* Cambridge, MA: Harvard University Press, 1979.

Goran Morris. *The Story of Fritz Haber.* Norman, OK: University of Oklahoma Press, 1967.

Gross, Rachel and Werner Renz, *Der Frankfurter Auschwitz-Prozess (1963-1965),* 2 Volumes. Frankfurt: Campus Verlag, 2013.

Hayes, Peter. *From Cooperation to Complicity: Degussa in the Third Reich.* Cambridge: Cambridge University Press, 2007.

Higham, Charles. *Trading with the Enemy: The Nazi-American Money Plot 1933-1949.* New York: Barnes and Noble Books, 1983.

Hilberg, Raul. *The Destruction of the European Jews.* Chicago: Quadrangle Books, 1961.

Rudolf, Höss. *Commandant of Auschwitz.* New York: World Publishing Co, 1960.

Jeffreys, Diarmuid. *Hell's Cartel: IG Farben and the Making of Hitler's War Machine.* New York: Henry Holt and Co., 2008. Kindle Edition.

Kraus, Ota and Erich Kulka, *Tovarna na smrt* (Death Factory). Prague: Nase Vojsko, 1957.

Langbein, Herman. *Der Auschwitz-Prozess. Eine Dokumentation*. Frankfurt: Europäische Verlagsanstalt, 1965, 2 vols.

People in Auschwitz. Chapel Hill, NC: University of North Carolina Press, 2004.

Laternser, Hans. *Die andere Seite im Auschwitz-Prozess 1963/65. Reden eines Verteidigers*. Stuttgart: Seewald Verlag, 1966.

Levi, Primo. *Survival in Auschwitz*. Chicago, IL: BN Publishing, 2007.

Lifton, Robert Jay. *The Nazi Doctors: Medical Killing and the Psychology of Genocide*. New York: Basic Books, 1986.

Naumann, Bernd (translated by Jean Steinberg). *Auschwitz: A Report on the Proceedings Against Robert Karl Ludwig Mulka and Others Before the Court at Frankfurt*. New York: Frederick A. Praeger, 1966.

Moeller, Robert. *War Stories: The Search for a Usable Past in the Federal Republic of Germany*. Berkeley: University of California Press, 2001.

Nyiszli, Miklós. *I Was Doctor Mengele's Assistant*. Kraków, Poland: Frap-Books, 2000.

Pendas, Devin O. *The Frankfurt Auschwitz Trial, 1963-1965: Genocide, History, and the Limits of the Law*. Boston: Cambridge University Press, 2006).

Posner, Gerald, and John Ware. *Mengele: The Complete Story*. New York: McGraw-Hill, 1986.

– *God's Bankers: A History of Money and Power at the Vatican*. New York: Simon and Schuster, 2015.

Renz, Werner. *Fritz Bauer und das Versagen der Justiz. Nazi-Prozesse und ihre »Tragödie«*. Hamburg: Europäische Verlagsanstalt, 2015.

Rückerl, Adalbert. *The Investigation of Nazi Crimes, 1945-1978: A Documentation*, trans. Derek Rutter. Heidelberg: C. F. Müller, 1979.

Schlesak, Dieter. *The Druggist of Auschwitz: A Documentary Novel*. New York: Farrar, Straus and Giroux, 2011.

Solonari, Vladimir. *Purifying the Nation: Population Exchange and Ethnic Cleansing in Nazi-Allied Romania.* Baltimore, MD: Johns Hopkins University Press, 2009.

Steinke, Ronen. *Fritz Bauer: oder Auschwitz vor Gericht.* Gebundene Ausgaben, 2013.

Taylor, Telford. *Sword and Swastika: Generals and the Nazis in the Third Reich.* Chicago, IL: Quadrangle Books, 1969.

Wittmann, Rebecca. *Beyond Justice: The Auschwitz Trial.* Cambridge, MA: Harvard University Press, 2012.

Articles and Periodicals

"Auschwitz: 60 Year Anniversary – The Role of IG Farben-Bayer." Alliance for Human Research Protection, January 27, 2005.

"Auschwitz Druggist Tagged As Jekyll-Hyde Character." *Nevada State Journal* (Reno, NV), June 21, 1964.

Bauer, Fritz. "Zu den Naziverbrecher Prozessen." *Stirnrne der Gemeinde zum Kirchlichen Leben, zur Politik, Wirtschaft and Kultur*, Vol 18, 1963.

Bribe Allegations At Auschwitz Trial." *The Sydney Morning Herald,* Sydney, New South Wales, Australia, April 8, 1964.

"Chemist 'Stored Gold Teeth.'" *Sydney Morning Herald* (Sydney, New South Wales, Australia), June 20, 1964a

"Doctor Testifies Man He Aided Killed Family." *The Fresno Bee Republican,* Fresno, CA, August 18, 1964.

"Horror Loot of a Nazi Camp Told." *Independent* (Long Beach, CA), June 19, 1964.

"'Jekyll-And-Hyde' Described." *Tucson Daily Gazette* (Tucson, AZ), June 19, 1964.

"Mass Killer Also Accused of Theft." *Tucson Daily Gazette* (Tucson, AZ), August 27, 1964.

"Past Notes: SS Orderly Kills 250 Patients." *The Guardian* (London), January 31, 1995.

"Spectators At War Crimes Trial Call For Lynching Of 'Child-Killer.'" *The Lincoln Star* (Lincoln, NE), April 7, 1964.

"Summation and Replies of Friedrich Karl Kaul, legal representative of the co-plaintiffs in the German Democratic Republic in the criminal proceedings against Mulka and others before the criminal court at the Provincial Court in Frankfurt-am-Main. Dresden: Verlag Zeit im Bild, 1965.

"Survivor Of Auschwitz Labels Capesius 'Devil.'" *The Lincoln Star,* Lincoln, NE, August 25, 1964.

Day, Matthew. "SS Documents Discovered Near Auschwitz." *The Telegraph,* March 23, 1970.

Gutman, Yisrael and Michael Berenbaum. *Anatomy of the Auschwitz Death Camp.* Bloomington, IN: Indiana University Press, 1998.

Kellerhoff, Sven Felix. "Dokumente zu KZ-Ärzten in Auschwitz entdeckt," *Die Welt*, March 24, 2010.

Martin, Tom. "Nazi Scientist Stripped Me of Motherhood and I Still Need an Apology." *Sunday Express* (UK), August 17, 2003

Pendas, Devin O. "'I Didn't Know What Auschwitz Was': The Frankfurt Auschwitz Trial and the German Press, 1963-1965," *Yale Journal of Law and Humanities* 12, 2000.

"Displaying Justice: Nazis on Trial in Postwar Germany," Ph.D. dissertation. University of Chicago, 2000.

Phil, Miller. "Scots Holocaust Victim In Fight for Compensation." *Sunday Times* (London), December 30, 2001.

Solonari, Vladimir, "The Treatment Of The Jews Of Bukovina By The Soviet And Romanian Administrations In 1940–1944," *Holocaust and Modernity*, No. 2 (8) 2010.

Wittmann, Rebecca E. "Holocaust On Trial? The Frankfurt Auschwitz Trial In Historical Perspective," thesis submitted for Doctor of Philosophy, Graduate Department of History, University of Toronto, 2001.

"Telling The Story: Survivor Testimony and The Narration Of The Frankfurt Auschwitz Trial." Fritz Stern Dissertation Prize Presentation, November 15, 2002 and reprinted in *GHI Bulletin*, No. 32, Spring 2003.

"Legitimating the Criminal State: Former Nazi Judges on the Stand at the Frankfurt Auschwitz Trial," *Lessons and Legacies VI: New Currents in Holocaust Research*, ed. Jeffry Diefendorf. Chicago: Northwestern University Press, Spring 2004.

"The Wheels of Justice Turn Slowly: The Pre-Trial Investigations of the Frankfurt Auschwitz Trial, 1963-1965." *Central European History* 35, No. 3, 2002.

Zuppi, Alberto L. "Slave Labor in Nuremberg's I.G. Farben Case: The Lonely Voice of Paul M. Hebert." Louisiana Law Review, Volume 66, Number 2, Winter 2006.

Government Publications

"Elimination of German Resources for War," Hearings before a Subcommittee of the Committee on Military Affairs, United States Senate, 79th Congress, 1st Session, Part X, 1945.

"The Francolor Case in France," *Trials of the War Criminals Before the Nuremberg Military Tribunals,* Under Council 10, Vol. VIII, Section D, U.S. National Archives.

Trials of War Criminals before the Nuremberg Military Tribunals under Control Council Law No. 10. Washington D.C.: US Government Printing Office, 1949.

World War II Crimes and Prosecutions: Nuremberg Industrialists, Vol 1-2, and the Farben Trial, Vol. 8, U.S. National Archives.

Archive Sources

Archive Nationale Istorice Centrale România, Bucharest, Romania; Archive România Cluj Judet, Cluj-Napoca, Romania; Bundesarchiv, Koblenz, Germany; Bundesarchiv Außenstelle Ludwigsburg, Ludwigsburg, Germany; Bundesarchiv Dienststelle, Berlin; DPA Picture Alliance, Frankfurt; Federal Commissioner for the Records of the State Security Service of the former German Democratic Republic (BStU), Berlin; Fritz Bauer Institute, Frankfurt; Hessian Hauptstaatsarchiv, Wiesbaden, Germany; Hoover Institution of War, Revolution and Peace, Stanford, California; Howard Gotlieb Archival Research Center, Boston; International Auschwitz Committee, Berlin; Lastenausgleichsarchiv (War Indemnity Archives), Bayreuth, Germany;

Öffentlicher Ankläger (Public Prosecutor) Office, Frankfurt; Staatsarchiv München, Munich; UK National Archives, Kew, England; U.S. Holocaust Memorial Museum, Washington D.C.; U.S. National Archives and Records Administration, College Park, Maryland; Yad Vashem, Jerusalem.

Film and Television

183 Tage - Der Auschwitz-Prozess Deutschland, (183 days - The Auschwitz Trial Germany), written and directed by Janusch Kozminski, in association for "Jewish Media and Culture Munich," 2014.

Fritz Bauer: Gespräche, Interviews und Reden aus den Fernseharchiven 1961–1968 (Fritz Bauer: Conversations, Interviews and Speeches from the Television Archives) 2 DVDs. Berlin: Absolut Medien, 2014.

Auschwitz vor Gericht (The Auschwitz Trial), Rolf Bickell and Dietrich Wagner, directors, HR Productions, 2013.

Der Auschwitz-Prozess: Tonbandmitschnitte, Protokolle, Dokumente (The Auschwitz Trial: Tape Recordings, Records, Documents), edited and compiled by Fritz Bauer Institute. Berlin: Directmedia Publishing, 2004.

Kingreen, Monica, *Der Auschwitz-Prozess 1963-1965: Geschichte, Bedeutung und Wirkung: Materialien für die pädagogische Arbeit mit CD: Auschwitz-Überlebende sagen aus* (The Auschwitz Trial 1963-1965: History, Meaning and Effect: Materials for Educational Study with CD: Auschwitz survivors Tell All). Frankfurt: Fritz Bauer Institut, 2004.

"Verdict on Auschwitz: The Frankfurt Auschwitz Trial 1963-1965," documentary film by Rolf Bickell and Dietrich Wagner, First Run Films, 1993.

NOTES

CHAPTER 1 – "PHARMACIST UNCLE"

1. Testimony of Mauritius Berner in the presentation of the prosecution case against Robert Mulka, 4 Ks 2/63 District Court in Frankfurt am Main, testimony of August 17, 1964. See also testimony of Mauritius Berner, testimony in "Verdict on Auschwitz: The Frankfurt Auschwitz Trial 1963-1965," documentary film by Rolf Bickell and Dietrich Wagner, First Run Films, 1993.

   Until 1965, German trials did not have daily verbatim transcripts as do American and British courtroom cases. In some instances, testimony cited is from contemporaneous newspaper accounts, and audio recordings of the witnesses themselves. In addition, statements of witnesses and defendants taken prior to the trial by prosecutors are later submitted as part of the complete trial record.

   For general commentary on the eyewitness testimony provided by witnesses such as Berner, see generally Rebecca E. Wittmann, "Telling The Story: Survivor Testimony And The Narration Of The Frankfurt Auschwitz Trial," Fritz Stern Dissertation Prize Presentation, November 15, 2002, Marquette University. Also Paul Hoffmann, letter to the Auschwitz Committee (Berlin), November 22, 1950, Bielefeld. StA b. LG Osnabrück, 4 Ks 2/52, Hauptakten, Vol. II, p. 17R.

   The tape recordings of the witness testimony are in 4Ks 2/63. "Strafsache gegen Mulka . . ." (Criminal Proceedings against Mulka and Others), Hessisches Staatsarchiv, Wiesbaden, Germany.

2. Berner cited in "Doctor Testifies Man He Aided Killed Family," *The Fresno Bee Republican* (Fresno, CA) August 18, 1964, 31. See also Testimony of Mauritius Berner, in the presentation of the prosecution case against Robert Mulka, 4 Ks 2/63 District Court in Frankfurt am Main, testimony of August 17, 1964.

3. Berner cited in "Doctor Testifies Man He Aided Killed Family," *The Fresno Bee Republican*, 31. See also Testimony of Mauritius Berner in the presentation of the prosecution case against Robert Mulka, 4 Ks 2/63 District Court in Frankfurt am Main, testimony of August 17, 1964.

4. Testimony of Mauritius Berner, 4Ks 2/63, Hessisches Staatsarchiv. Also "Verdict on Auschwitz: The Frankfurt Auschwitz Trial 1963-1965." Also

Berner cited in "Doctor Testifies Man He Aided Killed Family," *The Fresno Bee Republican*, 31.

5   Testimony of Dr. Gisela Böhm as recounted in Bernd Naumann (translated by Jean Steinberg), *Auschwitz: A Report on the Proceedings Against Robert Karl Ludwig Mulka and Others Before the Court at Frankfurt* (New York: Frederick A. Praeger, 1966), 305; 4Ks 2/63, Hessisches Staatsarchiv.

6   Testimony of Ella Salomon (née Böhm), 4Ks 2/63, Hessisches Staatsarchiv and as recounted in Naumann *Auschwitz*, 304-305

7   Testimony of Ella Salomon (née Böhm), in the presentation of the prosecution case against Robert Mulka, 4 Ks 2/63 District Court in Frankfurt am Main, testimony of November 19, 1964.

CHAPTER 2 – THE FARBEN CONNECTION

1.   Agfa was Aktiengesellschaft für Anilinfabrikation, or Company for Aniline Production and BASF was Badische Anilin und Soda Fabrik.

2.   See Joseph Borkin, *The Crime and Punishment of I. G. Farben* (New York: The Free Press, 1978), 6-7.

3.   "Elimination of German Resources for War," Hearings before a Subcommittee of the Committee on Military Affairs, United States Senate, 79th Congress, 1st Session, Part X, 1945.

4.   Borkin, The Crime and Punishment of I. G. Farben, 54, 57-58.

5.   Quoted in Morris Goran, *The Story of Fritz Haber* (Norman, OK: University of Oklahoma Press, 1967), 39.

6.   See generally Peter Hayes, *Industry and Ideology: IG Farben in the Nazi Era* (New York: Cambridge University Press, 1987).

7.   Diarmuid Jeffreys, *Hell's Cartel: IG Farben and the Making of Hitler's War Machine* (New York: Henry Holt and Co.). Kindle Edition, p. 170, 172.

8.   Letter of Heinrich Gattineau, I.G. Farben, to Dr. Karl Haushofer, June 6, 1931, World War II Crimes and Prosecutions, U.S. National Archives.

9.   Affidavit of Heinrich Gattineau, World War II Crimes and Prosecutions: Nuremberg Industrialists, 4833, 1-2, U.S. National Archives.

10.   See Goran, The Story of Fritz Haber, 38-39.

11.   See Josiah E. DuBois, Jr., The Devil's Chemist: 24 Conspirators of the International Farben Cartel Who Manufacture Wars (Boston: The Beacon Press, 1952), 264-69.

12.   Chart of I.G. employees and officers and memberships in National Socialist organizations, World War II Crimes and Prosecutions: Nuremberg Industrialists, 12,042 and Chart of I.G. Farben Supervisory Board, World War II Crimes and Prosecutions: Nuremberg Industrialists, 7957, U.S. National Archives.

13.   Jeffreys, *Hell's Cartel*, 229.

14. Charles Higham, *Trading with the Enemy: The Nazi-American Money Plot 1933-1949* (New York: Barnes and Noble Books, 1983), 133.

15. For details on the Skodawerke takeover see DuBois, Jr., *The Devil's Chemist,* 219-21; also Raul Hilberg, *The Destruction of the European Jews* (Chicago: Quadrangle Books, 1961), 61.

16. Borkin, The Crime and Punishment of I. G. Farben, 98; see also DuBois, Jr., *The Devil's Chemist,* 113-15.

17. "The Francolor Case in France," *Trials of the War Criminals Before the Nuremberg Military Tribunals,* Under Council 10, Vol. VIII, Section D; see also "Elimination of German Resources for War," Hearings before a Subcommittee of the Committee on Military Affairs, United States Senate, 79th Congress, 1st Session, Part X, p. 1387, 1945; see also DuBois, Jr., *The Devil's Chemist,* 287-98.

18. Higham, Trading with the Enemy, 133.

19. DuBois, Jr., *The Devil's Chemist,* 143-47.

20. The Poles called it Oswiecim., Jeffreys, *Hell's Cartel,* Kindle Edition), 281. File note on conference held with Ambros, ter Meer and Krauch, February 6, 1941, *Trials of the War Criminals Before the Nuremberg Military Tribunals,* Under Council 10, Vol. VIII, p. 349-51 (Washington DC: U.S. Government Printing Office); See also letter from Dr. Otto Ambros to Fritz ter Meer, Director of I. G. Farben, regarding SS assistance to construct the Farben camp at Auschwitz, 1941, reproduced in Telford Taylor, *Sword and Swastika: Generals and the Nazis in the Third Reich* (Chicago, IL: Quadrangle Books, 1969).

CHAPTER 3 – I. G. AUSCHWITZ

1. The History Department of the University of California at Santa Barbara provides a "Historical Dollar-to-Marks Currency Conversion" chart at http://www.history.ucsb.edu/faculty/marcuse/projects/currency.htm#tables. The last wartime year in which there was a RM to US dollar comparison was 1941, at which point 2.5 RM equaled $1.

2. DuBois, Jr., *The Devil's Chemist,* 219; see Jeffreys, Kindle Edition, *Hell's Cartel,* 4591 of 9525.

3. Benjamin B. Ferencz, *Less Than Slaves: Jewish Forced Labor and the Quest for Compensation* (Cambridge, MA: Harvard University Press, 1979), 9-10.

4. Ambros to ter Meer, cited in DuBois, Jr., *The Devil's Chemist,* 172.

5. See Jeffreys, *Hell's Cartel,* 4638 to 4654 of 9525, Kindle Edition.

6. Ferencz, *Less Than Slaves,* 15.

7. Quoted in Jeffreys, *Hell's Cartel,* 293.

8. DuBois, Jr., The Devil's Chemist, 179.

9. Jeffreys, *Hell's Cartel,* Kindle Edition, 4898 of 9525.

10. Alberto L. Zuppi, "Slave Labor in Nuremberg's I.G. Farben Case: e Lonely Voice of Paul M. Hebert," *Louisiana Law Review*, Volume 66, Number 2, Winter 2006, 509, n. 57; Yisrael Gutman and Michael Berenbaum, *Anatomy of the Auschwitz Death Camp* (Bloomington, IN: Indiana University Press, 1998), 17-18.

11. Jeffreys, *Hell's Cartel*, Kindle Edition, 4928 of 9525.

12. Ferencz, *Less Than Slaves*, 24-25.

13. DuBois, The Devil's Chemist, 223.

14. Jews were often treated worse than other prisoners when it came to diet. See DuBois, *The Devil's Chemist*, 221.

15. Ferencz, *Less Than Slaves*, xvii.

16. Robert Jay Lifton. *The Nazi Doctors: Medical Killing and the Psychology of Genocide*. (New York: Basic Books, 1986), 187.

17. C. Krauch to Reichsfüher SS, July 27, 1943, Nuremberg Trial, Vol. VIII, p. 532.

18. Primo Levi, *Survival in Auschwitz* (Chicago, IL: BN Publishing, 2007), 72.

19. Some early estimates were that upwards of 200,000 died, but that was based on erroneous early information cited by Allied investigators. See generally DuBois, *The Devil's Chemist*, 220-21, 224.

CHAPTER 4 – ENTER CAPESIUS

1. Naumann, *Auschwitz*, 22.

2. Judicial Hearing Transcript, District Court, Frankfurt, Viktor Capesius in person before Examining Magistrate Judge Heinz Düx, 8 pages, 4 Js 444/59, January 24, 1962, courtesy of Fritz Bauer Institut, 5, 4; The Military Government of Germany Fragebogen (Questionnaire), December 27. 1946, 6 pages, Landesarchiv Baden-Württemberg.

3. Dieter Schlesak, "Fragwürdiger Holocaustworkshop in Siebenbürgen/ Hermannstadt," *Zeit Online*, June 1, 2010.

4. Hans Nogly, "Die Mörder sind wie du und ich," *Stern*, No. 10, 1965. 58.

5. Letter of Victor Capesius, May 12, 1947, regarding the Spruchkammer des Interniertenlagers 74, Article/Case 895/J/74/1213, in reference to Klageschrift of May 2, 1947, 2 pages, Landesarchiv Baden-Württemberg, p. 1- 4.

6. The Military Government of Germany Fragebogen (Questionnaire), December 27. 1946, 6 pages, Landesarchiv Baden-Württemberg; see also Letter of Victor Capesius, May 12, 1947, regarding the Spruchkammer des Interniertenlagers 74, Article/Case 895/J/74/1213, in reference to Klageschrift of May 2, 1947, 2 pages, Landesarchiv Baden-Württemberg, p. 1.

7. Nogly, "Die Mörder sind wie du und ich," 58.

8.   The Military Government of Germany Fragebogen (Questionnaire), December 27. 1946, 6 pages, Landesarchiv Baden-Württemberg.

9.   "Statistics of Income for 1934," Part 1, U.S. Treasury Department, Income Tax Unit, Government Printing Office, 1936, 23, 78.

10.   Schlesak, *The Druggist of Auschwitz,* Hardcover Edition, 232, 236.

11.   "After my graduation as Dr. of Philosophy I was hired, beginning Feb. 1, 1934, as manager of "Romigrefa" SAR, Bukarest, to represent all over Rumania the Bayer-Medicamente, and after a 3-months course in my new professional specialty assigned to Leverkusen." Much of the biographical material about Capesius is from his own letters and submissions during his 1947 denazification proceedings in Germany, Letter of Victor Capesius, May 12, 1947, regarding the Spruchkammer des Interniertenlagers 74, Article/Case 895/J/74/1213, in reference to Klageschrift of May 2, 1947, 2 pages, Landesarchiv Baden-Württemberg, p. 1- 4; and also the presentation of the case against the defendants by the prosecutor Joachim Kügler, Frankfurt Auschwitz Trial, "Criminal case against Mulka et al", 4 Ks 2/63, Landgericht Frankfurt am Main, May 13, 1965; also see generally Dieter Schlesak, *The Druggist of Auschwitz: A Documentary Novel* (New York: Farrar, Straus and Giroux, 2011).

12.   Nogly, "Die Mörder sind wie du und ich," 60 – 61.

13.   Presentation of the case against the defendants by the prosecutor Joachim Kügler, Frankfurt Auschwitz Trial, "Criminal case against Mulka et al", 4 Ks 2/63, Landgericht Frankfurt am Main, May 13, 1965; see also Capesius 4-page handwritten letter to the Prosecutor, Ludwigsburg, January 3, 1947, p. 1, Landesarchiv Baden-Württemberg.

14.   Nogly, "Die Mörder sind wie du und ich," 61.

15.   Capesius interviewed in Schlesak, *The Druggist of Auschwitz,* Hardcover Edition, 271.

16.   Roland Albert interviewed in Schlesak, *The Druggist of Auschwitz,* Hardcover Edition, 206.

17.   Capesius interviewed in Schlesak, *The Druggist of Auschwitz,* Hardcover Edition, 271.

18.   Roland Albert interviewed in Schlesak, *The Druggist of Auschwitz,* Hardcover Edition, 235.

19.   Roland interviewed in Schlesak, *The Druggist of Auschwitz,* Hardcover Edition, 236.

20.   Capesius in Schlesak, *The Druggist of Auschwitz,* Kindle Edition, 1580 of 5519.

21.   The two were Dr. Alexandro Bardeanu (formerly Rotbart) and Dr. Mortiz Scheerer.

Letter of Victor Capesius, May 12, 1947, regarding the Spruchkammer des Interniertenlagers 74, Article/Case 895/J/74/1213, in reference to Klageschrift of May 2, 1947, 2 pages, Landesarchiv Baden-Württemberg, p. 1- 4.

22. Hans Nogly, "Die Mörder sind wie du und ich," *Stern*, No. 10, 1965. 61.

23. Naumann, *Auschwitz*, 22-23.

24. Karl Heinz Schuleri quoted in Schlesak, *The Druggist of Auschwitz*, 141-42.

25. Nogly, "Die Mörder sind wie du und ich," 62.

26. Ibid.

27. Helge Krempels, "Kreisgruppe Ludwigsburg: In Erinnerung an Melitta Capesius," *Siebenbürgische Zeitung*, December 3, 2013.

28. Naumann, *Auschwitz*, 23; see also Hans Nogly, "Die Mörder sind wie du und ich," *Stern*, No. 10, 1965. 60.

29. Schlesak, *The Druggist of Auschwitz*, Hardcover Edition, 174.

30. There had been some confusion in earlier published accounts about Capesius as to whether or not he had the SS tattoo. The author confirmed it by obtaining the previously classified file pursuant to a Freedom of Information Request: "War Crimes Central Suspect and Witness Enclosure," Headquarters, Civilian Internment Enclosure, APO 205, US Army, December 20, 1946, page 8, maintained in Dossier 76950, May 17, 1951, Subject, "Capesius, Victor Ernst," declassified April 1, 2016, NARA.

31. Schlesak, *The Druggist of Auschwitz*, Hardcover Edition, 175.

32. Naumann, *Auschwitz*, 22-23.

33. Roland Albert interviewed in Schlesak, *The Druggist of Auschwitz*, Hardcover Edition, 204.

34. Paul Georgescu, "Volksdeutsche in der Waffen-SS," *Südostdeutsche Vierteljahreshefe*, 53(2), 2004, 117-123.

35. Paul Meskil, *Hitler's Heirs; Where are They Now?* (New York: Pyramid Books, 1961), 36.

36. Meskil, *Hitler's Heirs*, 36-37.

37. Yisrael Gutman and Michael Berenbaum, *Anatomy of the Auschwitz Death Camp* (Bloomington, IN: Indiana University Press, 1998), 6, 8-9.

38. The five major battles that resulted in the most Russian POWs during the early months of fighting were Vyazma and Bryansk, 512,000; Kiev, 452,000, Smolensk, 300,000; Bialystok/Minsk, 290,000; and Uman, 103,000.

39. Thilo quoted in September 5, 1942 entry of Dr. Johann Paul Kremer, The Holocaust Education & Archive Research Team.

40. Capesius quoted in Schlesak, *The Druggist of Auschwitz*, Hardcover Edition, 174.

41. Schlesak, *The Druggist of Auschwitz*, Hardcover Edition, 175.

CHAPTER 5 – WELCOME TO AUSCHWITZ

1. Gerald Posner and John Ware, *Mengele: The Complete Story* (New York: McGraw-Hill, 1986), 11-13.

2. Lingens quoted in Schlesak, *The Druggist of Auschwitz,* Hardcover Edition, 269-70.

3. September 5, 1942 entry of Dr. Johann Paul Kremer, The Holocaust Education & Archive Research Team.

4. As for König getting drunk before the selections, see Herman Langbein, *People in Auschwitz* (Chapel Hill, NC: University of North Carolina Press, 2004), 353, and Naumann, *Auschwitz*, 93. As for Mengele at the selection ramp see Posner and Ware, *Mengele,* 26-27.

5. DuBois, Jr., The Devil's Chemist, 213.

6. Höss testimony in Trial of Major War Criminals before the International Military Tribunal, Nuremberg 1947, Vol XI, 348.

7. John Cornwell, Hitler's Pope: *The Secret History of Pius XII* (New York: Viking, 1999), 281.

8. Jeffreys, *Hell's Cartel,* Kindle Edition, 5161-5183 of 9525.

9. Posner, *God's Bankers: A History of Money and Power at the Vatican* (New York: Simon and Schuster, 2015, 91-92.

10. Capesius quoted from Schlesak, *The Druggist of Auschwitz,* Kindle Edition, 1259 of 5519.

11. Capesius quoted from Schlesak, *The Druggist of Auschwitz,* Hardcover Edition, 84.

12. Matthew Day, "SS Documents Discovered Near Auschwitz," *The Telegraph,* March 23, 1970.

13. Schlesak, *The Druggist of Auschwitz,* Kindle Edition, 2862 of 5519.

CHAPTER 6 – THE DISPENSARY

1. Gutman and Berenbaum, *Anatomy of the Auschwitz Death Camp*, 382.

2. Ibid., first photo insert, diagram of Auschwitz I.

3. Staatsanwaltschaftliche Vernehmung (Public Prosecutor's Interrogation), District Court, Göppingen, Viktor Capesius in person before Senior Judge Dr. Trukenmüller, 14 pages, 4 Js 444/59, December 4, 1959, courtesy of Fritz Bauer Institut, 6; see also Capesius quoted from Dieter Schlesak, *The Druggist of Auschwitz: A Documentary Novel* (New York: Farrar, Straus and Giroux, 2011), Kindle Edition, 1220 of 5519.

4. Naumann, *Auschwitz*, 191.

5. Staatsanwaltschaftliche Vernehmung, 6.

6. Jan Sikorski, testimony sworn statement and testimony at the Auschwitz Trial, District Court, Frankfurt am Main, June 19, 1964.

7. Naumann, *Auschwitz*, 191.

8. Jan Sikorski sworn statement and testimony at the Auschwitz Trial, District Court, Frankfurt am Main, June 19, 1964; quoted in Schlesak, *The Druggist of Auschwitz: A Documentary Novel* 1287-1293 of 5519.

9. Capesius's height and weight came from his answers to The Military Government of Germany Fragebogen (Questionnaire), December 27. 1946, 6 pages, Landesarchiv Baden-Württemberg.

10. Ludwig Wörl quoted in "Spectators At War Crimes Trial Call For Lynching Of 'Child-Killer,'" *The Lincoln Star* (Lincoln, NE), April 7, 1964, 2.

11. Capesius quoted from Dieter Schlesak, *The Druggist of Auschwitz*, Kindle Edition, 1245 of 5119.

12. Sikorski quoted in Schlesak, *The Druggist of Auschwitz: A Documentary Novel,* Kindle Edition, 1488 of 5519.

13. Capesius documents prepared for his defense at the Auschwitz Trial, District Court, Frankfurt am Main, June 19, 1964, cited in Schlesak, *The Druggist of Auschwitz*, Kindle Edition, 191 of 5519.

14. The SD, Sicherheitsdienst, security police.

15. Wilhelm Prokop testimony in 4Ks 2/63, Hessisches Staatsarchiv and cited in Naumann, *Auschwitz*, 190.

16. Capesius quoted from Dieter Schlesak, *The Druggist of Auschwitz*, Kindle Edition, 1245 of 5119.

17. Sikorski testimony in 4Ks 2/63, Hessisches Staatsarchiv and cited in Naumann, *Auschwitz,* 191-92.

18. Wörl was honored after the war as a Righteous Gentile by Israel's Holocaust Museum, Yad Vashem. Ludwig Wörl quoted in *The Bridgeport Telegram* (Bridgeport, CT), April 7, 1964, 11; Josef Klehr quoted in *Pittsburg Post-Gazette* (Pittsburg, PA), April 7, 1964; also Klehr quoted in *Kingsport News* (Kingsport, TN), January 31, 1963, 23, and in "Past Notes: SS Orderly Kills 250 Patients," *The Guardian* (London), January 31, 1995, T3.

19. Jan Sikorski sworn statement and testimony at the Auschwitz Trial, District Court, Frankfurt am Main, June 19, 1964.

20. Capesius quoted by Sikorski, sworn statement and testimony at the Auschwitz Trial, District Court, Frankfurt am Main, June 19, 1964; see also Prokop in Schlesak, *The Druggist of Auschwitz,* Kindle Edition, 1928 of 5519.

21. Prosecutor interrogation of Victor Capesius, Frankfurt am Main, December 7, 1959, quoted in Schlesak, *The Druggist of* Auschwitz, Kindle Edition, 1314 of 5519.

22. Although after the war his memory was fuzzy. He claimed the Zyklon B storage was "very mysterious" and he "can't say" with any specificity how much was stored exactly where. Victor Capesius, questioning of during

judicial investigation pursuant to Auschwitz trial, December 7, 1959, cited in Schlesak, *The Druggist of Auschwitz,* Kindle Edition, 1311 of 5519.

23. Jan Sikorski sworn statement and testimony at the Auschwitz Trial, District Court, Frankfurt am Main, June 19, 1964, 4Ks 2/63, Hessisches Staatsarchiv.

24. Testimony of Władysław Fejkiel 4Ks 2/63, Hessisches Staatsarchiv and in Naumann, *Auschwitz,* 156.

25. Ludwig Wörl quoted in "Bribe Allegations At Auschwitz Trial," *The Sydney Morning Herald* (Sydney, New South Wales, Australia), April 8, 1964, 3.

26. Tadeusz Szewczyk testimony cited in Naumann, *Auschwitz,* 225.

27. Peter Hayes, *From Cooperation to Complicity: Degussa in the Third Reich* (Cambridge: Cambridge University Press, 2007), 298.

28. Zdzisław Mikolajski testimony cited in Naumann, *Auschwitz,* 253.

29. Klehr interviewed in Schlesak, *The Druggist of Auschwitz,* Kindle Edition, 1054 of 5519.

30. Testimony of Paisikovic Frankfurt Auschwitz Trial, "Criminal case against Mulka et al", 4 Ks 2/63, Landgericht Frankfurt am Main, August 6, 1964.

31. Capesius quoted in Schlesak, *The Druggist of Auschwitz,* Kindle Edition, 861 of 5519.

32. Wilhelm Prokop testimony 4Ks 2/63, Hessisches Staatsarchiv and cited in Naumann, *Auschwitz,* 189.

33. Capesius quoted in Schlesak, *The Druggist of Auschwitz,* Kindle Edition, 1190 of 5519.

34. Ibid., 1174 of 5519.

35. Miklós Nyiszli, *I Was Doctor Mengele's Assistant* (Kraków, Poland: Frap-Books, 2000), 88.

36. Hermann Langbein, testimony before the Auschwitz Trial, District Court, Frankfurt am Main, 4Ks 2/63, Hessisches Staatsarchiv and cited in *Democrat and Chronicle* (Rochester, NY), March 7, 1964, 1. See also Miklós Nyiszli, *I Was Doctor Mengele's Assistant* (Kraków, Poland: Frap-Books, 2000), 90-92.

37. Miklós Nyiszli, *I Was Doctor Mengele's Assistant* (Kraków, Poland: Frap-Books, 2000), 92.

38. Ibid.

39. DuBois, The Devil's Chemist, 221.

40. Prokop quoted in Schlesak, *The Druggist of Auschwitz,* Kindle Edition, 1916-1926 of 5519.

41. Wilhelm Prokop testimony 4Ks 2/63, Hessisches Staatsarchiv and cited in Naumann, *Auschwitz,* 190.

CHAPTER 7 – "GET TO KNOW THE DEVIL"

1. Capesius and Röhde quoted in Naumann, *Auschwitz,* 68-69; see also Fejkiel quoted on 155.

2. Capesius quoted in Naumann, *Auschwitz,* 69.

3. Capesius quoted in Schlesak, *The Druggist of Auschwitz,* Kindle Edition, 356 of 5519.

4. Roland Albert interviewed in Schlesak, *The Druggist of Auschwitz,* Kindle Edition, 1637 of 5519.

5. Jan Sikorski testimony 4Ks 2/63, Hessisches Staatsarchiv and cited in Naumann, *Auschwitz,* 193.

6. Schlesak, *The Druggist of Auschwitz,* Kindle Edition, 2299 of 5519.

7. Naumann, *Auschwitz,* 124.

8. Erich Kulka testimony 4Ks 2/63, Hessisches Staatsarchiv and cited in Naumann, *Auschwitz,* 125.

9. Testimony of Hermann Langbein, Frankfurt Auschwitz Trial, "Criminal case against Mulka et al", 4 Ks 2/63, Landgericht Frankfurt am Main, June 3, 1964, 58, reference 4Ks 2/63, Hessisches Staatsarchiv; Capesius in Schlesak, *The Druggist of Auschwitz,* Kindle Edition, 821 of 5519.

10. *Täter Helfer Trittbrettfahrer: NS-Belastete aus dem östlichen Württemberg* Vol. 3, "Der Apotheker Dr. Victor Capesius und die Selektionen in Auschwitz-Birkenau" Dr. Werner Renz, (Reutlingen: Wolfgang Proske Verlag, 2014), 67.

11. Raphael Gross, Werner Renz, Sybille Steinbacher, Devin O Pendas and Johannes Schmidt, *Der Frankfurter Auschwitz-Proses (1963-1965): kommentierte Quellenedition* (Frankfurt: Campus Verlag, 2013).

12. Raphael Gross, et al, *Der Frankfurter Auschwitz-Prozess*; Pajor testimony cited in Naumann, *Auschwitz,* 301.

13. Krausz quoted in Schlesak, *The Druggist of Auschwitz,* Kindle Edition, 600 of 5519.

14. Sarah Nebel testimony cited in Naumann, *Auschwitz,* 263.

15. See Sarah Nebel testimony in "Verdict on Auschwitz: *The Frankfurt Auschwitz Trial* 1963-1965," documentary film by Rolf Bickell and Dietrich Wagner, First Run Films, 1993; Sarah Nebel testimony cited in Naumann, *Auschwitz,* 263.

16. Lajos Schlinger testimony 4Ks 2/63, Hessisches Staatsarchiv and cited in Naumann, *Auschwitz,* 243.

17. Lajos Schlinger testimony cited in Naumann, *Auschwitz,* 242-43.

18. Ibid., 243; see also Peter Weiss, *The Investigation: Oratorio in 11 Cantos* (London: Marion Boyars, 1996), 18-19.

19. Raphael Gross, Werner Renz, Sybille Steinbacher, Devin O Pendas and Johannes Schmidt, *Der Frankfurter Auschwitz-Proses (1963-1965): Kommentierte Quellenedition* (Frankfurt: Campus Verlag, 2013), 475.

20. Ibid., 475-476.

21. Ibid., 476.

22. Jan Sikorski quoted in "Auschwitz Druggist Tagged As Jekyll-Hyde Character," *Nevada State Journal* (Reno, NV), June 21, 1964, 13; see also Sikorski quoted in "'Jekyll-And-Hyde' Described," *Tucson Daily Gazette* (Tucson, AZ), June 19, 1964, 12.

23. Ibid., 579, 610 of 5519.

24. By the time she testified at the Auschwitz trial, Ella Böhm had married and she is listed in those records as Ella Salomon.

25. Salomon (née Böhm) in Schlesak, *The Druggist of Auschwitz*, Kindle Edition, 717 of 5519.

26. Josef Glück testimony 4Ks 2/63, Hessisches Staatsarchiv and cited in Naumann, *Auschwitz*, 217-218.

27. Josef Glück testimony cited in Naumann, *Auschwitz*, 218; Ota Kraus and Erich Kulka, "Tovarna na smrt" (Death Factory), (Prague: Nase vojsko, 1957), 200.

28. Josef Glück testimony 4Ks 2/63, Hessisches Staatsarchiv and cited in Naumann, *Auschwitz*, 217; see also letter from Glück to Langbein, cited in Schlesak, *The Druggist of Auschwitz*, Kindle Edition, 2255-2266 of 5519.

29. Magda Szabó testimony cited in Naumann, *Auschwitz*, 222.

30. "Survivor Of Auschwitz Labels Capesius 'Devil,'" *The Lincoln Star* (Lincoln, NE), August 25, 1964, 19; "Death Camp Defendant Was 'Devil,'" *The Troy Record* (Troy, NY), August 25, 1964, 17; Magda Szabó testimony cited in Naumann, *Auschwitz*, 223.

31. "Nazi Called Self The Devil, Witness Says," *Democrat and Chronicle* (Rochester, NY), August 25, 1964, 9; Magda Szabó testimony cited in Naumann, *Auschwitz*, 223.

CHAPTER 8 – "BAYER'S POISON"

1. Hoven quoted in "Auschwitz: 60 Year Anniversary – The Role of IG Farben-Bayer," Alliance for Human Research Protection, January 27, 2005.

2. For details on the Farben directed experiments see DuBois, *The Devil's Chemist*, 207-227.

3. Jeffreys, *Hell's Cartel*, 327.

4. DuBois, Jr., *The Devil's Chemist*, 125-26.

5. Jeffreys, *Hell's Cartel*, 327.

6. Jeffreys, *Hell's Cartel*, Kindle Edition, 5252 of 9525.

7. Capesius interviewed in Schlesak, *The Druggist of Auschwitz,* Hardcover Edition, 22.

8. Presentation of the case against the defendants by the prosecutor Joachim Kügler, Frankfurt Auschwitz Trial, "Criminal case against Mulka et al", 4 Ks 2/63, Landgericht Frankfurt am Main, May 13, 1965.

9. Robert Lifton, The Nazi Doctors: Medical Killing and the Psychology of Genocide, (New York: Basic Books, 1986).

10. Testimony of Victor Capesius in the Judicial Hearing Transcript, District Court, Frankfurt, Viktor Capesius in person before Examining Magistrate Judge Heinz Düx, 15 pages, 4 Js 444/59, January 10, 1962, courtesy of Fritz Bauer Institut, 13-14.

11. Phil Miller, "Scots Holocaust Victim In Fight for Compensation," *Sunday Times* (London), December 30, 2001, Section Home News; Tom Martin, "Nazi Scientist Stripped Me of Motherhood and I Still Need an Apology," *Sunday Express* (UK), August 17, 2003, 49.

CHAPTER 9 – "AN UNAMBIGUOS SMELL"

1. Rudolf Höss, *Commandant of Auschwitz* (New York: World Publishing Co, 1960), 175–176; Gerald L. Posner and John Ware, *Mengele: The Complete Story* (Kindle Edition), New York: Cooper Square Press, 6328.

2. Höss quoted in Allan Hall, "My Beautiful Auschwitz Childhood," *The Daily Mail*, June 16, 2015.

3. Posner and Ware, *Mengele*, Kindle Edition, 726-733.

4. Ibid., 714.

5. Roland Albert interviewed in Schlesak, *The Druggist of Auschwitz,* Hardcover Edition, 236.

6. Op. Cit., Posner and Ware, *Mengele*, Kindle Edition, 822-823.

7. Böhm quoted in Schlesak, *The Druggist of Auschwitz,* Hardcover Edition, 275.

8. Posner and Ware, *Mengele*, Kindle Edition, 1322.

9. Naumann, *Auschwitz*, 334.

10. Fabritius disliked his new home in the Beskidy Mountains, considering it an "enforced exile" from his native Romania. Overview of The Foreign Organization of the Nazi Party, "The Nazi Foreign Organization and the German Minorities ('Ethnic Groups')," Chapter IV, United Nations publication, undated, 8485; see also Schlesak, *The Druggist of Auschwitz,* Kindle Edition, 2435, 2695 of 5519.

11. Dr. Fritz Klein, Testimony in the Bergen Belsen Trial, 1945, transcript at Yad Vashem archives.

12. Dampf-Kraft-Wagen was a German car and motorcycle manufacturer that was eventually folded into Audi. Hans Stoffel testimony cited in Naumann, *Auschwitz*, 334.

13. Albert interviewed in Schlesak, *The Druggist of Auschwitz,* Hardcover Edition, 65.

14. Capesius in Schlesak, *The Druggist of Auschwitz,* Kindle Edition, 1497 – 1498 of 5519.

15. Testimony of Zdzislaw Mikolajski 4Ks 2/63, Hessisches Staatsarchiv and in Naumann, *Auschwitz*, 252.

16. Hans Stoffel testimony in 4Ks 2/63, Hessisches Staatsarchiv and cited in Naumann, *Auschwitz*, 334; and part of Capesius diary as reported in Schlesak, *The Druggist of Auschwitz,* Kindle Edition, 2021-2043.

17. Hildegard Stoffel in Schlesak, *The Druggist of Auschwitz,* Kindle Edition, 2488 of 5519 and testimony cited in Naumann, *Auschwitz*, 335.

18. Hans Stoffel testimony in 4Ks 2/63, Hessisches Staatsarchiv cited in Naumann, *Auschwitz*, 334.

19. Schlesak, *The Druggist of Auschwitz,* Kindle Edition, 2043, 2463 of 5519.

20. Naumann, *Auschwitz*, 334.

21. A translation of "Dorna-Watra", *Geschichte der Juden in der Bukowina,* {History of the Jews in the Bukovina} Edited by: Dr. Hugo Gold, Written by: Prof. Dr. H. Sternberg, Tel-Aviv, Published in Tel Aviv, 1962; Vladimir Solonari, The Treatment Of The Jews Of Bukovina By The Soviet And Romanian Administrations In 1940–1944, *Holocaust and Modernity*, No. 2(8), 2010, 152-158; See Vladimir Solonari, *Purifying the Nation: Population Exchange and Ethnic Cleansing in Nazi-Allied Romania* (Baltimore, MD: Johns Hopkins University Press, 2009).

22. Capesius in Schlesak, *The Druggist of Auschwitz,* Kindle Edition, 1696 of 5519.

23. Sternberg, Geschichte der Juden in der Bukowina.

24. Notes by Capesius cited in Schlesak, *The Druggist of Auschwitz,* Kindle Edition, 2048.

CHAPTER 10 – THE HUNGARIAN JEWS

1. The Auschwitz-Birkenau State Museum, Oswiecim "Diary of Paul Kremer."

2. Libuša Breder quoted in "Auschwitz: Inside The Nazi State, Corruption: Episode 4, PBS, 2005.

3. Gröning quoted in "Auschwitz: Inside The Nazi State, Corruption: Episode 4, PBS, 2005.

4. Konrad Morgen sworn statement and testimony at the Auschwitz Trial, District Court, Frankfurt am Main, 1964

5. Testimony of Gerhard Wiebeck, Frankfurt Auschwitz Trial, "Criminal case against Mulka et al", 4 Ks 2/63, Landgericht Frankfurt am Main, 1964.

6. Nyiszli, I Was Doctor Mengele's Assistant.

7. Schlesak, *The Druggist of Auschwitz,* Kindle Edition, 785 of 5519.

8. Roland interviewed in Schlesak, *The Druggist of Auschwitz,* Hardcover Edition, 178.

9. Schlesak, *The Druggist of Auschwitz,* Kindle Edition, 591 of 5519.

10. Prokop testimony quoted in Schlesak, *The Druggist of Auschwitz,* Kindle Edition, 1543-1544 of 5519.

11. Capesius in Schlesak, *The Druggist of Auschwitz,* Kindle Edition, 1466 of 5519.

12. Testimony of Hermann Langbein, Frankfurt Auschwitz Trial, "Criminal case against Mulka et al", 4 Ks 2/63, Landgericht Frankfurt am Main, June 3, 1964, 62, reference 4Ks 2/63, Hessisches Staatsarchiv.

13. Grosz letter to Langbein, November 21, 1962, made an exhibit of the Frankfurt Auschwitz Trial, "Criminal case against Mulka et al", 4 Ks 2/63, Landgericht Frankfurt am Main.

14. Wörl quoted in Schlesak, *The Druggist of Auschwitz,* Hardcover Edition, 174.

15. Tadeusz Szewczyk testimony cited in Naumann, *Auschwitz,* 225; also Tadeusz Szewczyk quoted in "Mass Killer Also Accused of Theft," *Tucson Daily Gazette* (Tucson, AZ), August 27, 1964, 36.; see Langbein, *People in Auschwitz,* citing testimony of Szewczyk, 348-49.

16. Langbein, *People in Auschwitz,* 350-51.

17. Prokop testimony quoted in 4Ks 2/63, Hessisches Staatsarchiv cited in Schlesak, *The Druggist of Auschwitz,* Kindle Edition, 1544-1550 of 5519.

18. Wilhelm Prokop testimony in 4Ks 2/63, Hessisches Staatsarchiv cited in Naumann, *Auschwitz,* 190.

CHAPTER 11 – DENTAL GOLD

1. Jeffreys, Hell's Cartel: IG Farben and the Making of Hitler's War Machine, 339.

2. See Richard H. Levy, *The Bombing of Auschwitz Revisited: A Critical Analysis* (New York, St. Martins Press, 2000); William D. Rubinstein *The Myth of Rescue* (London: Routledge, 1997).

3. After the war, Capesius claimed he had a four week leave, but it was more likely three at the most. He had an incentive to exaggerate the length of time he was away from the camp, since that reduced the number of incriminating accounts of his actions by eyewitness survivors. Judicial Hearing Transcript, District Court, Frankfurt, Viktor Capesius in person

before Examining Magistrate Judge Heinz Düx, 8 pages, 4 Js 444/59, January 24, 1962, courtesy of Fritz Bauer Institut, 5, 6.

4.   Hans Nogly, "Die Mörder sind wie du und ich," *Stern*, No. 10, 1965, 64; Letter of Victor Capesius, May 12, 1947, regarding the Spruchkammer des Interniertenlagers 74, Article/Case 895/J/74/1213, in reference to Klageschrift of May 2, 1947, 2 pages, Landesarchiv Baden-Württemberg, 2.

5.   *The Druggist of Auschwitz,* Kindle Edition, 4506 of 5519.

6.   Capesius quoted in Schlesak, *Druggist of Auschwitz*, Hardcover Edition, 31; see Robert Karl Ludwig Mulka and Others Before the Court at Frankfurt.

7.   Albert interviewed in Schlesak, *The Druggist of Auschwitz,* Kindle Edition, 4491 of 5519.

8.   Capesius to Stoffel, quoted in Schlesak, *The Druggist of Auschwitz,* Hardcover Edition, 136-38.

9.   Langbein, *People in Auschwitz*, 409-11; Schlesak, *Druggist of Auschwitz*, Hardcover Edition, 97.

10. Capesius declaration in Judicial Hearing Transcript, District Court, Frankfurt, Viktor Capesius in person before Examining Magistrate Judge Heinz Düx, 8 pages, 4 Js 444/59, January 24, 1962, courtesy of Fritz Bauer Institut, 5, 7-8.

11. Roosevelt letter cited in Higham, *Trading with the Enemy*, 211.

12. According to eyewitness testimony by Miklós Nyiszli in Nyiszli, *I Was Doctor Mengele's Assistant*s.

13. Posner, *God's Bankers*, 131.

14. Yakoov Gabai in Schlesak, *The Druggist of Auschwitz,* Kindle Edition, 1498 of 5519

15. Tadeusz Iwaszko, Hefte von Auschwitz 16 (Auschwitz: Verlag Staatliches Auschwitz-Museum, 1978), 71.

16. Zdzislaw Mikolajski testimony cited in Naumann, *Auschwitz*, 252.

17. Capesius in Schlesak, *The Druggist of Auschwitz,* Kindle Edition, 1488 of 5519.

18. Capesius statement in Judicial Hearing Transcript, District Court, Frankfurt, Viktor Capesius in person before Examining Magistrate Judge Heinz Düx, 15 pages, 4 Js 444/59, January 10, 1962, courtesy of Fritz Bauer Institut, 9-10.

19. Capesius in Schlesak, *The Druggist of Auschwitz,* Kindle Edition, 1466 of 5519; Prokop, Schlesak, *The Druggist of Auschwitz,* Kindle Edition, 1498 of 5519.

20. Wilhelm Prokop quoted in "Chemist 'Stored Gold Teeth'" *Sydney Morning Herald* (Sydney, New South Wales, Australia), June 20, 1964, 3; and Prokop testimony quoted in Schlesak, *The Druggist of Auschwitz*, Kindle Edition, 1550-1552 of 5519.

21. Jan Sikorski sworn statement and testimony at the Auschwitz Trial, District Court, Frankfurt am Main, June 19, 1964 and in Schlesak, *The Druggist of Auschwitz,* Kindle Edition, 1498 of 5519.

22. Ibid.

23. Wilhelm Prokop testimony cited in Naumann, *Auschwitz*, 190-91 and in Langbein, *People in Auschwitz*, 349-51; Wilhelm Prokop quoted in "Chemist 'Stored Gold Teeth'" *Sydney Morning Herald* (Sydney, New South Wales, Australia), June 20, 1964, 3; also Prokop "Horror Loot of a Nazi Camp Told," *Independent* (Long Beach, CA), June 19, 1964, 15; Prokop in Schlesak, *The Druggist of Auschwitz*, Kindle Edition, 1515 of 5519.

24. Daniel Bard quoted in "Eichmann Accused Anew at Nazi Crimes Trials," *The Cincinnati Enquirer* (Cincinnati, OH), August 18, 1954, 17.

CHAPTER 12 – IMPENDING END

1. Trials of War Criminals before the Nuremberg Military Tribunals under Control Council Law No. 10 (Washington D.C.: US Government Printing Office), 1949, Vol. 5, 445.

2. Puzyna quoted in Posner and Ware, *Mengele*, 58.

3. Sikorski quoted in "Auschwitz Druggist Tagged as Jekyll-Hyde Character," *Nevada State Journal* (Reno, Nevada), June 21, 1964, 13.

4. Sikorski quoted in *The Druggist of Auschwitz,* Kindle Edition, 1507 of 5519.

5. Capesius writing in the third person as the Stoffels, in a letter to them from prison, cited in Schlesak, *The Druggist of Auschwitz,* 139.

6. Staatsanwaltschaftliche Vernehmung, 3.

7. Ibid.; see also Judicial Hearing Transcript, District Court, Frankfurt, Viktor Capesius in person before Examining Magistrate Judge Heinz Düx, 8 pages, 4 Js 444/59, January 24, 1962, courtesy of Fritz Bauer Institut, 5, 6.

8. Written Statement of Victor Capesius, August 22, 1946, included in "War Crimes Central Suspect and Witness Enclosure," Headquarters, Civilian Internment Enclosure, APO 205, US Army, page 9, December 20, 1946, maintained in Dossier 76950, May 17, 1951, Subject, "Capesius, Victor Ernst," declassified April 1, 2016 at request of author, NARA.

9. Schlesak, *The Druggist of Auschwitz,* Kindle Edition, 4976 of 5519.

10. Jeffreys, *Hell's Cartel*, Kindle Edition, 5455 of 9525

11. Ibid., 342.

12. The U.S. Third Army set up its own central operations at Farben's headquarters.

13. Jeffreys, *Hell's Cartel*, 355.

14. Ibid., 350-51.

15. Written Statement of Victor Capesius, August 22, 1946, included in "War
     Crimes Central Suspect and Witness Enclosure," Headquarters, Civilian
     Internment Enclosure, APO 205, US Army, page 9, December 20, 1946,
     maintained in Dossier 76950, May 17, 1951, Subject, "Capesius, Victor
     Ernst," declassified April 1, 2016 at request of author, NARA.

16. Capesius quoted in Schlesak, *The Druggist of Auschwitz,* Hardcover
     Edition, 352.

CHAPTER 13 – "UNDER AUTOMATIC ARREST"

1.   The information about Capesius and his British detention is from
     answers he provided in detailed questionnaires to U.S. and German
     authorities during his denazification proceedings in 1946 and 1947, as
     well as information from the 1964 Frankfurt Auschwitz trial, and finally
     from some interviews Capesius gave after the war. In an effort to uncover
     possible British government and military documents about his detention,
     the author undertook a search in the National Archives and Records Centre
     in Kew, England. The following wartime record groups were searched
     but no Capesius references were discovered: Home Office (HO) 215,
     Internment, UK and abroad, conditions etc. and release and in some cases
     repatriation; HO 214, Personal case files, specifically by B3 division, on
     enemy aliens who were interned in WW2; Foreign Office (FO) 1039/874,
     Control Commission (British element) WE, Schleswig-Holstein 1946; FO
     1006/309, Conditions in Schleswig-Holstein; FO 1039/930, Monthly
     reports, Schleswig-Holstein, 1946-47; FO 1051/6755, Inspection reports,
     Schleswig-Holstein; FO 208/4661, MOD, Auschwitz POW section -
     interrogations by London District Cage of enemy POWs. June 1945-Oct
     1946; FO 939/32, German POWs - administration 1946-47; FO
     1024/75, Control Commission, prisoners' personal records 1946-1954;
     FO 938/78, Allegations of starvation in internment camps; FO 939/444,
     Correspondence of Control Commission in Germany 1945-47; FO
     939/23, War criminals - 1945-47; CO 537/132 Repatriation of German
     POWs, and; FO 945/453 Repatriation of German POWs in British hands
     outside the UK 1946-47.

2.   Simon Rees, "German POWs and the Art of Survival," *Military History,*
     July 2007.

3.   "A German POW Remember," Epping Forest District Museum, contributed
     on December 5, 2005, Article ID A7564548.

4.   Handbook for the Military Government in Germany: Prior to Defeat or
     Surrender, Supreme Headquarters, Allied Expeditionary Force, Office of
     the Chief of Staff, 385 pages, U.S. Army Military History Institute, p. 90.

5. See generally Merritt, Richard L. Democracy Imposed: U.S. Occupation Policy and the German Public, 1945-1949 (Yale University Press, 1995).

6. Hans Nogly, "Die Mörder sind wie du und ich," *Stern*, No. 10, 1965. 66.

7. Ibid., 64.

8. Notations made by Capesius while in custody awaiting his 1964 trial in Frankfurt, cited in Schlesak, *The Druggist of Auschwitz,* Kindle Edition, 2332 of 5519.

9. Author review of archive backup to prosecution case of Bergen-Belsen War Crimes Trial – Vol II, Evidence for Kraft.

10. Capesius quoted in Schlesak, *The Druggist of Auschwitz,* Kindle Edition, 2332 of 5519.

11. Presentation of the case against the defendants by the prosecutor Joachim Kügler, Frankfurt Auschwitz Trial, "Criminal case against Mulka et al", 4 Ks 2/63, Landgericht Frankfurt am Main, May 13, 1965; see also Schlesak, *The Druggist of Auschwitz,* Kindle Edition, 1377, 2557 of 5519, which lists the release date by the British as May 23, instead of the May 20 as set forth by the Frankfurt prosecutor. Capesius himself once gave a more generic date of June 1946 in Staatsanwaltschaftliche Vernehmung, 4. In fact, documents submitted in Capesius's denazification trial in 1947 confirm the release date was May 25.

12. Written Statement of Victor Capesius, August 22, 1946, included in "War Crimes Central Suspect and Witness Enclosure," Headquarters, Civilian Internment Enclosure, APO 205, US Army, page 9, December 20, 1946, maintained in Dossier 76950, May 17, 1951, Subject, "Capesius, Victor Ernst," declassified April 1, 2016 at request of author, NARA.

13. Written Statement of Victor Capesius, August 22, 1946, included in "War Crimes Central Suspect and Witness Enclosure," Headquarters, Civilian Internment Enclosure, APO 205, US Army, page 9, December 20, 1946, maintained in Dossier 76950, May 17, 1951, Subject, "Capesius, Victor Ernst," declassified April 1, 2016 at request of author, NARA.

14. The author obtained for the first time the 112-page file of the Cluj-Napoca court case from the National Archives, Ministry of the Interior, Bucharest. The court took witness statements against the defendants, most of whom were not present. No defense was presented for Capesius.

15. November 16, 1964 statement of Marianne Adam, née Willner4Ks 2/63, Hessisches Staatsarchiv.

16. Hans Nogly, "Die Mörder sind wie du und ich," *Stern*, No. 10, 1965. 66.

17. Friederike Capesius quoted in Schlesak, *The Druggist of Auschwitz,* Hardcover Edition, 343.

18. Staatsanwaltschaftliche Vernehmung, 4. See Presentation of the case against the defendants by the prosecutor Joachim Kügler, Frankfurt Auschwitz

Trial, "Criminal case against Mulka et al", 4 Ks 2/63, Landgericht Frankfurt am Main, May 13, 1965.

19. Meldebogen, Stuttgart, June 4, 1946, 2 pages, from Landesarchiv Baden-Württemberg.

20. Ibid.

21. See for instance assorted letters in support of Victor Capesius application for denazification, pp 30-39 of Spruchkammer, 37/40644, In Sachen, "Capesius, Viktor," Landesarchiv Baden-Württemberg.

22. Capesius writing in the third person as the Stoffels, in a letter to them from prison, cited in Schlesak, *The Druggist of Auschwitz*, 139.

23. Presentation of the case against the defendants by the prosecutor Joachim Kügler, Frankfurt Auschwitz Trial, "Criminal case against Mulka et al", 4 Ks 2/63, Landgericht Frankfurt am Main, May 13, 1965.

24. "War Crimes Central Suspect and Witness Enclosure," Headquarters, Civilian Internment Enclosure, APO 205, US Army, December 20, 1946, maintained in Dossier 76950, May 17, 1951, Subject, "Capesius, Victor Ernst," declassified April 1, 2016 at request of author, NARA.

25. The Auschwitz Trial. Tape Recordings, Protocols and documents on the DVD-ROM, from the collection of The Fritz Bauer Institute, Direct Media Publishing GmbH, 2nd revised edition, Berlin 2005, S. 3535.

26. "War Crimes Central Suspect and Witness Enclosure," Headquarters, Civilian Internment Enclosure, APO 205, US Army, December 20, 1946, maintained in Dossier 76950, May 17, 1951, Subject, "Capesius, Victor Ernst," declassified April 1, 2016 at request of author, NARA.

27. CI Arrest Report, "War Crimes Central Suspect and Witness Enclosure," Headquarters, Civilian Internment Enclosure, APO 205, US Army, page 9, December 20, 1946, maintained in Dossier 76950, May 17, 1951, Subject, "Capesius, Victor Ernst," p. 8, declassified April 1, 2016 at request of author, NARA.

28. Written Statement of Victor Capesius, August 22, 1946, included in "War Crimes Central Suspect and Witness Enclosure," Headquarters, Civilian Internment Enclosure, APO 205, US Army, page 9, December 20, 1946, maintained in Dossier 76950, May 17, 1951, Subject, "Capesius, Victor Ernst," declassified April 1, 2016 at request of author, NARA.

CHAPTER 14 – "WHAT CRIME HAVE I COMMITTED?"

1. Wirths letter quoted in Schlesak, *The Druggist of Auschwitz*, Hardcover Edition, 353.

2. Capesius interviewed in Schlesak, *The Druggist of Auschwitz*, Hardcover Edition, 260,

3. Roland Albert interviewed in Schlesak, *The Druggist of Auschwitz*, Hardcover Edition, 238-39.

4. Jeffreys, *Hell's Cartel*, 350.

5. Posner, *God's Bankers*, Simon & Schuster. Kindle Edition, 592-593.

6. Capesius letter to the Stoffels, cited in Schlesak, *The Druggist of Auschwitz*, 139.

7. The case number was 31G-6632-452. "War Crimes Central Suspect and Witness Enclosure," Headquarters, Civilian Internment Enclosure, APO 205, US Army, December 20, 1946, maintained in Dossier 76950, May 17, 1951, Subject, "Capesius, Victor Ernst," declassified April 1, 2016 at request of author, NARA.

8. 3-3 Work Sheet" in "War Crimes Central Suspect and Witness Enclosure," Headquarters, Civilian Internment Enclosure, APO 205, US Army, page 9, December 20, 1946, maintained in Dossier 76950, May 17, 1951, Subject, "Capesius, Victor Ernst," p. 17, declassified April 1, 2016 at request of author, NARA.

9. Arrest Report, "War Crimes Central Suspect and Witness Enclosure," Headquarters, Civilian Internment Enclosure, APO 205, US Army, page 9, December 20, 1946, maintained in Dossier 76950, May 17, 1951, Subject, "Capesius, Victor Ernst," p. 10, declassified April 1, 2016 at request of author, NARA.

10. Military Government of Germany, Fragebogen, "War Crimes Central Suspect and Witness Enclosure," Headquarters, Civilian Internment Enclosure, APO 205, US Army, page 9, December 20, 1946, maintained in Dossier 76950, May 17, 1951, Subject, "Capesius, Victor Ernst," pp. 2-3, declassified April 1, 2016 at request of author, NARA.

11. Ibid.

12. Ibid., pp. 5-6.

13. Capesius letter to the Stoffels, cited in Schlesak, *The Druggist of Auschwitz*, 139.

14. Meldebogen, Stuttgart, December 24, 1946, 2 pages, from Landesarchiv Baden-Württemberg.

15. Fragebogen of Victor Capesius, December 27, 1946, Part D, Question 29, Landesarchiv Baden-Württemberg.

16. All references to Capesius's letter are to his 4-page handwritten letter to the Prosecutor, Ludwigsburg, January 3, 1947, Landesarchiv Baden-Württemberg.

17. See for instance assorted letters in support of Victor Capesius application for denazification, pp 30-39 of Spruchkammer, 37/40644, In Sachen, "Capesius, Viktor," Landesarchiv Baden-Württemberg.

18. Letter of Karl Heinz Schuleri, December 17, 1946, 1 page, and letter of Mentzel and Braun, February 11, 1947, 1 page, from the Landesarchiv Baden-Württemberg.

19. Klageschrift, Spruchkammer, Interniertenlager 74, May 2, 1947, Ludwigsberg-Ossweil, 2 pages, from the Landesarchiv Baden-Württemberg.

20. Ibid.

21. The basis for this argument appears to be that the agreement between the governments of Romania and Germany left all ethnic Germans as Romanian citizens. That alone would have prevented him from the more elite elements of the SS. See flyer re Volks-Deutsche, November 17, 1943, Landesarchiv Baden-Württemberg.

22. Letter of Victor Capesius, May 12, 1947, regarding the Spruchkammer des Interniertenlagers 74, Article/Case 895/J/74/1213, in reference to Klageschrift of May 2, 1947, 2 pages, Landesarchiv Baden-Württemberg, p. 1- 4.

23. Ibid.

24. Koch cited Dr. Alexandro Bardeanu as the Jewish director that had a good relationship with Capesius. Eidesstattliche Erklarung, May 12, 1947, from Dr. H. Koch, 1 page, Landesarchiv Baden-Württemberg.

25. Protokoll, Lager 74, 895/J/74/1213, Viktor Ernst Capesius, May 22, 1947, Judges Dr. Hoffman, Klein, Krieg, Bächtle, and Müller, 3 pages, Landesarchiv Baden-Württemberg.

26. Spruch, Lager 74, 895/J/74/1213, May 22, 1947, Judges Dr. Hoffman, Klein, Krieg, Bächtle, and Müller, 2 pages, Landesarchiv Baden-Württemberg.

27. Spruch acknowledgement, challenged and tested, June 30, 1947, John D. Austin, Captain, 1 page, Landesarchiv Baden-Württemberg.

28. Entlassungsschein (Discharge Certificate), Ministry for Political Liberation in Württemberg-Baden, Lagr. 74, 1 page, Landesarchiv Baden-Württemberg; see also Op. Cit., Staatsanwaltschaftliche Vernehmung, 4.

29. Ray Salvatore Jennings, "The Road Ahead: Lessons in Nation Building from Japan, Germany and Afghanistan for Postwar Iraq," United States Institute of Peace, Washington D.C., April 2003, 14.

30. Andornung, Ministerim für politische Befreiung Württemberg-Baden, Int. Lag. 74, Ludwigsburg-Ossweil, In dem Verharen gegen Viktor Ernst Capesius, August 1, 1947, Landesarchiv Baden-Württemberg, 1.

CHAPTER 15 – NO ONE KNEW ANYTHING

1. A complete transcript of the trial, in English, of Vol VII of the Nuremberg Military Tribunal is available online at https://web.archive.org/web/20130601070552/http://www.mazal.org/archive/nmt/07/NMT07-C001.htm

2. Kevin Jon Heller, The Nuremberg Military Tribunals and the Origins of International Criminal Law (Oxford, UK: Oxford University Press, 2011), 35.

3. Rankin quoted in Congressional Record, November 28, 1947, 10938; Heller, The Nuremberg Military Tribunals and the Origins of International Criminal Law, 35.

4. Taylor quoted at Jeffreys, *Hell's Cartel,* 194.

5. Borkin, *The Crime and Punishment of I. G. Farben*, 137. Only Twenty-three were in the courtroom on the day the trial started since Max Brüggemann, Farben's chief legal counsel, was dismissed because of poor health. See The IG Farben Trial

6. The United States of America vs. Carl Krauch et al., *US Military Tribunal Nuremberg, Judgment of 30 July 1948,* http://werle.rewi.hu-berlin.de/IGFarbenCase.pdf.

   The judges were Grover Shake, ex-Indiana State Supreme Court justice; James Morris, a North Dakota Supreme Court justice; and Paul Hebert, dean of the Louisiana State University Law School. Clarence Merrell, a noted Indiana lawyer, was chosen as the alternate in case one of the three lead judges could not finish the trial for any reason.

7. Taylor quoted in Scott Christianson, *Fatal Airs: The Deadly History and Apocalyptic Future of Lethal Gases* (New York: Praeger Press, 2010), 70.

8. Minskoff quoted in Borkin, The Crime and Punishment of I. G. Farben, 141.

9. Morris quoted in DuBois, *The Devil's Chemist*, 82.

10. Dr. Hans Braus testimony about Ambros, DuBois, *The Devil's Chemist*, 169.

11. Fritz ter Meer quoted in DuBois, *The Devil's Chemist*, 156.

12. Ibid., 157.

13. Christian Schneider quoted in DuBois, *The Devil's Chemist*, 162.

14. DuBois, *The Devil's Chemist*, 163.

15. Bütefisch testimony cited at DuBois, *The Devil's Chemist*, 164-66.

16. Borkin, *The Crime and Punishment of I. G. Farben*, 145-46.

17. Ibid., 148.

18. DuBois, *The Devil's Chemist*, 219.

19. Strafprozeß-Vollmacht (Power of Attorney), Capesius to Rudolf Pander, Seidenstrasse 36, Stuttgart, September 8, 1947, Landesarchiv Baden-Württemberg.

20. Rudolf Pander, interrogation report, December 7, 1945, Military Intelligence Center USFET, CI–IIR/35, RG 165, Entry (P) 179C, Box 738 (Location: 390: 35/15/01), pp. 5–6, NARA.

21. Presentation of the case of Viktor Capesius, by Dr. Rudolf Pander, Aktenzeichen 37/40644, 3 pages, October 7, 1947, Landesarchiv Baden-Württemberg.

22. Protokoll, Aktenzeichen 37/40644, Viktor Ernst Capesius, October 9, 1947, Judges Palmer, Reuss, Schlipf, Zaiss, Entenmann, 3 pages, Landesarchiv Baden-Württemberg.

23. Spruch, Aktenzeichen 37/40644, Viktor Ernst Capesius, October 9, 1947, Judges Palmer, Reuss, Schlipf, Zaiss, Entenmann, 3 pages, Landesarchiv Baden-Württemberg.

24. Staatsanwaltschaftliche Vernehmung, 4.

25. Ibid., 5.

26. Five months after the court rendered its verdicts, Judge P. M. Herbert issued a bitter dissent on the majority ruling on slave labor and mass murder. He would have held most of the defendants responsible on that count. See The IG Farben Trial, The United States of America vs. Carl Krauch et al., *US Military Tribunal Nuremberg, Judgment of 30 July 1948,* 168, http://werle.rewi.hu-berlin.de/IGFarbenCase.pdf. Also, Borkin, *The Crime and Punishment of I. G. Farben*, 155.

27. Trials of the War Criminals Before the Nuremberg Military Tribunals, Under Council 10, Vol. VIII, 1134-36, 1153-1167, 1186-87.

28. DuBois quoted in Kevin Jon Heller and Gerry Simpson, *The Hidden Histories of War Crimes Trials* (Oxford: Oxford University Press, 2013), 186.

CHAPTER 16 – A NEW BEGINNING

1. Capesius listing of his net worth under Section H, Income and Assets on The Military Government of Germany Fragebogen (Questionnaire), December 27. 1946, 6 pages, Landesarchiv Baden-Württemberg.

2. Capesius quoted in Schlesak, *The Druggist of Auschwitz,* Kindle Edition, 1961 of 5519.

3. The Reichsmark had been replaced in 1948 with the Deutschemark.

4. Staatsanwaltschaftliche Vernehmung, 5.

5. Ladislas Farago, *Aftermath: Martin Bormann and the Fourth Reich* (New York: Simon & Schuster, 1974), 20-21.

6. Fritz ter Meer quoted in Farago, *Aftermath*, 20.

7. See generally Jeffreys, *Hell's Cartel,* 407-408.

8. Borkin, The Crime and Punishment of I. G. Farben, 157-61.

9. Nine smaller companies were also spun off, including Agfa, Kalle, Cassella, and Huels,

10. See generally Jeffreys, *Hell's Cartel,* 407-408.

11. DuBois, The Devil's Chemist, 359.

12. Peter Schneider, "Der Anwalt Des Bösen; Fritz Steinacker Hat Sein Leben Lang Die Schlimmsten Nazi-Verbrecher Verteidigt. Ist Er Stolz Auf Seine Erfolge?" *Die Zeit,* October 29, 2009, 26-33; Wolfgang Messner, "Man hat nichts getan, man hat nichts gewusst; Zwei Reporter erinnern sich an den Auschwitz-Prozess, vierzig Jahre nach der Urteilsverkündung," *Stuttgarter Zeitung,* August 15, 2005, 3.

13. Hans Nogly, "Die Mörder sind wie du und ich," *Stern,* No. 10, 1965. 66.

14. Helge Krempels, "Kreisgruppe Ludwigsburg: In Erinnerung an Melitta Capesius," *Siebenbürgische Zeitung,* December 3, 2013.

15. Hans Nogly, "Die Mörder sind wie du und ich," *Stern,* No. 10, 1965. 66. Capesius claimed immediately after his arrest he had only 12 employees, see Staatsanwaltschaftliche Vernehmung, 5.

16. Devin O. Pendas, *The Frankfurt Auschwitz Trial,* 1963-1965: Genocide, History, and the Limits of the Law (Cambridge: Cambridge University Press, 2006), 11-12.

17. Ingo Müller, *Furchtbare Juristen,* (Munich: 1987), 242.

18. Karl Heinz Seifert and Dieter Hömig, eds., *Grundgesetz für die Bundesrepublik Deutschland: Tachenkommentar,* 4th Edition (Baden-Baden: Nomos Verlag, 1991), 200-02, 464-68.

19. Oberländer resigned in 1960 after East Germany sentenced him to death for his World War II crimes.

20. Pendas, *The Frankfurt Auschwitz Trial,* 15.

21. "Between 1950 and 1962, the West Germans investigated 30,000 former Nazis, indicted 12,846, tried 5,426, and acquitted 4,027. . . . Of those sentenced, only 155 were convicted of murder." Rebecca Wittmann, *Beyond Justice: The Auschwitz Trial* (Cambridge, MA: Harvard University Press, 2005), Kindle Edition, 178 of 3837.

22. Pendas, *The Frankfurt Auschwitz Trial,* 52, n. 121.

23. Lilje quoted in Farago, *Aftermath,* 317.

24. Farago, *Aftermath,* 318; *Ofer Aderet. Secret Life of the German Judge Who Brought the Mossad to Eichmann,* Hareetz, October 18, 2014

25. Ibid., Farago, 319

26. Wittmann, *Beyond Justice,* Kindle Edition, 354 of 3837.

CHAPTER 17 – "INNOCENCE BEFORE GOD"

1. Ibid., 639 of 3837; Pendas, *The Frankfurt Auschwitz Trial*, 26-27.

2. Wittmann, *Beyond Justice*, Kindle Edition, 482 of 3837.

3. Both Boger quoted in "Verdict on Auschwitz: *The Frankfurt Auschwitz Trial* 1963-1965," documentary film by Rolf Bickell and Dietrich Wagner, First Run Films, 1993.

4. Posner and Ware, *Mengele*, Kindle Edition, 2601of 7525.

5. "Holocaust: Der Judenmord bewegt die Deutschen," *Der Spiegel*, May 1979

6. Wittmann. *Beyond Justice*, Kindle Edition, 791-93 of 3837.

7. Preliminary observations on the criminal case against Mulka et al, 4 Ks 2/63. DVD ROM "Der Auschwitz Prozess: Tonbandmitschnitte Protokolle, Dokumente; Herausgegeben vom Fritz Bauer Institut Frankfurt, und dem Staatlichen Museum Auschwitz-Birkenau, The First Frankfurt Auschwitz Trial, 995.

8. Judicial Hearing Transcript, District Court, Göppingen, Viktor Capesius in person before Senior Judge Dr. Trukenmüller, 5 pages, Register Gs. 385/59, December 4, 1959, courtesy of Fritz Bauer Institut.

9. Schlesak, *The Druggist of Auschwitz*, Kindle Edition, 2557 of 5519.

10. Capesius interview in Schlesak, *The Druggist of Auschwitz*, Hardcover Edition, 95.

11. Grosz letter to Langbein, November 21, 1962, made an exhibit of the Frankfurt Auschwitz Trial, "Criminal case against Mulka et al", 4 Ks 2/63, Landgericht Frankfurt am Main.

12. Ibid.

13. Letter of Ferdinand Grosz to Hermann Langbein, November 21, 1962, reproduced in Schlesak, *The Druggist of Auschwitz*, Kindle Edition, 1413 of 5519.

14. Stoffel testimony cited in Schlesak, *The Druggist of Auschwitz*, Hardcover Edition, 167-68.

15. Preliminary observations on the criminal case against Mulka et al, 4 Ks 2/63. DVD ROM "Der Auschwitz Prozess: Tonbandmitschnitte Protokolle, Dokumente; Herausgegeben vom Fritz Bauer Institut Frankfurt, und dem Staatlichen Museum Auschwitz-Birkenau, The First Frankfurt Auschwitz Trial, 51.

16. Staatsanwaltschaftliche Vernehmung, 1-2.

17. Ibid., 3, 5.

18. Ibid., 7.

19. Ibid., 8.

20. Ibid., 7.

21. Ibid., 8, citing Dr. Gisella Perl, *I Was A Doctor in Auschwitz* (New York: International Universities Press, 1948), 13-17.

22. Perl, I Was a Doctor in Auschwitz, 16-17.

23. Capesius interviewed in Schlesak, *Druggist of Auschwitz,* Hardcover Edition, 371.

24. Nadine Brozan, "Out of Death, A Zest for Life," *New York Times*, November 15, 1982.

25. Op. Cit., Staatsanwaltschaftliche Vernehmung, 9.

26. Ibid.

27. Ibid., 10.

28. Ibid., 8.

29. Ibid., 12.

30. Ibid., 11.

31. Ibid., 14.

32. Before 1965, pretrial interrogations in Germany were not transcribed verbatim, but instead summarized by the judicial officials and then signed by the witness. Rebecca Elizabeth Wittmann, "Holocaust On Trial? *The Frankfurt Auschwitz Trial* In Historical Perspective," thesis submitted for Doctor of Philosophy, Graduate Department of History, University of Toronto, 2001, p. 49.

33. Private letters of Capesius cited in Schlesak, *The Druggist of Auschwitz,* Hardcover Edition, 157-58.

34. Judicial Hearing Transcript, District Court, Göppingen, Viktor Capesius in person before Senior Judge Dr. Trukenmüller, 5 pages, with additional coverage of hearing of December 7, 1959 in District Court, Court Clerk Leonhardt, Register Gs. 385/59, December 4, 1959, 3, courtesy of Fritz Bauer Institut.

35. Ibid., 1 – 2.

36. Ebd., Bd. 48, BI. 8.61 O sowie Bd. 60, BI. 11.115 und DVD-ROM, S. 3.566.

37. Op. Cit, Judicial Hearing Transcript, District Court, Göppingen, Viktor Capesius in person before Senior Judge Dr. Trukenmüller, 5 pages, Register Gs. 385/59, December 4, 1959, 3, courtesy of Fritz Bauer Institut.

38. Ibid., 3.

39. Ibid., 4.

40. Capesius quoted in Schlesak, *The Druggist of Auschwitz,* Hardcover Edition, 170.

41. Capesius letter to Eisler cited in Schlesak, *The Druggist of Auschwitz*, Kindle Edition, 2008 of 5519.

CHAPTER 18 – "BANALITY OF EVIL"

1. *Täter Helfer Trittbrettfahrer: NS-Belastete aus dem östlichen Württemberg* Vol. 3, "Der Apotheker Dr. Victor Capesius und die Selektionen in Auschwitz-Birkenau" Dr. Werner Renz, (Reutlingen: Wolfgang Proske Verlag, 2014), 65-66.

2. Posner and Ware, *Mengele,* Hardcover Edition, 140.

3. Isser Harel interviewed by Gerald Posner and John Ware, August 1985, reported in Posner and Ware, *Mengele*, Kindle Edition, 2750 of 7525.

4. Posner and Ware, *Mengele,* Kindle Edition, 2757-2761, 2761-2769, 2791-2794 of 7525. 'Ofer Aderet. *Secret Life of the German Judge Who Brought the Mossad to Eichmann*, Hareetz, October 18, 2014

5. "The Judiciary and Nazi Crimes in Postwar Germany," by Henry Friedlander, Museum of Tolerance Wiesenthal Learning Center, Annual 1, Chapter 2.

6. *Völkermord als Strafsache*, Werner Renz, http://www.fritz-bauerinstitut.de/texte/essay/0800_renz.htm

7. Letter Victor Capesius to Gerhard Gerber, June 1960, exhibit to Frankfurt Auschwitz Trial, in the presentation of the prosecution case against Robert Mulka, 4 Ks 2/63 District Court in Frankfurt am Main.

8. See Ernst Klee, Auschwitz. Täter, Gehilfen und Opfer und was aus ihnen wurde. Ein Personenlexikon (S. Fischer Verlag, Frankfurt, 2013).

9. Pendas, *The Frankfurt Auschwitz Trial*, 265.

10. Vermerk, Kügler (December 21, 1960), FFSTA HA 4 KS 2/63, Bd. 4,Bl. 659-63, cited in Pendas, *The Frankfurt Auschwitz Trial,* 48, n 105.

11. Wittmann, "Holocaust On Trial?", p. 111.

12. Hannah Arendt. *Eichmann in Jerusalem: A Report on the Banality of Evil.* New York: Viking, 1964.

13. Judicial Hearing Transcript, District Court, Frankfurt, Viktor Capesius in person before Senior Judge Opper, 3 pages, Register 931 Gs. 2240/61, April 13, 1961, 2, courtesy of Fritz Bauer Institut.

14. Ibid., 1- 2.

15. Ibid., 2- 3.

16. Op. Cit., Staatsanwaltschaftliche Vernehmung, 12.

17. Bauer's office had submitted its first motion to open a preliminary judicial inquiry on July 12, 1961. The second formal phase of the Auschwitz investigation started on August 9, 1961, when the court officially began its inquiry. Wittmann, *Beyond Justice*, Kindle Edition, 503 of 3837.

18. Christa Piotroski, "Die Unfähigkeit zur Sühne: Vor 25 Jahren Urteilsverkündung im 'Auschwitz'Prozeß' in Frankfurt," *Weltspiegel*, August 19, 1990; Wittmann, *Beyond Justice*, Kindle Edition, 492 of 3837.

19. Düx quoted in Guy Walters, *Hunting Evil: The Nazi War Criminals Who Escaped and the Quest to Bring Them to Justice* (New York: Broadway Books, 2010), 313.

20. Walters, *Hunting Evil*, 313-14.

21. Posner and Ware, *Mengele: The Complete Story* (Kindle Edition), 3086-3090).

CHAPTER 19 – "I HAD NO POWER TO CHANGE IT"

1. In the document relating this incident, the date for the confrontation is listed as January 11, 1962, during the proceeding summary, but the signature of the clerk correctly reflects that the date this was discussed before the court was, in fact, January 10. Vermerk UR IV, Dux, 4 Js 444/59, 11129, Note, 2 pages, courtesy of Fritz Bauer Institut.

2. Vermerk UR IV, Dux, 4 Js 444/59, 11129, Note, 2 pages, courtesy of Fritz Bauer Institut.

3. Judicial Hearing Transcript, District Court, Frankfurt, Viktor Capesius in person before Examining Magistrate Judge Heinz Düx, 15 pages, 4 Js 444/59, January 10, 1962, courtesy of Fritz Bauer Institut, 1, 4.

4. Ibid., 8-10.

5. Ibid., 4.

6. Ibid., 3.

7. Capesius quoted in Schlesak, *The Druggist of Auschwitz,* Hardcover Edition, 154.

8. Op. Cit., Staatsanwaltschaftliche Vernehmung, 10.

9. Op. Cit., Judicial Hearing Transcript, District Court, Frankfurt, Viktor Capesius in person before Examining Magistrate Judge Heinz Düx, 15 pages, 4 Js 444/59, January 10, 1962, 6.

10. Capesius interviewed in Schlesak, *The Druggist of Auschwitz,* Hardcover Edition, 155.

11. Op. Cit., Judicial Hearing Transcript, District Court, Frankfurt, Viktor Capesius in person before Examining Magistrate Judge Heinz Düx, 15 pages, 4 Js 444/59, January 10, 1962, 5.

12. Ibid., 11.

13. Ibid., 14.

14. Capesius declaration in Judicial Hearing Transcript, District Court, Frankfurt, Viktor Capesius in person before Examining Magistrate Judge Heinz Düx, 8 pages, 4 Js 444/59, January 24, 1962, courtesy of Fritz Bauer Institut, 5, 1.

15. Ibid., 5, 3 Capesius quoted in Schlesak, *The Druggist of Auschwitz,* Kindle Edition, 1576 of 5519.;

16. Capesius declaration in Judicial Hearing Transcript, District Court, Frankfurt, Viktor Capesius in person before Examining Magistrate Judge Heinz Düx, 8 pages, 4 Js 444/59, January 24, 1962, courtesy of Fritz Bauer Institut. 5, 4.

17. Preliminary observations on the criminal case against Mulka et al, 4 Ks 2/63. DVD ROM "Der Auschwitz Prozess: Tonbandmitschnitte Protokolle, Dokumente; Herausgegeben vom Fritz Bauer Institut Frankfurt, und dem Staatlichen Museum Auschwitz-Birkenau, The First Frankfurt Auschwitz Trial, 1001.

18. Capesius letters cited in Schlesak, *The Druggist of Auschwitz,* Hardcover Edition, 158.

19. Op. Cit., Judicial Hearing Transcript, District Court, Frankfurt, Viktor Capesius in person before Examining Magistrate Judge Heinz Düx, 8 pages, 4 Js 444/59, January 24, 1962, 5, 7.

20. Vermerk, Kügler (June 27, 1962), FFStA HA 4Ks 2/63 Bd. 8, Bl. 1547.

21. Capesius to Eisler, quoted in Schlesak, *The Druggist of Auschwitz,* Hardcover Edition, 133.

22. Capesius to Stoffel, quoted in Schlesak, *The Druggist of Auschwitz,* Hardcover Edition, 136.

23. See statements of Stoffel, January 7, 1965, part of the trial record criminal case against Mulka et al", 4 Ks 2/63, Landgericht Frankfurt am Main.

CHAPTER 20 – "PEPETRATORS RESPONSIBLE FOR MURDER"

1. Wittmann, *Beyond Justice*, Kindle Edition, 569-621 of 3837

2. Acklageschrift, FFStA 4 Ks 2/63, 273-74, Bundesarchiv.

3. Herbert Ernst Müller quoted in Pendas, *The Frankfurt Auschwitz Trial*, 117.

4. Acklageschrift, FFStA 4 Ks 2/63, 35, Bundesarchiv.

5. Pendas, *The Frankfurt Auschwitz Trial*, 49.

6. Section 47 of Militärstrafgesetzbuch cited in Pendas, *The Frankfurt Auschwitz Trial*, 119.

7. The charges were reduced against Breitwieser, Frank, Hantl, Höcker, Lucas, Mulka, Schatz, Scherpe, Schlage, Schoberth and Stark.

8. Acklageschrift, FFStA 4 Ks 2/63, 46-48, Bundesarchiv.

9. Bauer quoted in Wittmann, *Beyond Justice*, Kindle Edition, 763 of 3837.

10. Twenty of the twenty-two indicted were to stand trial. Besides Baer's June death, Nierzwicki had been dropped because of poor health.

CHAPTER 21 – UNINSPIRED BUREAUCRATS

1. Pendas, *The Frankfurt Auschwitz Trial*, 229-30, 270.
2. "Prozeß gegen SS-Henker von Auschwitz," *Neues Deutschland*, December 21, 1963, 1, 10.
3. Pendas, Devin O. (2000) ""I didn't know what Auschwitz was": *The Frankfurt Auschwitz Trial* and the German Press, 1963-1965," *Yale Journal of Law & the Humanities*: Vol. 12: I. 2, Article 4, 425.
4. Pendas, *The Frankfurt Auschwitz Trial*, 86.
5. Ibid., 123-30.
6. "21 on Trial for Murder of Millions," *The Bridgeport Post* (Bridgeport, CT), December 20, 1963, p. 60.
7. Arthur Miller, "Facing Up to Murder of Millions," *St. Louis Post-Dispatch* (St. Louis, Missouri), March 22, 1964, p. 80.
8. Rebecca Wittmann, "Legitimizing the Criminal State: Former Nazi Judges and the Distortion of Justice at the Frankfurt Auschwitz Trial, 1963-1965," Diefendorf, ed., *Lessons and Legacies*, VI, 352-72; see also Pendas, *The Frankfurt Auschwitz Trial*, 123-30.

CHAPTER 22 – "NO CAUSE FOR LAUGHTER"

1. The prosecution used ten historians as its expert witnesses, four of whom were the primary scholars; Helmut Krausnick, Hans-Adolf Jacobsen, Hans Buchheim, and Martin Broszat. Subsequently, the information from those four scholars served as the basis for a 1968 book, *Anatomy of the SS State*, the first thorough historical study of the SS based on its own records. See Preliminary observations on the criminal case against Mulka et al, 4 Ks 2/63. DVD ROM "Der Auschwitz Prozess: Tonbandmitschnitte Protokolle, Dokumente; Herausgegeben vom Fritz Bauer Institut.
2. The entire episode with Langbein and the court is recounted in "Nazis Rage in Dramatic Confrontation," *Democrat and Chronicle* (Rochester, NY), March 7, 1964, 1; see also "Points Out His Auschwitz Captors," *The Kansas City Times*, March 7, 1964. 1.
3. Wittmann, *Beyond Justice*, Kindle Edition, 2167 of 3837
4. Pendas, *The Frankfurt Auschwitz Trial*, 216.
5. See the instance of Laternser accusing the witness, Erwin Olszowka, of being a communist and coordinating his testimony with Langbein. Pendas, *The Frankfurt Auschwitz Trial*, 164, 188-90.
6. Preliminary observations on the criminal case against Mulka et al, 4 Ks 2/63. DVD ROM "Der Auschwitz Prozess: Tonbandmitschnitte Protokolle, Dokumente; Herausgegeben vom Fritz Bauer Institut.
7. Ella Salomon (née Böhm) quoted in Schlesak, *The Druggist of Auschwitz*, Hardcover Edition, 8.

8.   Ella Salomon (née Böhm) in 4Ks 2/63, Hessisches Staatsarchiv and also cited in Schlesak, *The Druggist of Auschwitz*, Hardcover Edition, 8-9.

9.   "Defendant at Auschwitz Trial Displays Indifference to Murder Charges," *Jewish Telegraphic Agency*, May 12, 1964.

10.   Henry Ormond, "Plädoyer im Auschwitz-Prozeß," *Sonderreihe aus Gestern und Heute* 7(1965), 41.

11.   See Capesius testimony cited in Naumann, *Auschwitz*, 72; Mulka et al, 4 Ks 2/63. DVD ROM "Der Auschwitz Prozess: Tonbandmitschnitte Protokolle, Dokumente; Herausgegeben vom Fritz Bauer Institut Frankfurt, und dem Staatlichen Museum Auschwitz-Birkenau, The First Frankfurt Auschwitz Trial, 963.

12.   Mulka et al, 4 Ks 2/63. DVD ROM "Der Auschwitz Prozess: Tonbandmitschnitte Protokolle, Dokumente; Herausgegeben vom Fritz Bauer Institut Frankfurt, und dem Staatlichen Museum Auschwitz-Birkenau, The First Frankfurt Auschwitz Trial, Vol VII and Vol VIII, 1095.

13.   Statement of Joachim Kügler on the 162nd day of the Auschwitz Trial proceedings (May 24, 1965), 4Ks 2/63, Hessisches Staatsarchiv.

14.   Kulka testimony 4Ks 2/63, Hessisches Staatsarchiv and quoted in Naumann, *Auschwitz*, 125.

15.   Prokop testimony and Hofmeyer admonition in 4Ks 2/63, Hessisches Staatsarchiv and quoted in in Naumann, *Auschwitz*, 190.

16.   Kaduk testimony 4Ks 2/63, Hessisches Staatsarchiv and cited in Naumann, *Auschwitz*, 201-02.

17.   Wittmann, "Holocaust On Trial?", p. 11.

18.   Ludwig Wörl quoted in "Bribe Allegations At Auschwitz Trial," *The Sydney Morning Herald* (Sydney, New South Wales, Australia), April 8, 1964, 3.

19.   "Auschwitz Druggist Tagged as Jekyll-Hyde Character," Associated Press, *Nevada State Journal* (Reno), June 21, 1964, 13.

20.   Chemist 'Stored Gold Teeth'" *Sydney Morning Herald* (Sydney, New South Wales, Australia), June 20, 1964, 3; "Horror Loot of a Nazi Camp Told," *Independent* (Long Beach, CA), June 19, 1964, 15.

21.   "Auschwitz Story Written in Blood," *Detroit Free Press*, August 27, 1964, 14.

22.   "Doctor Testifies Nazi He Aided Killed Family," UPI wire service, *The Fresno Bee* (Fresno, CA), August 18, 1964, 31.

23.   "Nazi Called Self The Devil, Witness Says," *Democrat and Chronicle* (Rochester, NY), August 25, 1964, 9; Magda Szabó testimony cited in Naumann, *Auschwitz*, 223.

24.   "Nazi Called Self The Devil, Witness Says," Associated Press, *Democrat and Chronicle* (Rochester, NY), August 25, 1964, 9.

25. Hofmeyer 4Ks 2/63, Hessisches Staatsarchiv and in Naumann, *Auschwitz*, 224.

26. Mulka et al, 4 Ks 2/63. DVD ROM "Der Auschwitz Prozess: Tonbandmitschnitte Protokolle, Dokumente; Herausgegeben vom Fritz Bauer Institut, 1145-54.

27. Capesius, Pajor and Hofmeyer in Naumann, *Auschwitz*, 300-01.

28. Ormond quoted in Naumann, *Auschwitz*, 73.

29. Dr. Ella Lingens, Mulka et al, 4 Ks 2/63. DVD ROM "Der Auschwitz Prozess: Tonbandmitschnitte Protokolle, Dokumente; Herausgegeben vom Fritz Bauer Institut, 2743.

30. Viktoria Ley testimony in 4Ks 2/63, Hessisches Staatsarchiv and cited in Naumann, *Auschwitz*, 344-46.

31. Capesius testimony quoted in Naumann, *Auschwitz*, 73.

32. Pendas, *The Frankfurt Auschwitz Trial*, 2162; "'Auschwitz Trial' Enters Sixth Week; Says Archbishop Said to Obey Orders," *The Wisconsin Jewish Chronicle* (Milwaukee, WI), January 31, 1964, 1.

33. Opening argument Preliminary observations on the criminal case against Mulka et al, 4 Ks 2/63. DVD ROM "Der Auschwitz Prozess: Tonbandmitschnitte Protokolle, Dokumente; Herausgegeben vom Fritz Bauer Institut, 1243; 4Ks 2/63, Hessisches Staatsarchiv.

34. As for Capesius laughing and then stopping, see "Horror Loot of a Nazi Camp Told," *Independent* (Long Beach, CA), June 19, 1964, 15; testimony at Mulka et al, 4 Ks 2/63. DVD ROM "Der Auschwitz Prozess: Tonbandmitschnitte Protokolle, Dokumente; Herausgegeben vom Fritz Bauer Institut, 1321.

35. Capesius notes, May 20, 1964, cited in Schlesak, *The Druggist of Auschwitz*, Hardcover Edition, 187.

36. Capesius notes, undated, cited in Schlesak, *The Druggist of Auschwitz*, Hardcover Edition, 251.

CHAPTER 23 – THE VERDICT

1. Wittmann, *Beyond Justice*, Kindle Edition, 754-759 of 3837.

2. Naumann, *Auschwitz*, 388.

3. Pendas, *The Frankfurt Auschwitz Trial*, 216.

4. Mulka et al, 4 Ks 2/63. DVD ROM "Der Auschwitz Prozess: Tonbandmitschnitte Protokolle, Dokumente; Herausgegeben vom Fritz Bauer Institut, 1601.

5. Capesius statement in Naumann, *Auschwitz*, 409-10.

6. 1964 DIVO-Institute survey cited in Pendas, *The Frankfurt Auschwitz Trial*, 216.

7. The first 80 pages was a summary of the history of Auschwitz, a shorter version of the 195 pages the prosecutors had set forth in their original indictment. Verdict in Mulka et al, 4 Ks 2/63. DVD ROM "Der Auschwitz Prozess: Tonbandmitschnitte Protokolle, Dokumente; Herausgegeben vom Fritz Bauer Institut.

For full citations reference is 4 Ks 2/63, "Das Urteil im Frankfurter Auschwitz-Prozess" (Auschwitz Trial Judgment), Lanclgericht Frankfurt am Main, August 1965.

8. 4 Ks 2/63, "Das Urteil im Frankfurter Auschwitz-Prozess," August 1965; August 19, 1965, 182nd Session, in Verdict in Mulka et al, 4 Ks 2/63. DVD ROM "Der Auschwitz Prozess: Tonbandmitschnitte Protokolle, Dokumente, T10-11; Herausgegeben vom Fritz Bauer Institut; Hofmeyer statement in Naumann, *Auschwitz*, 414-15.

9. Verdict in Mulka et al, 4 Ks 2/63. DVD ROM "Der Auschwitz Prozess: Tonbandmitschnitte Protokolle, Dokumente; Herausgegeben vom Fritz Bauer Institut; see 4 Ks 2/63, "Das Urteil im Frankfurter Auschwitz-Prozess," August 1965.

10. Rückerl, Investigation of Nazi Crimes, 64-66.

11. Mulka et al, 4 Ks 2/63. DVD ROM "Der Auschwitz Prozess: Tonbandmitschnitte Protokolle, Dokumente; Herausgegeben vom Fritz Bauer Institut; see also Naumann, *Auschwitz*, 424.

12. See generally Schlesak, *Druggist of Auschwitz*, XXXX.

13. "Former Guards at Auschwitz Get Life Terms," *St. Louis Post-Dispatch* (St. Louis, MO), August 19, 1965, 24.

14. Hofmeyer summary in 4 Ks 2/63, "Das Urteil im Frankfurter Auschwitz-Prozess," August 1965 and cited in in Naumann, *Auschwitz*, 425.

15. Fritz Bauer, "Im Namen des Volkes: Die strafrechtliche Bewaltigung der Vergangenheit," In Helmut Hammerschmidt, ed. *Zwanzig Jahre danach: Eine Deutsche Bilanz, 1945-1965* (Munich: Desch Verlag, 1965), 301-302, 307.

16. Ibid., 307-08.

17. "Prosecutors Ask for New Trial of 8 in Nazi Death Camp Trial," *The Bridgeport Post* (Bridgeport, CT), August 25, 1965.

18. Bulletin des Comité International des Camps, No. 10 (September 15, 1965), 4.

19. Wittmann, *Beyond Justice*, Kindle Edition, 3020-3036 of 3837.

20. Dr. K. "Das Urteil von Frankfurt," *Neues Deutschland*, August 20, 1965.

21. Capesius quoted in Schlesak, *The Druggist of Auschwitz*, Kindle Edition, 2832 of 5519.

22. "Sybille Bedford, "Auschwitz – Did A Nation Learn From the Millions of Deaths," *The Courier-Journal* (Lexington, KY), March 14, 1965, Section 1, 8.

CHAPTER 24 – "IT WAS ALL JUST A BAD DREAM"

1. Letter, Attention: Nazi Criminal Victor Capesius Auschwitz," from E. Brand, File 0.33, page 8; Letter, Dr. Y. Martin to Mr. Braner, Yad Vashem, re Victor Capesius, July 11, 1965; Letter, Mr. Brand to A. L. Kobobi, re Victor Capesius, August 11, 1965, written on 21.11.65; Letter, Emmanuel Brand re Langbein and Ambassador to Austria, November 19, 1965; Collection of Archival Documents Regarding Victor Capesius, Yad Vashem.

2. "Nazi Convicted of Auschwitz Murders, Released After Three Years of Prison," *Jewish Telegraph Agency*, January 25, 1968; "Nazi Free on Appeal," *The Kansas City Times* (Kansas City, MO), January 24, 1968, 70.

3. Karen Schnebeck, "Neue Ausstellung zum 25-Jahr-Jubiläum; Jüdisches Museum in Göppingen," *Stuttgarter Zeitung*, April 28, 2016, 22.

4. Capesius interviewed in Schlesak, *The Druggist of Auschwitz*, Hardcover Edition, 23.

5. Ibid., 123.

6. Friederike Capesius interviewed in Schlesak, *The Druggist of Auschwitz*, Kindle Edition, 2832 of 5519.

7. Ibid., 143.

8. Henry Ormond quote in Schlesak, *The Druggist of Auschwitz*, Hardcover Edition, 227-28.

EPILOGUE

1. Pendas, Devin O. *The Frankfurt Auschwitz Trial, 1963-1965: Genocide, History, and the Limits of the Law*, (Boston: Cambridge University Press, 2006) and Wittmann, Rebecca. *Beyond Justice: The Auschwitz Trial*, (Cambridge, MA: Harvard University Press, 2012).

2. Melissa Eddy, "Chasing Death Camp Guards With New Tools," *The New York Times*, May 5, 2014.

3. Kharunya Paramaguru, "70 Years Later, German Prosecutors to Hold Nazi Death-Camp Guards to Account," TIME, April 16, 2013.

4. Melissa Eddy, "Germany Sends 30 Death Camp Cases to Local Prosecutors," *The New York Times*, September 3, 2013.

5. Ibid.

6. Eliza Gray, "The Last Nazi Trials," *TIME*.

7. Ibid.

8. Philip Oltermann, "Ex-Auschwitz Guard Talks of Shame During Trial Over Mass Killings," *The Guardian*, April 26, 2016.

9. Melanie Hall, "Former Auschwitz Guard Convicted in one of Germany's Last Holocaust Trials," *The Telegraph*, June 17, 2016.

INDEX

Lightning Source UK Ltd.
Milton Keynes UK
UKHW041824150819
348037UK00001B/111/P